A HIGHER FORM
OF POLITICS:

The Rise of a Poetry Scene,
Los Angeles, 1950–1990

Sophie Rachmuhl

Translated from the French
by Mindy Menjou & George Drury Smith

OTIS BOOKS | SEISMICITY EDITIONS

The Graduate Writing program
Otis College of Art and Design

Beyond Baroque Foundation
Venice, CA

LOS ANGELES ● 2015

Book design and typesetting: Rebecca Chamlee

ISBN-13: 978-0-9860173-5-3
ISBN-10: 0-9860173-5-3

OTIS BOOKS | SEISMICITY EDITIONS
The Graduate Writing program
Otis College of Art and Design
9045 Lincoln Boulevard
Los Angeles, CA 90045

http://www.otis.edu/graduate-writing/seismicity-editions
seismicity@otis.edu

TABLE OF CONTENTS

In memoriam, Wanda Coleman (1946–2013),
for George Drury Smith,
& for all Los Angeles poets, dead, alive and to be
& for my mother

Untitled L.A. Poem

The palms flatten
against chance hot winds
we bore in
for the duration
rigid
the palms yield
to our touch
oh Los Angeles
we are your spawn
whim and hope
our eyes pan
one another
for the right side
the solid profile

Your face
screens huge
I cannot reach behind
for the yes
the hungry yes
we need so much
we cannot even touch
the palms
of our hands
tight fists
we hold it in
we hold it in

—LAUREL ANN BOGEN

INTRODUCTION

This book has been more than 20 years in the making.

First came *Innerscapes, 10 Portraits of L.A. Poets*, an hour-and-a-half documentary I made in 1988 on the Los Angeles poets of the 1980s and which is included with the present book. This came about after I was chosen in 1986 by a jury that Pierre Salinger chaired to receive the Tocqueville Award for a video documentary project – originally conceived to be about the Los Angeles poet Charles Bukowski and the literary underground he was a part of.

After a lot of reading, interviewing and attending poetry readings, with UCLA film student Willie Dawkins I filmed 30 hours of interviews, poets, poetry readings, events and locales, including Los Angeles' poetry center, Beyond Baroque Foundation.

Two years and many hours of editing later, the final documentary I screened at UCLA was not the moving panorama of the scene I had originally envisioned, but rather ten intimate portraits of nine individual poets and one group who, together, conveyed the diversity and energy of the poetry scene. These were Wanda Coleman (1946–2013), Laurel Ann Bogen, Marisela Norte, *Youthless* (a "little magazine" that gathered teenagers Beck and Channing Hansen, Rain Smith and Mario Acosta), Dr. Mongo, Leland Hickman (1934–91), Dave Alvin, Jack Grapes, Kamau Daáood and La Loca – black, brown and white, young and old, publishers, actors, organizers, wanderers or musicians.

Then after another decade that included sifting through the material I had accumulated (local "little magazines," poetry books, articles, interviews, tape-recordings of events, flyers), reading criticism, and finally writing intensely for four years, I produced a 600-page analysis of the L.A. poetry scene, written in French, with quotes and poems in English, entitled *Los Angeles 1950–1990 – The Rise of an Arts Scene and a Poetic Discourse on the*

City. This was my doctoral dissertation, directed by Université Paris 7 Professor Geneviève Fabre.

And now, after two sons and two partners and a long period of intellectual burn-out and motherly investment, I have the opportunity to see my book translated and published in the United States, thanks to a publishing partnership originally between Paul Vangelisti, chair of Otis College of Art and Design Graduate Writing program, and Fred Dewey, who was then director of Beyond Baroque Foundation; and on the initiative of Beyond Baroque founder George Drury Smith.

Why did I spend so many years analysing a scene that I am not a part of, studying an art I do not practice, in a city where I lived three years?

Listening to the poetry; looking at the amazingly creative small presses; seeing all the locales, the energy, the people; reading the poetry; talking to the poets who shared their unique perspective on their city with me; crisscrossing Greater Los Angeles going to readings, then later digging the history out in small press literary magazines; forming hypotheses; meeting the challenge of defining the broad scene and establishing some of its history over a period of 40 years, I felt like an explorer and a discoverer, ceaselessly amazed at this bold way of embracing an art form that I thought off-limits.

Being an "outsider" was very useful, too, for it enabled me to write with some kind of neutrality and serenity about a poetry that was both intensely personal and intensely public, yet mostly ignored by the literary establishment (universities and the East Coast literary world) and the entertainment industry that so dominated Los Angeles culture, where fame and power were so significant that they could blind the players to certain aspects of the scene.

I was struck too by the prominence of oral readings, a format virtually unknown at the time in France, and the dynamic network of events and places that developed, allowing people to meet and share.

Though Los Angeles poets displayed great diversity, openness, quality and continuity, and many had produced a significant body of work, I wondered, as did they themselves, why they generally went unrecognized even locally and certainly nationally and internationally.

Was it true, as some poets claimed, that Los Angeles poetry was uniquely isolated from the rest of the country and that the area provided unique conditions for writing?

And why didn't the poetry scene reflect much ethnic diversity?

I decided that the best way to answer these questions would be to do a study of the poetry scene that would:

–look at diverse Los Angeles communities from multiple angles, thus taking stock of its complexity (unless otherwise specified, when I say "Los Angeles" or even "city" I often mean the complex Greater Los Angeles urban area, which includes Los Angeles County and its nearly 90 incorporated cities);

–follow three main threads: the city, the poetry scene and the poetry itself–and their interrelationships;

–intermingle poems; quotations from interviews, "little magazines," recorded events and other source materials; and social, anthropological, sociological and literary analysis; and

–have one or several theoretical models to organize and give meaning to the profuse multidimensional phenomena on which I had accumulated literally hundreds of pounds of material that I carried around in boxes wherever I moved.

The basic theoretical models and principles of organization I used are to be found in the work of French sociologist Pierre Bourdieu, which provided me with a way to analyse the politics of poetic production; understand poets as groups and their attitudes and interests; and study the strategies they employed to achieve visibility and legitimacy.

And Mike Davis's stimulating *City of Quartz: Excavating the Future in Los Angeles* gave me a framework to place these poets within the city's cultural history.

The last step was to define and delineate the subject of my study, i.e., what I meant by "Los Angeles poetry scene," what it was and what it was not, who belonged to it and who did not. I decided that the "scene" included anyone who, a) created what they themselves called "poetry," b) made it public, mainly through poetry readings, and c) who was active in the local network of writing, publishing and reading.

Thus I have excluded, for example, "closet poets" who do not make their writings public, as well as academic poets (associated with universities), other well-known poets who were not really involved with the local scene, and finally rappers, who did not say their words were "poems" (though they could be considered to have poetic qualities) and used different production and distribution channels.

This book analyses the Los Angeles poetry scene in four chapters. I start with a description of the national poetry scene and its evolution in order to situate Los Angeles poetry in the national context. I then move on to the local scene from the 1950s and the Venice West Beat scene (Chapter 2); to some of the Watts writers in the 1960s and black poets who later became prominent (Chapter 3); and finally to the larger scene in the 1970s and 1980s, which built on the two earlier phases and truly developed after the creation of L.A.'s own poetry center, Beyond Baroque.

I focused mostly on the '70s generation of poets, especially poets who were particularly active or representative in the poetry community and who were facilitators between different poet groups. They were the ones who, through a conscious collective effort to build up the local scene, gave it a firm foundation to rise and grow from.

I have considered the poets who were newcomers to the scene in the 1980s as a group, and have not dwelled on important poets from that period individually.

My documentary *Innerscapes,* which features a cross-section of poets from that "generation," is an essential complement to the written analysis presented here of this period. This is precisely why it has been included with the book.

I must add that my original work included additional chapters—a chapter on Los Angeles history and another on L.A.'s symbolic history, which had a number of poems on the city and its history.

I envision the present book as the second part of a triptych that includes the documentary as well as a projected third part which would be an anthology of poetry by some of the poets I am sorry I had to omit from this English version of the book.

This book is translated from an academic analysis originally written in French academic style, and thus can sound awkward or abstract at times and make for arduous reading, but I hope this approach is rewarding in the end. George Drury Smith and I have certainly worked hard on alleviating the academic jargon and making the English "readable." I must say I am very pleased with the end result.

I have retained some footnotes from the original French work, which in the original version nearly made up a second, parallel book. Readers can find in these notes complementary material on the Los Angeles poetry scene, as well as contextual information and theoretical explanations and observations.

Many new poets have surged on the Los Angeles scene since I began this journey, and there are many who have disappeared. Some have died, some have stopped writing poetry, others have moved away. But there are many more who have carried on.

Since the period this book covers, the Internet has given poets a new medium in which circulate their works and establish contact.

Many of the older poets have been recognized and the oral character of poetry has been confirmed with the rise of slams and performance poetry.

Los Angeles has started to take a look at itself, as the development of the "L.A. Studies" field since the 1990s shows. New books and articles on the arts/literature/poetry scene have been published, in particular Julian Murphet's *Literature and Race in Los Angeles;* and *The Sons and Daughters of Los*, a collection of articles on "Culture and Community in L.A." The prestigious Cambridge University Press devoted a book of its Companion to Literature and Classics collection to Los Angeles Literature in 2010. Numerous anthologies have appeared, among which Estelle Gershgoren Novak's *Poets of the Non-Existent City*, a collection of poets from the 1950s literary magazines *California Quarterly* and *Coastlines*; and David L. Ulin's monumental anthology on *Writing Los Angeles*, which includes some poets. Finally, Bill Mohr's *Hold-Outs: The Los Angeles Poetry Renaissance, 1948–1992*, University of Iowa Press, 2011, is an insider's look at the Los Angeles poetry scene over the same period I am studying.

My own analysis – that of a French outsider scholar and poetry lover – should complement Mohr's history of Los Angeles poetry, seen through the eyes of a veteran poet and editor, as well as those of an academic. The (few) poets I chose to focus on are symbolic of something greater than themselves though they cannot be representative of the whole scene. This study does not claim to be comprehensive. In particular, the chapters about community poets treat only a few significant poets and anthologies. I am aware that many poets have been left out. I hope my choices will create no controversies or feelings of exclusion, though I think the work of the scholar as well as that of the director of a documentary is precisely to select. Los Angeles' energy and multiplicity certainly cannot be grasped in one study. This is in the end my personal journey through Los Angeles, some of its poets and their poetry. Despite careful readings from various friends and poets, I am sure some mistakes remain, due to the amount of material, time and space I am covering, as well as lack of written documentation concerning some parts, the wealth of new research since the 1990s, and finally the distance between Bordeaux, France and Los Angeles, USA.

I am still hoping that this will be a worthy contribution to the growing body of critical work on Los Angeles writing and be a base for the poets and future L.A. poetry scholars to build on. All I can say is that it was done with care, love, determination, curiosity, sympathy, and a lot of endurance.

—SOPHIE RACHMUHL,
Bordeaux, September 2014

CHAPTER ONE

The American Poetic Field: From Modernism to the 1980s

The Split

The notion of American literature was born at the same time as that of political independence, leading to a literary nationalism after the 1783 Treaty of Paris. It showed in the new use of the term "American literature" – almost unknown before then – and the militancy of magazine editors calling for "the creation of a 'national' literature" (Golding 1983, 281).

The literary and political projects were always close, as can be seen in the first anthology of American poetry, Elihu Hubbard Smith's *American Poems, Selected and Original*, published in 1793:

> Smith's Federalism underlies what he saw as the use of his anthology: to build America's sense of identity by gathering an independent national literature to match and strengthen the country's newly achieved political independence (ibid., 281).

Spurred on by the same patriotic flame some fifty years later, the Transcendentalists arrived at the first collective formulation of a philosophical and poetic American credo. In Whitman's eyes, the poet was the herald of egalitarian democracy, the liberator of the masses and the individual, paving the way for a "new order [to] arise and [the poets] shall be the priests of man, and every man shall be his own priest" ("Preface" *Leaves of Grass*). Thus the writer was a citizen first and foremost. He was duty-bound to participate in the life of the nation and to watch over and safeguard its values as they were written in its founding documents. Early 20th century anthologies commonly highlighted this "Americanness" (Golding 1983, 295–6).

With the advent of modernism, the early years of the second decade of the 20th century were in more ways than one transitional for American poetry. Unlike their predecessors, Modernists "used their anthologies to propose a canon written in defiance of inherited poetic forms." These were often "aimed at a small audience, [and] mainly influenced other poets" (Golding 1983, 295–6).

At the same time, the number of "little magazines" grew phenomenally, led by *Poetry*. This "probably had more to do with the promotion of modern American poetry than any other medium," wrote Richard J. Gray (Gray 1990, 39).

In the field of art, 1913 was marked by the resounding success, touched by scandal, of the *Armory Show* in New York, which revolutionized the scene by presenting the most innovative European paintings since Impressionism – including Marcel Duchamp's famous *Nude Descending a Staircase*. Of this work, William Carlos Williams said, "I do remember how I laughed out loud when I first saw it, happily, with relief" (quoted in Gray 1990, 43). Williams' famous precept, "No ideas but in things," as well as his verses modeled on the rhythms of American speech and his allegiance to Walt Whitman, made him, in the eyes of the rebellious Beat poets of the 1950s, "the oldest living poet among [our] ancestors" (Lipton 1959, 235). His remark expresses what a lot of poets and artists felt upon first viewing this painting: a feeling of liberation from the conventions of tradition, as well as a sense of belonging to an international community, united in its yearning to experiment. From Imagism to Vorticism, from radical poetry to the art of the Harlem Renaissance, explorations of these new horizons filled the pages of British and American small press publications. Founded in Chicago in 1912, *Poetry* published many of the important American poets of the early 20th century, and in a sense it inaugurated and symbolized a split in the American literary world.

Poetry, however, was confined to a very limited dissemination, through a medium at the margins of commercial publishing – the little magazines. Thus, unlike earlier poets, who had been judged according to their popularity and fidelity to society's moral values, a number of modernist poets deliberately sought to break with the larger public. They wrote difficult poetry, from which sentiment was banned. They favored innovation and rejected the aesthetic and social norms of the day. They wrote above all for their peers, with whom they shared a specific tradition.

Bourdieu has studied this phenomenon and described it thus:

> The field of production...owes its own structure to the opposition between...on the one hand, *the field of restricted production*, as a system that produces cultural goods...objectively destined... for a public consisting of producers of cultural goods who themselves produce for producers of cultural goods, and, on the other hand, *the field of large-scale cultural production*, which is organized specifically to produce cultural goods destined for non-producers of cultural goods, i.e., "the general public."[1]

American poetry was split between writers writing for writers and writers writing for non-writers.

But the universities slowly monopolized the field of restricted production, freezing modernism's creative exuberance into an academic formalism. The New Criticism's reading of T.S. Eliot had a dominating influence on this process. This interpretation of Eliot's poetry and criticism (particularly of the essay "Tradition and the Individual Talent") shaped the reading lists and critical approaches of university curricula at a time when professors of American literature were seeking to establish their discipline as a specialty. Apart from the necessity of studying the poetic tradition, the New Criticism argues that the poem is an autonomous, discreet and universal entity detached from its historical and personal origins. Only the links of the poem with the whole of the poetic tradition count, not those with the life or the personality of the author.

The rise of the New Critics coincided with the taming of modernism and the growing role of the university. The spectacular increase in student population led the university to play an ever more important role in the intellectual and artistic life of the country. The university little by little found itself to be the arbiter of cultural legitimacy. It assumed every literary function, for it was at once the authority on creation, dissemination and conservation. Consequently, the university had a quasi-monopoly on poetry, imposing a "hierarchy of legitimacy" and standards for the evaluation of poems and poets. As Ron Silliman says, "the primary institution of American poetry is the university." It mediates and legitimatizes poetry for the academic as well as the non-academic world, thus providing "the context in which the majority of all poems in the u.s. are both written and read" (Silliman 1990, 151).

The Establishment of an Independent Poetry

Two anthologies published in the late 1950s exemplified this fracture. *New Poets of England and America* (1957), edited by Donald Hall, Robert Pack and Louis Simpson, represented the poets appreciated by academic criticism; and *New American Poetry* (1960), edited by Donald Allen, covered the dissident movements (Beats, the New York school, the Black Mountain school, etc.). This last anthology featured poets who shared a "distaste for what they identified as academic poetry, and a commitment to the relationship between poetry and speech" (Silliman 1990, 157).

The division of poetry into two camps began with a revolt against the New Critical establishment by the Beats, who "challenged nearly everything previously pious in poetry," as Richard Kostelanetz writes:

By the late fifties, the American poetry scene became split... into two warring camps known variously as square and beat, raw and refined, academic and antiacademic, each of which had its magazines, its critics, its publishers, its students, and inevitably, its anthologists (Kostelanetz 1981, 27–8).

Or, as Robert Lowell said in his 1960 National Book Award Acceptance Speech:

Two poetries are now competing, a cooked and a raw. The cooked, marvelously expert, often seems laboriously concocted to be tasted and digested by a graduate seminar. The raw, huge blood-dripping gobbets of unseasoned experience are dished up for midnight listeners. There is a poetry that can only be studied, and a poetry that can only be declaimed, a poetry of pedantry and a poetry of scandal. I exaggerate, of course" (quoted in Golding 1983, 299).

In light of classical 19th century precepts of democracy and Whitman's claim that the poet was the nation's natural guide, this poetic rupture appears more clearly, as the academy did not necessarily promote these values. Little by little, the anti-academic current set up a counter-tradition with its own institutional authorities, publication, dissemination, modes of evaluation, models, continuities and values.

In the late 1960s Jerome Rothenberg saw himself and his generation as embodying precisely that which was pushed aside by the academic canon. He first spoke of ethnopoetics as an alternative tradition characterized by experimentation and the exploration of all cultures. Indeed, he said the poet must be free to "reconsider and review the common sources" and "mak[e]-it-new at every step," in a poetry whose "root idea" is "metamorphosis" (Rothenberg 1975, 525). [2] In this quest, poetry must seek out influences and inspiration in all civilizations, oral and written, Western and Eastern.

From World War I on, the development of a continuous movement toward the exploration of consciousness, language & poetic structure–what we can see & say & make. This latter movement...explodes circa 1914 in a series of transformative moves, then continues unbroken to our own time (ibid., 528).

The poets who shared this anti-academic attitude sought to enlarge the concept and the role of poetry. They wanted to thwart the separation of poetry from the social or political world as well as its detachment from history and daily life, and make it once again relevant and involved. They revitalized poetry by exploring "a performance model of the poem, for which the written versions serve as the notation or the score" (ibid., 519).

Recitation was brought back into fashion in the United States by Welsh poet Dylan Thomas whose three American tours in the 1950s were notorious and triumphant. "Because he was the fashionable college poet of his day..., contemporary poetry started to be identified with the poetry reading.... For it was right after his successful tours that poetry readings began to multiply" (Hall 1984/85, 64).

Inspired by Thomas's example, the Beats popularized the public reading, making it accessible to all–known and unknown authors, educated and uneducated audiences. Once again poets simply adopted an older tradition, recitation. In declamatory literary anthologies called "readers" or "speakers," children had once learned to read. "Elocution" [or "Speech"] was a full-fledged discipline, taught in public schools as well as universities. Between 1850 and World War I, this family pastime of the Victorian era even became a separate theatrical art, the "platform performance." Performances were professionally organized on a national scale and their success was so phenomenal that the popularity of certain famous writers like Charles Dickens in the late 1860s, Oscar Wilde in the 1870s, or Mark Twain in the 1880s could be compared to that of the Beatles in the 1960s.[3]

After a pause in the late 1950s, poetry readings were presented in an ever-growing number of cafes throughout the 1960s and they benefited from a new popularity. With the rise of folk music and then rock and the successes of singer-poet stars like Bob Dylan and Jim Morrison, poetry continued to be performed on stage, and this led to its acceptance by a large audience. The revival of this oral form has constantly grown in importance ever since, to the point of becoming what Hall called "the chief form of publication for American poets" (Hall, ibid., 63) since the 1950s, surpassing "the audience for written poetry by a factor of ten or twenty or even one hundred" (Austin 1981, 248).

The counterculture and its underground publishing also stimulated independent poetry, which was abundantly seen in its pages. The anti-establishment youths of the 1960s knew how to use the technical advances in printing that made publishing much easier. Small presses and alternative magazines and newspapers combined eclectic inventiveness with defiant energy and reflected a rebellion as political as it was aesthetic, and they consequently experienced a veritable boom in the mid-1960s – a boom that would never die down.[4] And dissident poetry in all its forms found a favorable terrain here that reinforced its outreach and its independence, as Len Fulton described:

In the early sixties, poetry was still struggling to escape the aesthetic regulations of the "formulists" (Eliot, Ransom, etc.). Language in general was still struggling for a full measure of freedom against suppressive social forces as well as academic ones. The Beats had made gains in both these matters in the fifties, but it truly remained for the little magazines and underground newspapers of the sixties to take up the cause with their sheer number and diversity (Fulton 1978, 431).

With principal modes of dissemination being readings and the independent presses, poetry was an art that was eminently public and authentically democratic, because the "producers" possessed the "means of production," and it was thus easily converted into a weapon that was mobilized to change the world, from the civil rights movement to the Vietnam War opposition, by breaking with convention and lowering interdisciplinary boundaries.

The State of Poetry after the 1960s

In the late 1960s, the American poetry field appeared to be tripartite. On one hand was the "field of large-scale production," or mass culture, in which poetry had almost no place; on another the "restricted field," within which the university predominated; and a third, more independent field that was developing in part its own networks of production, dissemination and validation.

There are three distinct groupings in autonomous or independent poetry–which some call "outsider poetry," "alternative poetry," or "marginalized poetics" (Silliman 1990, 157)–that interests us here. The first of these is an experimental avantgarde, which reacted against the dominating influence of elite literary "scholars" and was based on a personal reading of the common cultural world heritage; this heritage becomes the subject matter of an inventive, learned and iconoclastic poetry. The second is the Beat and the underground bohemia, or "meat poets," whose figurehead was Charles Bukowski (1920–94). They opposed the dominant values of society as well as elite culture, and attacked conformism. And lastly, there is identity and ethnic poetry, symbolically opposed to a mainstream tied to the white Anglo-Saxon male.

ONE IMPORTANT AVANT-GARDE poetic movement to appear after the late 1970s was L=A=N=G=U=A=G=E poetry. This school, falling into the first vein, experimental, included poets such as Charles Bernstein, Bruce Andrews, Ray DiPalma, Douglas Messerli, Ron Silliman, Lyn Hejinian and Barrett Watten, was based mainly in New York and San Francisco. Their poetry opposed the conception of language as a tool of communication, responsible for transmitting a message from a speaker to a listener. For them, no human reality existed outside language: the subject and the world that one inhabits are always already constructed. Thus a poetic idea is "not the expression in words of an individual speaking subject, but the creation of that subject by the particular set of discourses (cultural, social, historical) in which he or she functions," wrote Marjorie Perloff (1985, 219–20). They were Marxists and theorists who established a parallel between the belief in a "referential dimension" to language, which is translated by realism, on the one hand, and on the other by the domination of "capitalist functioning" which transforms everything including language into "merchandise."

The L=A=N=G=U=A=G=E poets were at the center of many controversies. The bohemian and community poets saw L=A=N=G=U=A=G=E poets as a group of predominantly white writers who were attempting to pass themselves off as more oppressed than they really were, and whose works were inaccessible to a non-specialist and non-intellectual audience. This contradicted their radical or revolutionary aspirations. Their high visibility, in the 1980s and especially the '90s, fueled resentment against them, and in the eyes of their independent peers sometimes made them a symbol of heresy and not far removed from the academic poets.

Even so, Ron Silliman argued that both identity poets and avantgarde poets were outsiders, but based their work in different experiences of "historic subjectivity":

> *Writing meets the need of different communities differently.* Those groups which have been the subject (the *I* and *we*) of history are apt, for good reason, to tend toward a poetics which is, in practice, a critique of the subject itself, while others may long for precisely this experience of subjectivity ("we need to hear our stories told") (Silliman 1987, 30).

L=A=N=G=U=A=G=E poetry was occupied precisely with deconstructing identity, while minority poetry was in search of identity. Previously invisible and excluded from history, identity writers used the same method to affirm their existence within the nation during the decades of struggles for civil rights as had their country itself after independence. They sought to build a literary and poetic body of work "between memory and imagination" (Fabre 1990, 188), which outlined a symbology, a genealogy, a set of themes and a canon unique to their community, a proof of its civic reality. Yves-Charles Grandjeat said of Chicanos that the "group is born of a desire for representation which [...imposes] its own symbolic logic of unity. The group owes its existence to those who proclaim it, utter it, portray it, write it" (Grandjeat 1989, 18). But this also works for other ethnic and identity groups. Integrated little by little into popular and scholarly cultural discourse, this more and more intricately constructed belonging has evolved from being a disadvantage to "become an advantage, even a prerequisite, for access to the American identity" (Fabre 1990, 187).[10]

Ethnic minorities struggling for their rights found in poetry a weapon to be used against the oppressor and his language, and at the same time a tool to reinforce community cohesion and identity–a means for the exploration of a specific culture and history, especially oral. Other civil rights movements of oppressed groups such as those of feminists and queer people had a similar approach and sought to develop their own independent traditions and literature. This encouraged an increase in the number of their own creation and dissemination networks, along with their own institutions. In the same way as African Americans before them, the ethnic and sexual minorities carved out a third niche within the independent poetry field alongside those of bohemia and the avant-gardes.

ANOTHER CHARACTERISTIC touching the whole American poetic scene–both university and independent–is its orality. Although generally ignored, the oral and theatrical dimension of the poetry scene became more and more established over time, developing into almost a "restricted field of production" of its own, whose opposite and complementary "field of large-scale production" was the entertainment industry. The appearance in Los Angeles in the 1980s of a hybrid genre, christened "spoken word," that blended poetry, monologue, cabaret and music, is a proof of this. The influence of performance was to be more and more decisive for this new form, on the border between the "restricted field" and the "field of large-scale production," where we see poetic circles and marginalized fringes of the music industry such as alternative rock, punk and rap along with those of the entertainment industry, like stand-up comedy.

Thus, since the 1950s and '60s the American poetic scene has evolved toward more openness, increased flexibility and variety within the poetic genre, ultimately determined essentially by the mode of printed or theatrical presentation chosen by the poet. Thom Gunn's response, typical of the 1980s, to the question "Does an American poetry exist today?" shows the importance of the decentralization that had been taking place since the 1940s and '50s:

My answer is certainly no, there is not *an* American poetry. There are as many as twenty or thirty American poetries.... There is room for anarchy in the United States: a lot of interesting poets, a lot of boring ones, but none with any claim to be in a central line of tradition, because there ain't no such thing (Gunn 1987, 21).

The momentum created by decentralization resulted in fragmentation and regrouping:

The scene of American poetry is defined by the proliferation of parochial establishments which jell [sic] around various common ties – academic connection, geographical location, sexual persuasion, ethnic or religious or racial origins.... This kind of poetry scene encourages stylistic diversity and clearly defined position-taking, as well as competition among informally organized forces (Kostelanetz 1981, 41–2).

Although government funding, complemented by that of universities and independent organizations, helped establish and support for the first time a solid base from which a varied national poetic scene was able to develop, the fact remained that poetry was still mainly distributed by small presses, alternative literary magazines and public readings, all of which were rather ephemeral and random media of uncertain financing. Silliman was "haunted by...disappearances from the public discourse and consciousness of poetry.... A poetry without history strikes me as bordering on the unintelligible, its social value, its very use to us in our daily lives, seems to me questionable, and its fate a mere choice between oblivion and the still worse doom of perpetually repeating itself. Poetry, particularly in the United States, is a profoundly amnesiac discourse (Silliman 1990, 150).

Historical amnesia – or rather a selective and fragmented collective memory – is born of the tension between two contradictory forces in the American poetic scene. On the one hand, there is the competition for recognition, which is itself based on the accumulation of specific "cultural capital" (acquired or inherited culture, considered as an asset in social life); and on the other, there is an aspiration of the American poet to make of his art a tool of existential affirmation and participation in a nation that may seem hostile to all accumulated and inherited specific culture. Each American bears in himself his own poetic expression, Whitman wrote. Thus, guided by an ideal of constant renewal, the poet desires to sidestep the limitations imposed by literary criticism and rise above the need for recognition of his peers. American poetry being organized around two distinct sets of values: recognition, based on a hierarchy of poetic legitimacy decided by peers that extends from the local and the oral (the least valued) to the national and the written (the most valued); and Americanness, with criteria of authenticity, citizenship and freedom. The fact remains that recognition remains essential, even when it is decried or denied. A book of poetry was considered wildly successful if it sold between 5,000 and 10,000 copies with an investment of $10,000, while 500 copies was considered an acceptable loss, G. Blooston wrote in 1983 (Blooston 1983, 48–52). Consequently one could also consider the flowering of poetry as a means of cultural expression for the emerging class of Americans that had acquired some "cultural capital." This was a class whose members might often have attended a university but had no public place in which to exchange the "cultural capital" they'd acquired.

IN LOS ANGELES specific conditions shaped the local poetry scene. But unlike New York, the development of poetic activity was relatively recent in Los Angeles, which had long had a reputation as a cultural desert and which Mike Davis described as "unable to produce, to this day [1990], any homegrown intelligentsia," all the while being "the world capital of an immense Culture Industry" (Davis 1990, 17).

In the following pages we will look at the peculiar conditions under which a poetry scene emerged in Los Angeles and attempt to trace the steps of its maturation.

But it is useful as a preliminary step to locate Los Angeles in its regional context, calling on Mike Davis's *City of Quartz:*

Excavating the Future in Los Angeles. According to his analysis, the city has experienced "three major collectivized interventions by intellectuals in [its] culture formation" (ibid., 22) at three turning points in its history – the turn of the 20th century, the Great Depression, and the 1980s. He calls the first group "Boosters," those promoters, following the lead of *L.A. Times* owner General Harrison Gray Otis and the paper's editor-in-chief Charles Lummis, who used fiction as a publicity strategy to sell the city. The second "intervention" is that of the "Noirs," from the fiction genre; and the third is by the "Mercenaries," the 1980s neo-"Boosters" who worked for the partnership between business and the great cultural institutions. Together, they developed the principal mythologies of the city, which have been continually renewed and transformed since their conception.

These were complemented by two other more secondary "groups": "the Exiles," i.e., exiled Europeans; and "the Sorcerers," which included the members of various sects and cults as well as science fiction devotees.

Concomitantly, Davis detects what he calls "three attempts, in successive generations, to establish authentic epistemologies for Los Angeles" (ibid., 23), which responded to the three dominant mythic paradigms. There were first the "Debunkers," critical city chroniclers moved by the spirit of social reform who attacked the idyllic myth created by the "Boosters" and created a documented historiography of the city that was respectful of its social struggles and minority groups. Next there were the "Communards," eclectic avant-gardists like the Venice bohemians or South Central black artists who made up the Los Angeles cultural underground during the 1950s and '60s and who were "the first L.A.-bred bohemia..., unified by their autobiographical search for representative phenomenologies of daily life in Southern California" (ibid., 24). The last (unnamed) attempt embraced the often conflicting efforts during the 1980s to redefine and reappropriate the city's system of symbols, which was led simultaneously by Marxist academics at UCLA and gangster rappers of the ghetto and their theoreticians.

The Establishment of an Infrastructure in the 1960s and '70s

After the Beats, the poetry scene expanded without precedent and thus proceeded to become independent or "autonomous," as Bourdieu calls it in the three-tiered process described in his seminal article "The Market of Symbolic Goods" (Bourdieu 1971, 50). First, a larger, more and more diverse audience gave poets means of financial support as well as set up for them "a competing principle of legitimacy." Concurrently, an ever larger body of writers, poetry organizers and bookstore owners came into being. Finally, rival distribution and recognition networks multiplied, vying for cultural legitimacy. These included the various places where poetry could be read, as well as publishers and studios that would publish or record it, as well as "consecration authorities," all the forms of peer recognition, such as prizes, scholarships, residencies, subsidies, prestigious and paid readings, invitations to conferences and participation in juries awarding various prizes.

Government financial aid for the arts beginning in the mid-1960s gave the independent arts world a firmer base on which to build–while also benefiting academics. At the center of the system was the National Endowment for the Arts (nea). Created in 1965 with a budget of eight million dollars the first year, this agency saw its funds grow and its programs and its scope expand (it was $170 million in 1989 when it was near its peak). In the area of literary creation and publication, traditionally less lucrative and visible than other art forms, the nea had an essential role, by giving money directly to literary organizations and writers and financing specialized programs that were in turn responsible for redistributing the funds. Such was the case with the Coordinating Council of Literary Magazines (cclm), created in 1967 by the nea to help magazines and small literary presses, a large majority of which were dedicated at least in part to poetry. Many of these were not-for-profit publishers but they did not have the formal nonprofit "501(c)3" status required to receive grants directly from the government. Other organizations essential to the development of poetic professionalism outside the university were the Poets in the Schools (pits) programs, which came about around the same time. These were independent organizations in each state, funded by the nea, state arts councils and private foundations, which endeavored to send poets into schools to share their work with students of all backgrounds and ages, from preschool to high school. In these programs, poetry was viewed as a pedagogical tool, serving "to nurture and develop" in the child or adolescent "critical and creative thinking skills," the means for "self-expression and problem solving" and "a love for and fluency with language."[5] pits inspired the creation of other organizations that pursued some of the same goals in partnership with entities such as prisons, hospitals, psychiatric clinics, retirement homes and halfway houses.

This public financing system was rounded out, also during the 1960s, by the foundation of state arts councils which subsidized the arts with state funds, as well as municipal, regional and county cultural agencies. It is important to note here that the dual requirement that cultural organizations in most cases be nonprofit and at the same time find matching grants elsewhere in order to obtain public subsidies was a handicap for many small organizations oriented towards poetry. Scarcely visible, let alone prestigious, due to their size and chosen art, they had a hard time attracting private funding, and moreover could not afford to incorporate as a nonprofit organization. Thus, the system of public financing of the arts, although it stimulated much artistic activity in the United States and paved the way for important cultural organizations to develop and survive, did not especially favor the more modest, more numerous organizations (including those focused on poetry), which were more or less doomed to be short-lived despite their desire to survive or their quality.

A slightly later (1973) federal program, the Comprehensive Employment and Training Act (ceta), intended to facilitate the employment and training of unemployed and low-income people, including artists (thanks to a 1976 amendment), was essential to the expansion of many cultural, educational, alternative and community organizations. Together, all of these governmental programs set up a comprehensive support system that favored the development of cultural institutions and activities–among which was independent poetry.

WE HAVE ALREADY NOTED the widespread influence of the university, which, in addition to its functions of preservation and recognition of poetry, was also its principal patron in the United States. This came about through the many university creative writing programs (some 250 in 1981), which made the university the main employer of poets (King 1981, 10) and the primary market for books of poetry, as well as literary magazines. Other contributions of the university were active promotion of public readings, of which it was the most important organizer (ibid., 12), and which were the best paid and often also the most highly rated on the poetry circuit; and finally, university presses, which took over the poetry sector, which was almost entirely neglected by commercial publishers, and this brought credibility, commercial infrastructure and opportunities to the works they published.

Following the example of the Iowa Writers' Workshop, created in 1936, universities would later found creative writing programs on the fringe of English literature departments. These programs further contributed to the spread of academic poetic activity, which came to be divided into two distinct practices: a teaching program for students who intended to become instructors and which introduced them to theory and criticism, with the goal of "understanding poetry"[6]; and writing apprenticeships, guided by professional poets, often "in residence" at the institution. This flexible contractual "in residence" formula allowed educational and cultural institutions to take on recognized but non-academic artists for a given period. This form of financing became widespread in the 1980s, when other sources of public subsidies often stagnated or dried up. This was a means of paying individual artists in exchange for a service, and it in no small measure made up for the abolishment of the CETA program by the Reagan Administration in the early 1980s.

The spread of writing programs expanded the audience for poetry and the number of organizations involved. The workshop model was followed outside the university, too. The number of writing workshops of every kind—private, academic, community—grew constantly starting in the late-1960s. With the expansion of short-duration college programs, inexpensive higher education, community colleges and extension programs, especially within the large state university systems, independent poets now had the opportunity to lead workshops. In addition, private, public and university libraries bought poetry magazines and books and sometimes even the archives of independent poetry presses, thus ensuring a reliable base of subscribers for many publications.

The creation of ethnic and women's studies departments in universities, colleges and alternative educational institutions gave life to new critical movements and to new readings, challenging the dominance of the New Critics' canon while simultaneously providing a theoretical and institutional base for alternative poetic traditions. Under the pressure of ever more varied student audiences, which reflected the political and demographical evolution of the country, higher education became more open, and to adopt an increased number of theoretical points of view—old and new—if only to ensure its own survival.[7] However, the ubiquity of the university, and its increased openness and stratification, as well as the significant development of poetry institutions, blurred the boundaries between independent and university poets.

THE INCREASING INSTITUTIONALIZATION of independent organizations, the ever-growing number of students and the great rise in all of the resources of poetry creation, dissemination and recognition accentuated a decentralization already apparent. Regional arts centers around the big cities as well as other smaller centers throughout the country organized in a more and more independent manner starting in the 1960s, to the point that in 1979, in the introduction to his widely noticed anthology (precisely because of its regional presentation) Edward Field observed,

"Wherever I go now I come across an indigenous poetry scene with its own small presses, magazines, and poetry magazines" (quoted in Machan Aal 1984, 52). Local poetry networks were set up in most urban regions, including Los Angeles, encouraged first by the influence of the Beats and the popularization of readings in cafes, followed by the diverse movements of the 1960s – those of the younger generation, the underground press and rock culture, ethnic and sexual minorities and their cultural organizations.

The renewed favor enjoyed by poetry took different forms, depending on the literary past and the spaces available to be transformed or revived. New York and San Francisco had dominated the American poetry landscape and continued to do so, because they both had longstanding literary, intellectual and bohemian traditions. Furthermore, it was in these two cities that the Beats flourished, and that the movements of the 1960s found a receptiveness to radicalism and political militancy particularly favorable to their flowering. The two cities each had organizations that were dedicated to poetry. In New York, the Poetry Center of the 92nd Street Y offered readings by the most well-known writers as well as writing workshops. Poets & Writers, Inc., thanks to federal and state subsidies, financed readings and workshops in New York State and consolidated information concerning poetry by publishing *Poets & Writers Magazine* six times a year, among other things. The Poetry Project at St. Mark's Church-in-the-Bowery presented readings, workshops and conferences. In San Francisco, the Poetry Center, located in the buildings of San Francisco State College, combined various functions. It was a source of information for the city and the state, it hosted other organizations, such as California Poets; and it maintained an audiovisual archive. It also provided space for workshops, conferences and public readings in partnership with the university's creative writing programs. City Lights Bookstore, the home of Beat poet Lawrence Ferlinghetti's press had played a role in bringing San Francisco Bay Area poets together, as did KPFA, an alternative radio station in Berkeley. Thanks in large part to a policy of generous and well-thought-out municipal and state subsidization in the two cities,[8] various venues and organizations not only managed to survive, but to multiply, stimulating diversity and vitality in the local poetic scene.

In this respect it is significant that San Francisco and New York were among the first to print a monthly bulletin containing programs of the public readings in their area as well as other information and articles on poetry–in New York the *NYC Calendar* and in San Francisco *Poetry Flash*–signs that the volume and intensity of poetic activity had created the need for an organized regional network. Soon, other big cities saw the creation and enlargement of local poetry centers, the multiplication of poetry venues and activities, and the publication of monthly newsletters. Starting in the 1970s, these newsletters gathered and shared information about public readings–the true heart of the emerging poetry networks that encompassed both universities and independent organizations: "There are so many readings in Boston and New York, San Francisco and Los Angeles, Cleveland, Washington, and Detroit that it is difficult for the consumer to keep track of them" (Hall 1984/85, 67–8).[9]

It should be noted that independent poetry outside these educational institutions remained at a disadvantage, receiving the smallest share of both honors and funding (Lazer 1990, 64–72). The disparity was still greater with minority poets, whose organizations depended on public funds that were even more variable and therefore more vulnerable. Less well-off and often falling victim to reactionary forces, these minority poets also had living conditions which had continuously deteriorated since the 1970s, with the result that their communities had been cut off from the local poetic circuit in places like Los Angeles. Although the poetry community, in Southern California for example, was becoming more and more "multicultural," very few poetry activities were actually taking place in "ethnic" neighborhoods themselves after the fading away of the Black Arts Movement and Chicano activism.

CHAPTER TWO

The Venice West Beats

Venice Poems

the city itself, what it
is, a
city of walking at nite
city of old & ugly houses
city of real pain & real children
city of open sores & open eyes
city of doom & terror
city of ocean & animal lust
city of dying & stru[gg]le
city of Venice, my city, city within a city I do not know or love
 ...
what a city is/

           a vision, a

holy eye, a

           structure

what a city is/

           a face, a face of
           love, of the place, the real
            place ...
            yes, there is a kind of
            knowing, it can be called
            love

—STUART PERKOFF

Hostility towards culture and towards public and private support for it were particularly staunch in Los Angeles, a city imbued with the utilitarian sensibilities of Midwestern migrants, who were a vast majority until the 1960s. Moreover, in the ultra-conformist and repressive climate of the 1950s, art that might represent contemporary reality and deviate ideologically and aesthetically from the "official" viewpoint that celebrated materialism was predictably doomed to marginality. Despite the success of some modernist architects, "[o]n the whole...the younger generation interested in new forms and practices was driven towards bohemia," Mike Davis wrote (Davis 1990, 63). Bebop musicians, abstract or politically active painters, independent filmmakers and Beat poets in the 1950s,[10] as well as "minority" and/or underground artists in the 1960s, formed temporary alliances with their peers, connected by the solidarity of exclusion and shared experience. Their shared interest in "critically reworking and re-presenting subcultural experience...made them the first truly 'autobiographical' intelligentsia in Los Angeles history" (Davis 1990, 64).

The later Los Angeles poetry scene is directly descended the "communes" of the 1950s and '60s – particularly the Beat poets – who laid the groundwork for a dissenting tradition in Los Angeles.

Venice, California

Venice, a small coastal community, had been an independent city before being absorbed by the City of Los Angeles in the mid-1920s. It was the gathering place of an eclectic bohemia considered as the local Beat movement in the late 1950s. Often designated as Venice West, they were united by a rejection of a society of growing affluence, and the search for another way of life through art and brotherhood, rather than by a shared aesthetic tradition. The local Beats found in the dilapidated Venice neighborhood a place where they could put their ideas into practice and be detached from the indifferent outside world. In what Davis called "the supreme incarnation of the Mediterranean metaphor" (ibid., 28) envisioned by the first "Boosters," Venice of America, as it was originally called, was the fruit of the romantic imagination of Abbot Kinney. He was an enlightened turn-of-the-century millionaire who had the idea of reproducing the ultimate symbol of European refinement in Los Angeles. In 1905 he used his entire fortune to build a copy near Los Angeles, where previously there had been nothing but dunes and marshes. Sixteen miles of canals were dredged, weeping willows and gum trees were planted, and Italianate villas were built. Gondolas and singing gondoliers were brought from the old Venice, as were pigeons, whose descendants still begged popcorn near the dismantled pier a half-century later. The architecture of Windward Avenue, was intended to conform to that of St. Mark's Square. There was even a St. Mark's Hotel (Walker 1976, 237).

Like other visionary promoters of the period, Kinney believed he could create the regional intellectual center that Southern California lacked, by offering a blend of art and science, of Orient and Occident, in a sumptuous setting likely to attract people of taste.

> The art galleries included an Oriental building with a permanent Japanese display sponsored by the local Nisei; the aquarium was designed as a laboratory for studying Pacific marine life; the pier with its ship cafe was one of the best on the Coast, with a concert pavilion at its ocean end.... A Chautauqua was inaugurated, bringing men of letters and scientists and musicians (ibid., 237–8).

Kinney thought that he could foster what he called "creative reproduction" by allowing people of quality to multiply and thus improve the race in the healthy climate of Southern California, an unfortunate center of early twentieth century American eugenics. But upon his death the holiday city was almost abandoned. In order to reduce the costs of municipal services and assure a water supply, the city's inhabitants voted in the mid-1920s for its annexation to the City of Los Angeles. A good number of its canals were filled in; the Italianate façades gradually deteriorated, and, following the discovery of oil, derricks sprang up, juxtaposing their futuristic vertical silhouettes with the pseudo-Renaissance architecture. By the 1950s, Venice was a neighborhood with little to recommend it. It wasn't just, as Raymond Chandler labelled it a decade earlier, "a slum by the sea." Its exceptional facilities, architecture and location near the beach, offered a unique backdrop for its odd population of small businessmen, artisans, petty crooks, actors, students and the unemployed.

The place had a keen sense of its difference, symbolized by the Venetians' predilection for walking and bicycling as modes of transport, activities rarely seen in much of the rest of the megalopolis. Unlike most other neighborhoods, Venice forged an identity based on its history, which its inhabitants devoted themselves to preserving. Ironically, the cultural mecca dreamt of by Kinney would indeed see the light of day, albeit some fifty years later, and bohemian, rather than bourgeois. It had all the conditions needed to attract artists and ensure a creative, collective dynamic: modest rents, isolation, an ideal climate, a strong identity, a taste for eccentricity, and a heterogeneous population. Robert Kirsch wrote in the *Los Angeles Times*: "[The pattern] of renaissances [is well known]: to find a decaying place, with rents poor painters and poets could afford, a place with some beauty, some connection to nature, to invite the new and encourage the experimental" (Kirsch 1977, 4).

What came to be known as the third American Beat community, was, in reality, composed of a few dozen often penniless people who had been attracted to Venice at different times throughout the 1950s. They included the writers and poets Lawrence Lipton, Stuart Perkoff, Alexander Trocchi and Charlie Foster; painters like Tony Scibella (who was also a poet), John Altoon, Ben Talbert and Mike Angeleno; the folk singer Julie Meredith, impresario Jimmy Alonzi, sculptor Tati, and boxer Joe Greb, as well as various wives and girlfriends who hovered around them in this rather masculine world.[11] It was not an artists' colony in the traditional sense because most of them were artists simply because their friends were, or because they believed in creativity. For the most part they were not "professional" artists.

Counterculture Values
for a Generation Affected by War

A number of these artists were World War II or Korean War veterans who had become disenchanted with war, democracy and the anti-communist crusade. They belonged to the generation that had directly experienced the trauma of the atomic bomb and the crisis of conscience engendered by its possible use. As Tony Scibella put it:

> People would leave their families and move to the beach, in the back of their cars. The spirit. People worry about the bomb and all that but they don't know about the bomb in the '50s as far as fear goes. We had just gone through two wars. Now here is this other hostility, the bomb, and it got to be everything was so straight. Anything outside of that was lunacy (Scibella 1987, 18).

Like other rebellious young whites—as described in Norman Mailer's in 1957 essay "The White Negro: Superficial Reflections on the Hipster"—they identified with African American bebop music, embodied by Charlie Parker, whom they set up as the symbol of their own alienation. LeRoi Jones tells us in *Blues People* that in the 1940s certain whites began to imitate African American cultural codes (wearing "zoot suits" or using "bop talk" or "hip talk") to set themselves apart from their fellow citizens and to assert their opposition to mainstream American society. In the 1940s, this imitation remained somewhat superficial and one-way. But in the 1950s young blacks and whites came together socially and artistically. Analogous tendencies toward alienation in both American "high art"[12] and Bebop, which combined characteristics of African American music and what LeRoi Jones called "the canons of formal Western nonconformity" (Jones 1963, 201), furthered this sense of identification. In this way a "lateral synthesis," as it is called by Jones, between white and black American subcultures came to define a common form of non-conformity (the major difference lying in the fact that it was chosen freely by whites, whereas it was imposed on blacks). As Jones wrote:

> It was a lateral and reciprocal identification the young white American intellectual, artist, and Bohemian of the forties and fifties made with the Negro, attempting...to reap some emotional benefit from the similarity of their positions in American society.... But the reciprocity of this relationship became actively decisive during the fifties when scores of young Negroes and, of course, young Negro musicians began to address themselves to the formal canons of Western nonconformity, as formally understood refusals of the hollowness of American life (ibid., 231–3).[13]

FOLLOWING IN THE FOOTSTEPS of other bohemians, the Venice Beats drew inspiration from the bebop musicians' way of life in fashioning their own world. They borrowed the mythology of the damned artist, the hip language and the drug use, and sought to apply the principles of improvisation to their poetry.

These young white artists chose to live in what Lawrence Lipton termed a "voluntary poverty" (Lipton 1959, 151). Most of the Venice Beats benefited from the GI Bill of Rights (federal programs to provide funds for college educations, home-buying loans, and other benefits for World War II armed services veterans),[14] and they were content to live on little money, supplementing their income with temporary odd jobs. They opposed the "Protestant ethic," which finds in material wealth a sign of divine favor and in poverty a sin. They demonstrated that one could retire from "the rat race," in order to live a fulfilling life with their peers. Their communal spirit was all-embracing. Everything was shared – in a way of life they considered to be true communism, as Tony Scibella is quoted as saying:

> This was truly the spirit of communism, a communistic society. Everyone's pad was your own. You went from pad to pad. You pay your rent, you had a whole house for $36. Right there, like right here in Venice! (Scibella 1987, 20)

Success for the Venice Beats was self- and world exploration through art. They wanted to recover art's existential and sacred value, and to rediscover through it the deepest sources of human nature. Their artistic practice was polyvalent and exuberant, without respect for the conventional divisions between artistic disciplines or genres. They cultivated spontaneity in a libertarian spirit close to that of "assemblage."

Called "the first home-grown California modern art" by Peter Plagens, assemblage is the art of recycling, using materials that are "the cast-off, broken, charred, weathered, water-damaged, lost, forgotten, fragmentary remains of everyday life." Assemblage is created when the artist takes as a departure point not the history of an art form, but the scraps of consumer society, and fuses them, as for instance in Sabato Rodia's spontaneous proto-assemblage, the Watts Towers; Edward Kienholz's room-size assemblages of the 1950s and '60s; or Noah Purifoy's artworks made from the debris of the Watts riots. In Peter Plagens' words:

> Assemblage, in the end, is non-Duchampian anti-art; that is, it does not deal intellectually with what is or is not art, or with deliberate subversion of the bourgeoise [sic] production-distribution system of salable art objects. [It is] created with whatever means the artist has at hand in an urban world of consumer goods, trash, violence and poetry (Plagens 1974, 87).

The Venice Beats considered themselves in the Dada tradition, and saw themselves as its continuers. Abstract expressionism had seemed a true revelation at the time, and it became one of the Beats' major sources of inspiration and creative fervor. In this way they made use of all the liberating possibilities of the modernist aesthetic revolutions. In America, this revolution had been led in painting by Jackson Pollock and his practice of dripping, where the body and the material, more than the intellect, are the agents of the work, and where chance and movement stand in for premeditated composition. In music it was bebop's use of improvisation in the 1940s. The Beats interpreted these advances in modern art as an invitation to creative license, excusing them from the obligation of a scholarly apprenticeship. Liberation from formal constraints opened up the field of possibilities. Again, Tony Scibella describes the scene:

> The whole thing of doing a performance in a cafe, all that seems connected in the current literary scheme of things, the big thing is on, multiplicity, bringing many things together, the whole idea of collage itself is a symbol of so many things. Straight from dada. If you don't isolate dada, it's just the outpouring that comes with any kind of thing, action whatever you want to call the fifties. Dada is like all the stuff that spills over. The little collages, everybody, that's right, everybody did everything because there were no limits. It was all new. This whole feeling.... Anything is possible, because it didn't–you look at Rembrandt and you go I'd have to go to school for 35 years before I could ever draw this good. But Pollock, I got a lot of paint. Pollock started it (Scibella 1987, 27–8).

At the Heart of the Creative Process, Poetry

The Venice Beats applied this liberating approach to their poetry, but in their case it was liberation *from* the modernist aesthetic. The young poets of the post-war period had been shaped in universities by the second generation of modernist writers and critics. But they rebelled against their professors' conception of the well-written, impersonal poem, the value of which was its learned allusions and masterful versification. As we noted in Chapter 1, this rebellion resulted in a lasting schism in American poetry: on the one side, carefully crafted academic poetry preoccupied with aesthetics; and, on the other, those who, outside the university, wrote a more accessible and personal poetry. "Professor," by Michael C. Ford (one of the rare poets to bridge the gap between the Venice Beats and the later Los Angeles poetry scene), illustrates this long-standing split:

The college trained poet
conducting the poetry workshop says:
Since the heart is a pump,
a biological muscle,
your heart cannot be filled with love,
or pain,
or anything emotional.
The heart can't be full of anything
but blood.
Otherwise,
never use the word heart
in a poem.
Outside of its
clinical context of course.

All right! But
Let's pretend that
if the word heart
written on your income tax return
could be shredded into scattered heart-shaped shavings

Well then, heart
turns out to be stronger
than the commands coming from computerized

English department cowards
who are trying to put the bullet of compromise
through my heart.

Heart
is a rock you can hurl through a jewelry storefront window in
Paris.
Heart
is an egg you can crack open over Cairo.
Heart
is a bloody history of all our broken hearts
rushed at the ground in Nicaragua.
Heart
is ashes
you can sweep away
from raging, incomprehensible bonfires
in Johannesburg
under the skull-head of Africa.

I'd say it all
but I just haven't got the
heart
to tell you.

Ford rejects the repressive attitudes of the poet-professor who
frowns upon any emotional immediacy in poetic writing. He
pursues the metaphor of the heart throughout the poem to show
its human dimension and political resonance. He denounces the
conservative scholar who sees, where a tragedy is being played
out, nothing but a functional biological organ.

Similarly, Scibella records his personal experience of the break
with "university" or "professor" poetry:

As far as influences go, when I got to the beach ('53–'54), I
probably had read maybe two poems outside of school, high
school.... But on my own, I just had never read poetry. So,

on the other hand, Stuart [Perkoff] read everything. So in a way, I never really went back. I haven't read the classics.... Stuart would read stuff, like Emily Dickinson, like Poe, the people that influenced him, Patchen.... *Black Mountain Review* was out during that period.... The difference would be Patchen's passion with Creeley slang, Olson's punctuation and abbreviating and it kind of was, at the time if you don't have any background, then you are free to do anything (Scibella 1987, 1–2).

Unlike many of the poets of the San Francisco Renaissance, many Venice Beats had little formal education (and often none in the realm of arts and letters) or were self-educated, and they often possessed no knowledge of poetry except that imparted by some of their more educated peers. They interpreted the libertarian aesthetic of their contemporaries as an authorization for anyone–savant and neophyte alike–to create, without being inhibited by the fact that this new-found freedom was the result of a long historical cultural development.

The Venice Beats, like other Southern California artists, were disengaged from the history of art, according to Peter Plagens. Los Angeles lacked cultural institutions during this period, and those that did exist were indifferent to local artists. Additionally, the near-absence of any established culture excluded Los Angeles artists from modernism. Isolated, and confronted with an overwhelming mass culture and a rich Southern California popular culture, Los Angeles artists had difficulty adopting the classical roles of the artist–intellectuals, guardians of culture, prophets, rebels or iconoclasts; the "artist's role in Los Angeles is schizophrenic because it is constantly measured, not against ingrained 'fine art' tradition, but against the most salient facets of California culture: pop architecture and music, movies, and the garment industry" (Plagens 1974, 30). The Venice Beats exploited the potential of art with enthusiasm and innocence, without feeling obligated to possess all of its aesthetic historical traditions.

ALTHOUGH A GREAT NUMBER of Venice artists had little affinity for poetry in the beginning, poetry became a part of their artistic practice under the joint influence Venice West's most remarkable figures: Lawrence Lipton (1898–75) and Stuart Perkoff (1930–74).

Lawrence Lipton was the author of successful detective stories, radio and film scripts, and two little-known novels.[15] He was driven by a somewhat precarious financial situation to move to Venice in the late 1940s. Determined to dedicate himself entirely to "serious" literature, he set about writing a long prose poem, *Rainbow at Midnight*, which he then promoted. One of the small locally established literary magazines, *California Quarterly*, agreed to publish a long excerpt in 1953, and it was published as a whole in 1955. A veteran of radical literary and political movements in New York, Detroit and Chicago, he soon spotted the eclectic group of rebellious young people in Venice (Maynard 1991, 47–8).

Lipton got to know them, and he soon transformed his home into a salon for the discussion of poetry and literature. And he recorded these evenings. Having watched more than one bohemia come and go in his lifetime, he put his erudition at the service of his guests so they would feel that they were taking part in a venerable tradition, of which they were, he taught them, the modern heirs. He wanted a unified bohemia, of which he would be the patriarch and interpreter, explaining to the others their links with earlier bohemias and international avant-garde groups. Lipton found a way to recapture his own rebellious youth and confirm the ideas he had developed about commercialism, money, the role of art, and the revolutionary potential of youth–all ideas which he saw these (voluntarily) marginalized youths spontaneously embody in their lives.

Stuart Perkoff figured prominently among Lipton's guests. Philomene Long described him as the "voice and fire of Venice," and "inhabited by the Muse with a very shabby appearance, with a very large, what you would call a Moses complex" (interview with the author). Perkoff was from St. Louis, where he spent his youth dawdling around in the city, drinking, talking revolution and writing poems. He then followed his calling as a poet in New York, where in addition to writing poetry he spent time combing through library shelves. After a short stay in prison in 1948 for draft-dodging, several moves back and forth between the East and West Coasts, his marriage, and the birth of his first child, he settled in Venice in the early 1950s, less by choice than for economic reasons. He and his wife joined the local bohemia, adopting its way of life, and soon numbering among its principal characters. Following the 1956 publication of his first collection of poems, *The Suicide Room*, Perkoff resolved to take his art and its demands more seriously. This turning point is detailed in a journal excerpt from 1956:

> Now I see that the art & craft of poetry takes much more knowledge, discipline, time to become proficient at than I wd ever have suspected. Perhaps I never saw this before because I was incapable up till now of conceiving of myself, except in a kind of horror, as a way of torturing myself, as unformed. Now it is an excitement to me, the things I have to learn, looking at them. & every day now I learn more (& more consciously) about my craft (quoted in Maynard 1991, 67).

Perkoff's insistence on the long, rigorous and difficult aspect of apprenticeship–the necessary path for the acquisition of a "craft"–gives the twice-repeated term "learn" an initiatory, almost sacred meaning. For him, poetry was a gift and a mark of privilege, and it bestowed responsibilities and duties. Ignoring or betraying them could lead a poet to lose the powers. His poems were the fruits of daily writing and eclectic reading, that ranged from ancient and contemporary poetry to great religious (particularly Jewish) and esoteric texts, as well as anthropology, politics, history, mythology and psychoanalysis. He "knows all forms and sources that a poet living and trying to feed himself today may know," remarked fellow Beat poet William J. Margolis in an account he gave of a public reading (Margolis 1974, 2).

Tony Scibella, one of Perkoff's closest friends, marveled at Perkoff's versatility. "Look at that [poem], the little abbreviations, the slashes, the punctuation, it was that you were free to use anything. Some of Stuart's work is really classical, long line stanzas, rhymes, he did everything.... But the best ones were the ones where there was not even a change, no editing, correcting. Just free blown and it all comes out and its [*sic*] from journal writing" (Scibella 1987, 2).

For Perkoff, poetry, while integrating certain knowledge, had first to emanate from the intimate "me" and reveal its profound truths in simple and direct language. The raw material of life could be transmuted into vision and song by the grace of the Muse, who opened the "the doors of the bedrooms, & of the eye" (quoted in Margolis 1974, 1). He never failed to address a reverent invocation to his Muse in his poetry readings, books and personal journals. He was an outstanding performer, with a powerful and moving voice. In his eyes the poet's mission was to revive the oral tradition from which the art had grown. The poet needed to draw his principle inspiration from music, or more precisely, from the bebop improviser, as we see in the following excerpt from "Round About Midnite: A Poem for Sounding":

HIPSTERS
dig
this poet
sits at a piano
clanging fingers against each other
bonkdblonk bonkbonk

DEALER
is he hip?
does he swing?

HIPSTERS
he's been around before
at sessions up & down the street

always listening
always trying to dig

POET
dreams I've got
who'll lay some fingers
on my hand

HIPSTERS
the sound is the thing, man

This poem illustrates a facet of Perkoff's style that is directly inspired by jazz. The rapid cadence, resulting from the use of monosyllables, evokes the swing of jazz and the speech of the jazzman. And like the jazzman, the poet is a musician, a maker of sounds. His instruments are his words, his solos, his poems. Recited aloud, they must render his vision palpable to the audience—the third party indispensable for the restoration of poetry's ritual and sacred dimension.

sitting on the benches, bodies warm & throats filled

with
joy & love

we offered worship
sitting warm, eyes & skin touching, love flowing
we offered worship

we sang
& spoke languages & poems
offered worship & love
mixing the birds of passion & the swords of God
in our beautiful young eyes

This excerpt from "Feasts of Love, Feasts of Death" shows another, more lyrical and incantatory vein of his poetry, with its partial repetitions, sometimes regular and sometimes irregular meter, assonance, alliteration, a blend of unusual and banal expressions, and a religious vocabulary. He was a self-proclaimed follower of Blake, Villon, Dylan Thomas and Charles Olson, and like them he wanted to reaffirm the superiority of the poetic imagination and the power of creative energy through a poetry of intense and inspired lyricism.

waw

that which sees: the eye
that which is seen: the lite

that which hears: the ear
that which is heard: the wind, speaking

that which hungers: the need
that which tastes: the need

all are balanced on this precise
point, where eye & lite combine
to banish darkness
ear interlocks with the songs of the air
hungers feed

from darkness
              revelation
from silence
              revelation
from hunger
              revelation

its arithmetical number is 6

This excerpt, from the collection *Alphabet* (1973), in which each poem is a meditation on a letter of the Hebrew alphabet, shows Perkoff's ascetic austerity. The poet's meditation leads to the revelation of metaphysical truths. In a state of absolute receptivity, he is one with his sensory organs. The truths revealed take the form of timeless and incontestable facts, reduced to their simplest expression. The dynamics are generated by metrical and syntactic gaps that interrupt the regularity. Through repeated echoes and disruptions the entire poem is oriented to the last cryptic line, which goes back to the title of the poem, the Hebrew letter *waw*, which corresponds to the sixth character of the alphabet ("its arithmetical number is 6"). The text progresses toward its resolution in four movements. The immobility of the first three couplets in the first movement is followed by five lines that recapitulate the preceding elements in order to fuse them into a point of suspended equilibrium. This is followed by the introduction of a new element in its center, "darkness," which announces and initiates the flight of the third movement. These three indented lines bring the poem to its culmination with their incantatory sound before returning to the occult immutability of the last line, the key to an enigma. Beyond this balance of immobility and motion we see the polyvalence of words. This fading of the boundaries between body, soul and universe represents Perkoff's poetic experience: a mystical communion that enables the ascension to completion, bliss, unity and participation in man's age-old spiritual quest, in an almost religious manner.

In Perkoff, Lipton found something to bolster his own ideas about the poet's role as the shaman of modern society and the need to return to an oral, worshipful poetry—ideas that Lipton himself had set forth in *Rainbow at Midnight*. Perkoff listened to Lipton attentively, impressed by the extent of his knowledge, sometimes working entire days to integrate the fruits of their discussions into his poetry. In Perkoff, Lipton saw the qualities of a spiritual guide, thanks to his intensity, his demand for purity and his magnetism. And Perkoff had a decisive influence on a number of his friends as well.

Venice West: The Construction and Promotion of a Symbolic Community

Many a Venice West landlord has walked into an apartment just vacated by some beatnik...to find all the walls and sometimes even the floors and doors covered with abstract murals.... Everybody is always drawing everybody else, at readings and at parties, and everybody is writing a book.... None but a fraction of this artistic activity will ever see completion, let alone exhibition or publication, but it will have served its purpose just the same. It is simply a part of "making the scene."... The creative process is not an assault upon the materials of the art, a conquest, but an unfolding, a growth from within, as a tree grows (Lipton 1959, 255).

Like the other Beats, the Venice West poets were in favor of spontaneity and interested in process rather than the finished product. They resisted to the lure of worldly success, so esteemed by the market society from which they wished to distance themselves. They sought instead to express the self and to share a fleeting moment with an audience of friends. Furthermore, unlike their San Francisco or New York counterparts who were published, the Venice Beat poets did not benefit from a network of influential contacts. They therefore published very little, so little in fact that they reportedly described their endeavors as "the greatest drive for nonrecognition in the history of literature" (Maynard 1991, 2).

The exception to this was Lipton himself. "At his best, [he] was a very considerable poet," wrote *Los Angeles Times* critic Robert Kirsch, but, he added, "his talents [were] perhaps hindered rather than helped by his desire, his irresistible impulse, to be publicist, promoter, impresario in the cultural circus of Southern California." He continued: "Venice West was Lipton's last stand. He wanted to make it a center, fertile and creative, another Left Bank, another Bloomsbury, brought up to date, filled with excitement, ready to burst through" (Kirsch 1977, 11).[16]

To this end, Lipton sought out and succeeded in gaining the acceptance of the small circle of established Los Angeles poets, united around the literary magazines *Trace* (1952–70), *California Quarterly* (1951–56), and then *Coastlines* (1955–70) after *California Quarterly* ceased to be published. *Trace* editor James Boyer May put him in touch with other magazines and poets, including INTRO, which requested from Lipton and May an inventory of West Coast resources for the arts.

Lipton's response appeared in 1953 under the title *Secession: 1953 (The State of the Arts on the West Coast)*.[17] Relatively classical diatribe against the destructive effects of success and money on the creative faculties of writers and artists working for the film industry. What was new was his recommendation on how to escape. According to Lipton, the only solution was to reject the system entirely–to refuse to participate in any of it by living "a dedicated poverty." His article attracted a lot of attention, notably that of his old friend Kenneth Rexroth, one of the most influential figures in the entire San Francisco scene. From then on, the two men enjoyed a sustained correspondence, especially on Lipton's part.

UNDER REXROTH'S GUIDANCE, Lipton sought a new word to replace "alienation," which he found too hackneyed. He chose "disaffiliation," a term that leading unionist John L. Lewis had used.[18] In "Disaffiliation and the Art of Poverty," published in *Chicago Review* in the spring of 1956, as well as in numerous subsequent articles,[19] Lipton pursued his theorization of the new dissent. But Rexroth watched this with growing skepticism–particularly the amalgam he made of art, poverty and integrity–and in 1956 published his own article, "Disengagement: the Art of the Beat Generation." He spent at least a year preparing this text, without ever saying a word about it to Lipton. In it, he described the San Francisco Beats, but didn't specifically mention Venice. This marked a turning point for Lipton and the Venice Beat scene. Irritated at having been given the cold shoulder, Lipton started to think of Rexroth as a rival. In opposition to the San Francisco scene, Lipton would create his own Southern California Beat empire. In 1956 he wrote – but never mailed – a reproachful letter to Rexroth:

Is Big Sur the southern frontier beyond which lie the lands of the Barbarians? Evidently I can't belong by mail order. But I'm willing to negotiate before I set myself up as the anti-pope in these parts (quoted in Maynard 1991, 57).

It bears obvious witness to his bitterness and determination to create a competing artistic movement.

When Ginsberg, accompanied by Gregory Corso, made plans to pass through Los Angeles during the summer of 1956, Lipton organized a public reading in which "Howl" would be included. He wanted to make this event the Los Angeles counterpart of San Francisco's Six Gallery Reading. In her diary, Anaïs Nin mentions this memorable evening, when Ginsberg created a scandal by undressing after an altercation with a member of the audience, and finished his reading of "Howl" in the nude (Nin 1976, 64–5). In December 1957, following Rexroth's lead – he had organized wildly popular recitals in San Francisco that blended jazz and poetry – Lipton launched his own "First West Coast Poetry and Jazz Festival"[20] in Los Angeles (to which Rexroth was invited). He christened this mélange "jazz canto," hoping that this neologism would help him to make his mark on the new lyric form which, despite its imperfect debuts, he thought promised a beautiful future:

Poetry and jazz – or Jazz Canto, as I prefer to call it – will not be a viable art form until it solves its problems and becomes a part of the standard repertoire of public performance.... When poets learn more about music and musicians learn more about poetry it will be easier to make progress with this new idiom (Lipton 1959, 224–5).

While San Francisco's original Beat movement had already fragmented somewhat, the Beatnik became fashionable in

Hollywood and other areas of Southern California (cf. the goatee'd beatnik character Maynard G. Krebs in the the American network televison program *The Many Loves of Dobie Gillis,* which ran from 1959–63).

Lipton chose this moment to write and publish *The Holy Barbarians* in an attempt to gain fame for the Venice West bohemia – as well as for himself – equal to that of San Francisco or New York. From the hours of conversations he had tape-recorded over the course of his long evenings with the young Venetians, he attempted to create a profile of the small community. The book was a series of stereotyped portraits illustrating the various facets of Venice West, connected by philosophical explanations. A glossary of Beat vocabulary and a photo album rounded out the work. Beatnik characters had by then invaded television series, comic strips, film and radio, and long articles on the movement had appeared in national magazines such as *Time, Life, Look,* and *Newsweek;* so *The Holy Barbarians* was an immediate success when it was published in 1959. Lipton's manual in hand, tourists and young aspiring Beats flocked to Venice in search of the places and the characters cited in the book.

Lipton described a life based on art and the rejection of mercantile society. He elaborated on what he meant by disaffiliation in his earlier essays:

Disaffiliation is a voluntary self-alienation from the family cult, from Moneytheism and all its works and ways....

Why, then, disaffiliation in an era when *Time-Life-Fortune* pages are documenting an American Way of Life that is filled with color-matched stainless steel kitchens, bigger and faster cars, electronic wonders.... Because it is all being corrupted by the cult of Moneytheism.... Because underneath Henry Luce's "permanent revolution" – the New Capitalism, the People's Capitalism and Prosperity Unlimited – lies the ugly fact of an economy geared to war production, a design, not for living, but for death....

> The New Poverty is the disaffiliate's answer to the New
> Prosperity.
>
> It is important to make a living, but it is even more important
> to make a life.
>
> Poverty. The very word is taboo in a society where success is
> equated with virtue and poverty is a sin....
>
> The poverty of the disaffiliate is not to be confused with the
> poverty of indigence, intemperance [sic], improvidence or
> failure. It is simply that the goods and services he has to offer
> are not valued at a high price in our society....
>
> It is an independent, voluntary poverty.
>
> It is an art, and like all arts it has to be learned (Lipton 1959,
> 149–51).

This "voluntary poverty" was the best way to express rejection
of American society: it corresponded to the dissidents' delib-
erate violation of the "Protestant work ethic." Choosing poverty
was a blasphemous gesture in a nation dominated by this ethic.
"Voluntary poverty" was a way publicly to affirm one's disaf-
filiation. Lipton anticipated the views of Herbert Marcuse, who
placed the aesthetic dimension at the heart of liberation.

The book begins: "When the barbarians appear on the frontiers
of a civilization it is a sign of a crisis in that civilization." Lipton
develops his definition of the barbarians by comparing them
to what they are not. The holy barbarians resemble neither the
early twentieth century "expatriates in flight from New England
gentility and bluenose censorship," nor "the anti-Babbitt caper of
the twenties. Nor the politically-oriented alienation of the thir-
ties." The Beats made a real qualitative leap forward in rebellion,
truly distinguishing themselves from the others: "The alienation
of the hipsters from the squares is now complete."

As for Venice more particularly:

> I have chosen Venice, California, as the scene, the laboratory
> as it were, because I live here and have seen it grow up around
> me. Newer than the North Beach, San Francisco, scene or the

Greenwich Village scene, it has afforded me an opportunity to watch the formation of a community of disaffiliates from its inception. Seeing it take form I had a feeling of "this is where I came in," that I had seen it all happening before. But studying it closely, from the inside, and with a sympathy born of a kindred experience, I have come to the conclusion that this is not just another alienation. It is a deep-going change, a revolution under the ribs. These people are picking up where we – left off? – no, where we began. Began and lived it and wrote about it and waited for the world to catch up with us. I am telling their story here because it is *our* story, too. My story (Lipton, 1959, "Preface").

This undertaking is valid because he had seen and participated in the beginning of this new "community of disaffiliates" equal to the established bohemias of San Francisco and New York. Despite the apparent modesty of his project ("to tell a story") and of his motivations ("because I live here"), Lipton actually sought to launch a movement, following what he perceived as Rexroth's example in San Francisco's North Beach. He failed, however, in his first goal, which was to obtain literary and historic recognition for Southern California, for Venice West, and for himself.

Positioning in Relation to the City

Lipton's book also lets us analyze the position of poets with respect to the city. From this perspective, *The Holy Barbarians* is one of the first rare attempts by a bohemian artist in Los Angeles to construct a cultural identity based on place: Venice West. For the 1930s bohemia that congregated around the bookseller Jake Zeitlin, Los Angeles had been only a chance gathering place. In Zeitlin's eyes, this group incarnated a Los Angeles "renaissance," less a movement than kindred spirits united by circumstance:

Bohemianism thrives on adversity. It's not a movement but a consequence of certain conditions. You have to have a concentration of people practicing their arts, people with superior endowments who don't necessarily fit into society, and who are, in fact, often engaged in rebellions against convention, creating a symbiotic society where not only can they go and eat at each other's house when they're hungry, but where they can also spark each other and be each other's critical audiences (quoted in Rolfe 1991, 51).

The same was true of the Venice West Beats during the 1950s. But, by contrast, Lipton presents Venice as a romantic refuge, where those who felt compelled to flee from society's absurd and brutal demands, could come to be rejuvenated and reborn through their contact with the purity, creativity and tolerance that he found there:

Venice, USA Venice West, a horizontal, jerry-built slum by the sea, warm under a semitropical Pacific sun on a Sunday afternoon.... The regular weekend invasion has begun: all the impatient young-men-in-a-hurry, the lost, the seekers, the beat, the disaffiliated, the educated, diseducated, re-educated, in quest of a new vision; ...young girls in flight from unendurable homes in other, fancier, parts of town...; Hollywood writers dropping in to refresh their souls, hoping, perhaps, that some of the creative energy of dedicated artists will somehow rub off a little on them...; newsmen and radio people on the prowl for "experience," or just plain hungry for a taste of intellectual honesty and artistic integrity; ...and always the parade of weekday office and factory workers, Sunday refugees from the rat race, panting for a little music and poetry in their lives.... And the poets...and the painters...and the camp followers of the Muse freeloading and tailchasing on the lower slopes of Parnassus.... The clowns, the make-believers, the self-deceivers – and the mad. The talented mad (Lipton 1959, 17–8).

Lipton expressed his territorial ambitions for Venice West during a 1957 radio debate with Rexroth. Rexroth called San Francisco "a very free and easy city and very hospitable to the artist. Always has been," and Lipton responded that San Francisco's North Beach was nothing more than a "warmed-over, left-over Greenwich Village." He argued that only isolated, unknown and solitary artists – like the Venice artists – were open enough to novelty for an authentic artistic movement to be born among them.

> Only artists are hospitable to new art, and to one another. In Venice, in Los Angeles – "Venice West," *we* call it – such a community of poets and artists is working....Venice West is to Los Angeles what the Left Bank once was to Paris (quoted in Maynard 1991, 78).

For all this, one senses that his "we" was exclusive, for Lipton was the most fervent adherent of his own concept of Venice West, and most Venetians themselves were far from going along with this "territorial militancy."

ANOTHER GROUP OF LOS ANGELES POETS – those around the magazine *Coastlines*[21] – had a very different conception of the city. Unlike Lipton, the *Coastlines* editors did not believe in a Los Angeles movement at all and they barely believed in a West Coast (or Beat) one. In any case, if indeed a West Coast movement existed, in their view it had been born in San Francisco, their "big, loud brother up north," and it was San Francisco that ruled uncontested over the literary activity of California, to which their "own small [Los Angeles] community" (Frumkin, 1957–58, 48) contributed only very modestly. For those around *Coastlines,* whose objective was to promote local literary life, nothing distinguished Los Angeles especially. Only the fact of residing in the area connected these writers to Los Angeles, an attitude that recalls that of Jake Zeitlin's group. As a megalopolis with no well-defined limits or personality, Los Angeles inspired no particular loyalty, passion or poetry. In a word, Los Angeles was nonexistent, Lachlan MacDonald argued in "Poetry of the Non-Existent City." This long *Coastlines* article attempted to characterize Los Angeles poetry based on two collections of local poetry. In his eyes, Los Angeles poets were first and foremost isolated and varied individuals who could not be grouped under a single all-encompassing label:

> The selections [from a series of readings called "Poetry Los Angeles," made into a book (May, McGrath and Yates)] may be called *Poetry Los Angeles* chiefly through the fact that the writers are resident in this area and so were available for the readings. As one of the rare cultural meetings that might be expected to provide an image of Los Angeles the readings have been particularly free of any attempt to force this image into existence. The downtown ghost for tourists through which residents pass fleetingly on the freeways provides no actual community center – similarly the poets in this collection do not pause to identify themselves with the area.... The chief characteristic might be vaguely stated as *variety*, the tone as *awareness*, the styles and techniques as *versatile* (MacDonald 1959, 43).

MacDonald went on to argue that William Pillin, a poet of Russian Jewish origins who had lived in Los Angeles since 1946, was the typical Los Angeles poet:

> Perhaps it is Pillin, his poetry an even address of free verse, his concerns for affirmation in the face of assured defeat and destruction, and his individual glimpses into the shape of the city – for these qualities it is perhaps Pillin who typifies the Los Angeles poet (MacDonald 1959, 43).

MacDonald contended that for the Los Angeles poet the city could appear only in an indirect, underlying manner, as a form (free verse) or a general philosophy of life. When it is captured physically, it is represented only by fleeting and partial images.

To illustrate this, he discussed Pillin's "The Trip Home." Los Angeles is never named and is represented only by a series of discordant, kinetic, sonic and tactile concrete images. It is Gomorrah, a cacophonic and depraved hell, and the poet will have no rest until he has cut across it to get home to a tranquil clearing away from the tumult.

I came to you on a black span of asphalt
straining my lungs
against a downpour of torn newspapers,
running from cascades of broken glass,
from live coals glittering through darkness,
igniting restaurants, cinemas, shop windows.
...
I walked through percussion of death,
my nerves in tune with a thousand sirens.

I walked through terrible silences
punctuated by flutes of gloom;
past fear haunted houses
where people with ghostlike faces
spoke in strange tongues;
past pedestrians frozen by boredom on streetcorners;

past billboards of venereal roses;
past placards illustrating the profanation of the kiss,
past nudities on streetcorners
instigating youths to bacchanalian cakewalks.
I ran from maniacs crouching
in dimly lighted alleys.
I elbowed a snarling thug,
I kicked at a whining beggar.
I won free, I ran, I came to this clearing
hidden by poplars and moonlight....
and I was home again
in a clearing of pale stars
at the edge of Gomorrah.

Then, in the introduction to a special 1960 issue of *Coastlines* dedicated entirely to Los Angeles poets, MacDonald (the editor of the issue) pushed his theorization of the relationships – or, rather, the nonexistence – between poets and the city even further, contending that the geography of Los Angeles had become the principal cause of this lack of connection to the city.

MacDonald notes that the difficulty in representing Los Angeles is far from specific to this city. It simply reflects the drying up of specifically urban inspiration, due to the tendency toward standardization in the modern world. Thus, he refers to the predominant view of Los Angeles as a prototype for the modern megalopolis:

> It is unrewarding today to try to distinguish between what is characteristic of City and what is characteristic of a specific place, like Los Angeles. Traffic, suburbs, TV? Housing, hoods, education? These are but marginal differences – cities are different the way new models of automobiles are different (MacDonald 1960, 3).

Los Angeles, he remarks, has never attained poetic status; consequently, it is condemned to being indefinable and inexpressible. Language is incapable of grasping its boundless and multiple realities:

> It is a city praised, feared, joked about, promoted – but never quite identified. Not quite tangible enough to sustain a metaphor.... Of course we have all heard about Los Angeles – but the cat's meow is not quite the same as the cat.... It is as easy to believe that no such place exists as it is to try to visualize, to reconcile the myriad mental snapshots, to create the city. Better, maybe, to say that the city is nonexistent. To say "There is no city here." To say "What's this?" (ibid., 3–4)

MacDonald responded to his own question with the typical mythical view: Los Angeles is both dream and nightmare; a sprawling city that he called "the last great grazing range of the auto herd" (ibid., 4); it is the end of the World; its problems are those of all cities, and the only solution is prayer. Thus the editor presented this Los Angeles anthology as a collection of juxtaposed prayers, affording "some glimpses of life among the Angels," an "[e]ndless list, endless possibilities." Finally, he closed his article with the idea that nothing–"no school, clique or party"–united Los Angeles poets or designated them as Angelenos, except for the fact that they called Los Angeles home. Interestingly enough, MacDonad's view is echoed a decade later by Italo Calvino in his *Invisible Cities*:

> When the forms exhaust their variety and come apart, the end of cities begins. In the last pages of the atlas, there is an outpouring of networks without beginning or end, cities in the shape of Los Angeles...without shape. (139)

The difference between this approach to the city and Lipton's is apparent. For Lipton, the much smaller Venice community was at once an allegorical space, a refuge for the excluded, and a concrete, inhabited, living place. It is still more striking to compare MacDonald's introduction and Pillin's poem to Stuart Perkoff's poem on Venice (quoted at the beginning of this chapter). Perkoff's reasoning was like an inversion of MacDonald's. He started from Venice to arrive at the generic city, and for him human beings maintained a personal and intimate rapport with the city they inhabited even if, on another level, it incarnated metaphysical truths. Unlike Pillin, Perkoff spoke of the urban space with love. His emotional relationship with the city pours out from this poem.

The Open War Between Lipton and Coastlines

The differences in their understanding of the city highlight the literary differences between Lipton and *Coastlines,* and these would eventually lead to war.

Although Lipton recognized the seniority[22] of *Coastlines*, and even though the magazine had gladly published his writing starting in 1957, the friendship between them became strained. In a mocking article entitled "The Merchant of Venice," Mel Weisburd, one of the *Coastlines* editors, reproached Lipton for turning poetry into a commodity like any other, and for selling it as a way of life, "a package-deal of dissent, a whole underground way of life, complete with heroes." He accused Lipton of claiming a monopoly on "disaffiliation," and of practicing a policy of exclusion–unlike *Coastlines*, which sought to "represent as we can at least the writers of the Los Angeles area" (Weisburd 1957, 39). He did give Lipton credit for the stimulating quality of his work, and expressed a wish that *Coastlines* would one day welcome all of the region's talented poets–including those of Venice.

But Lipton's insulting description of the *Coastlines* editors in *The Holy Barbarians* stirred up conflict. In "The Great Promoter, A Hangnail Sketch of Lawrence Lipton," Gene Frumkin depicted Lipton as "a sort of encyclopedia salesman...with a quick Madison Avenue flow to his prose style" (Frumkin 1959b, 3). And he suggested that Lipton's book had done a disservice to those he had claimed to help by reducing them to a series of stock characters:

I think Mr. Lipton has been a mistake for the beatniks all the way.... In contrast to the more original influences of other key figures in the rise of the beatniks (mainly Miller, Rexroth, Ferlinghetti), Mr. Lipton has spent some years codifying the beat mores into what he would like to think of as the beat "ritual," harking back to the orgiastic rites of the Greeks and of primitive peoples.... What Mr. Lipton's book–his Napoleonic codification–does is to petrify individuals, turning them into molds which future beatniks must emulate (ibid., 6–7).

True to *Coastlines'* line of thought, Frumkin defined the Beats first and foremost as individuals, with varied talents, and he said the categories of Beats and "squares" – purportedly representing the whole of society – were inventions pure and simple, having no basis in reality. Frumkin ended his article:

> My own article, this one, is getting itself written not for money but to cast doubt, to the fullest extent I am able, on Mr. Lipton as an authoritative spokesman for Beat literature. He is rather their unsolicited advertising agent, I believe, a man who is using all the tricks of the trade...to sell a product, a way of life (ibid., 9).

After Frumkin's article, Lipton pulled the poets of Venice into his quarrel. As a result they were not published by *Coastlines*. The Venetians in fact were very critical of Lipton, who was alienating them little by little with his promotional methods.[23] The dispute with Lipton also pushed those in the *Coastlines* camp to dissociate themselves from the Beats. The *Coastlines* poets, "those silent and steady writers in Los Angeles" (Weisburd 1957, 40), sought to avoid media attention at any cost. They wanted poetry to be neither a commodity, nor an art of living, nor a fashion statement for immature and romantic young people.

Coastlines reproached the poets of the Beat movements for their claustrophobia, their intolerance and their herd mentality, championing instead an open and pluralistic approach. But beyond these differences, the two camps shared many values. They both believed in a living poetry, a poetry meant to be read, listened to, understood and appreciated by a public as wide and diverse as possible; they revolted against "creeping conservatism" (Weisburd 1957, 39) and preached dissent. In fact, *Coastlines* was the direct heir of *California Quarterly*, which had been founded by Hollywood radicals opposed to McCarthyism (some *Coastlines* regulars, including Thomas McGrath and Don Gordon, ran afoul of the House Committee on Un-American Activities). They also concurred in their hostility toward the East Coast, which they associated with dogmatic and intellectual poetry written by professors, for professors to dissect analytically.[24]

Despite their differences, the poets of Venice West and those of *Coastlines* dominated the poetic landscape of the early post-war years and left behind them a heritage of texts, attitudes, and people that fashioned the later poetic scene. The questions of geographical, group and aesthetic allegiance arose again in the 1980s. The responses to these issues ranged between the same poles: rejection, indifference, or loyalty; belonging to an exclusive clan of friends, or eclectic individualism; art and poetry as self-expression and way of life, or art for art's sake. However, the domination of the Los Angeles literary scene by these two antagonistic groups lasted only a short time. The mobility of the individuals involved caused old quarrels to be forgotten; other groups formed, and the Beats were integrated into the mass movements of the 1960s.

Evolution and Heritage

Following the enormous success of *The Holy Barbarians*, the media spotlight turned toward Venice and its bohemian Beats. In 1959 *Life* dedicated a long article to it, "Squareville USA vs. Beatville USA." It contrasted Venice with a small conservative city in Kansas. The poets Lipton had mentioned became veritable idols; Groucho Marx invited Stuart Perkoff to appear on *You Bet Your Life,* and several of Perkoff's poems were selected for publication in Donald Allen's 1960 anthology, *The New American Poetry.* The media attention ensured national visibility for Los Angeles bohemia. As artificial and incomplete as it was, this recognition forced the Venice poets and, consequently, other Los Angeles poets, to define themselves as such. The media coverage guaranteed that the Venice Beats would remain in the collective memory, because it made Venice the obligatory point of reference for future generations of bohemians and poets.

For the Venice Beats, this wave of publicity corresponded to a period of intense activity. Poetry readings and artists' cafés multiplied in Venice and Hollywood. *Coastlines* bore witness to the area's sudden infatuation with poetry in "Blunderbluss," an annotated calendar of poetic events in California:

> It is Los Angeles which, with its Hollywood predilections, has gone mad for the beatniks. More than twenty-five coffee houses in lean-tos, old store fronts, etc., have found expression on the billboard streets–like the Unicorn, Cosmo Alley, Les Enfants du Paradis, Café Fresco, Capriccio, Positano's, International, etc., where you can drink espresso at about $0.60 a cup, hear poetry and jazz by anybody, play chess, observe paintings and read the paperbacks and the big and little magazines (*Coastlines* II, 1958, 51).

By the early 1960s, the number of these venues had doubled. During a short period, the popularity of the Beats and of poetry was such that one tried to make a living from one's public readings. Anticipating the years to come, the Venice bohemia provided "communitarian" experiences, like those of the Gas House, an old building converted into an art gallery, café and community center for poets and artists; or the Grand Hotel, whose paying customers subsidized the free lodging of those artists.

But the Beat scene died due to a number of factors. Some residents of Venice–and the local police–were annoyed by the people who were invading their community, and by the creation of communal artist spaces. They used lawsuits, prohibitions and harassment, to force the closure of the Venice West Café, the Gas House and the Grand Hotel. The area deteriorated in other ways as well. With its licentious image, Venice had attracted a lot of criminals and drug addicts–and police officers. By the mid-1960s, many members of the initial Venice bohemia had left Los Angeles. Others had died. Drugs had contributed to the thinning of their ranks. Many used narcotics, and would go on to serve prison terms during the 1960s when repression was most severe. Stuart Perkoff, for example, who had become a heroin addict, was imprisoned on Terminal Island from 1967 to 1971.

The mark–both national and local–left by the Beats was hardly negligible. Their bohemian way of life in some ways foreshadowed that of their younger siblings, the hippies. Thus, many of their attitudes and much of their behavior would eventually influence the mores of the broader society. They also helped to open the field of possibilities for American writers by giving the oral tradition a vital role. Often taking the lyric "I" and its experiences as starting points, they considered poetry a tool of personal expression and liberation accessible to all–writers, readers, audiences. They tried to tear down the walls between art and life, and between various genres, as well as those that separated different media. They were enthusiasts of work that incorporated work from different disciplines, be it poetry, music, dance, painting or sculpture. In California, the Beat movement reaffirmed regional "Californian" literature. On the one hand, as Paul Vangelisti remarked in a retrospective interview on Los Angeles poetry, they aspired to "create a new poetic culture, that is both Californian and progressive politically"; and on the other, to "knowingly repudiate New York literary culture" (Vangelisti 1983, 69).

THE DISAPPEARANCE OF *Coastlines* in 1964 and the Beat movement's loss of momentum put an end to the contentiousness between the two clans. The poets formerly affiliated with the magazine continued to write and remained active in the poetry community of the 1960s and '70s, although sometimes in an indirect manner. There have been commemorative readings of their works organized by their peers upon their deaths, attesting to their importance in the collective history of local poetry. In addition to those poets mentioned above (McGrath, Gordon, Weisburd, Frumkin), these included Alexandra Garrett (1926–91), who worked at *Coastlines* and then, from the early '70s, worked with Beyond Baroque; William Pillin (1910–85); Henry Coulette (1928–88), a professor at California State University at Los Angeles; and Bert Meyers (1928–79), born in Los Angeles and at the end of his life a professor at Pitzer College in Claremont;

and Alvaro Cardona-Hine (1926), poet and translator, who at the end of the '70s relocated to New Mexico. Finally, a number of activities devoted to poetry inaugurated during the 1950s carried on into the 1960s and '70s, including writing workshops, private literary salons, public reading series and the independent Los Angeles Pacifica Radio station KPFK.

However, even if the tangible traces of certain Los Angeles poets remained, one should not overstate their importance. These traces are limited, because the poets lived on in the memory of only a few individuals and, as a general rule, they interested only a limited circle of people who had known them personally. Lipton's book, where it is still cited today, is more a reference for the Beat movement in general than for that of the Venice West poets. As for *Coastlines*, excerpts from its various issues were to be found in an anthology of Los Angeles poets from that period,[25] but few remember that the magazine ever existed. In poetry, as in other spheres in Los Angeles, populations were highly mobile. Although their constant comings and goings encouraged a certain dynamism, they discouraged continuity. The past, even the recent past, fell easily into oblivion, as Vangelisti explained:

Los Angeles is an open, vibrant city, which can communicate to you tremendous energy, but which even more so can discourage you. It is easy to undertake anything here, you can organize a grand, year-long poetry event, like "Specimen 73," [Pasadena Museum of Art, 1973–74], along with an extremely important catalogue, which today doesn't exist anymore and which nobody speaks about or even remembers – an event only 10 years old. In this way, ...Los Angeles can be an energetic charge and at the same time, it is a black hole, bottomless, spaceless and timeless (Vangelisti 1983, 81).

On the death in 1979 of Bert Meyers, one of the important figures of the 1950s, literary critic Kenneth Funsten noted the extent to which Los Angeles poetry needed a written history. Without such a written record, almost no proof of the past could survive. Each new generation, each freshly-arrived poet, imagined that he had landed in a poetic desert:

> If as much good and original poetry as is being written at present in L.A. were being written in any other city, like San Francisco or Minneapolis, for instance, the local press would be spouting off about a renaissance or movement or some other such nonsense.... Then the thought occurred to me why no one proclaims a rebirth of poetry in Los Angeles: it is because most people have no idea poetry or poets have ever existed here.... *Los Angeles needs a history* (Funsten 1979, 3).

In the end, the poets of the 1950s resembled the Los Angeles artists Plagens described in his *Sunshine Muse, Contemporary Art on the West Coast*. With neither institutional nor government support, the artist, along with his peers, creates and manages his own spaces of expression and publication, on the fringes; he neither respects nor is he necessarily familiar with high culture; and he feels free to do everything without either reference to the past or excessive self-reflection. Practicing poetry in a place nearly bereft of poetic tradition, writers are open to all influences. For these reasons, no recognizable school or style came out of the city. "In Los Angeles, poetry is much more diverse...the role of the poet does not exist, there is no common poetic language [whereas] everywhere else in America there is," said Vangelisti (Vangelisti 1983, 79). We will see that his remarks also apply in part to other "Communards," such as some of the black artists of South Los Angeles.

on returning to venice

I
time is confused on the streets of my city
returning, it is now & always as i walk
thru footsteps of memory

fog limits vision, & my eyes turn
inward, where birds fly the feet
over the paths of intricate memories

ghosts over my shoulder do not push or press
rather, their eyelessness peers to pierce
the veiled images of the future, or
the flowers ballooning from the clouds of mist

2
all is not voice
or vision, real walls
separate the rooms
within which movements
are limited by
space. & the bodies
within it

what endless histories
walk each separate flesh
each mind touching
its own
chronology
which goes beyond, encompasses
boundaries & isolations
within rigidity
the flow of continuity

3
o ghosts
o my past
the face I wear

o my city
my flesh
the space given

yr voices in my ears
yr tears in my eyes
hands touching
songs ringing
from room to rooms
in the houses of my mind

—STUART PERKOFF

CHAPTER THREE

The Trajectories of Some Black Poets
in South Central and Watts

Liberator of the Spirit

Life is a saxophone
Singing a sacred song

Rapture uphold the eyes
A cosmic view, a love supreme
Magic, magic music
Shining warrior dance
Leaping shooting star
Fire leap prancing sun
Rescue those lost in mirrors
And stuck in bubble gum

Wash the mind with music fresh as piss
From a brand new baby's bladder
Translate the nectar of scholars
Pondering the universe
Into music infants understand

Let us see the world that clearly
Let us know the world that well

It's a matter of believing
Beyond believing
Knowing

It's a matter of seeing the future materialize
As we see it
It's a matter of organizing
The raw materials of life into images as we will them
Not wish them to be

It's a matter of motion
It's a matter of discipline and sweat
It's a matter of developing the human potentials
In ourselves and others

As we organize our space
We organize our lives

As we organize our space
We organize our lives

The motion is the music
The energy is the music
The constant change is the music
The struggle is the music

Blowing, glowing, grooving, moving
Expressions, impressions
Pointing to a higher place

Break the silly staleness
The loud farts
The sound pollution
The lies

Bust the rat's ear drum
If you can't sing...Hummmmmmmmmmmmmmm

— KAMAU DAÁOOD

Harlem West and Central Avenue

From the 1920s through the '50s, the black neighborhoods of South Central and Watts[26] enjoyed a flourishing cultural life that nurtured the city's first generation of black poets. Just after World War I, as residential housing covenants were given sanction by the courts, black Angelenos were forced to retreat into their own neighborhoods in the face of toughening racial segregation. Then, during World War II, migrants attracted by work in war factories would, in the space of twenty years (from the 1940s to the 1960s), transform Watts and adjacent areas from a neighborhood where people of varied ethnic origins lived together (though within their own blocks), into a ghetto from which whites and more affluent black residents had fled. Los Angeles' black population went from some 15,500 in 1920 (or less than 3%) to 650,000 in 1965 (around 11%) within an unchanged perimeter.[27] According to the 2010 census, the figure dropped to 9.6%.

The nickname "Harlem West," first applied to the Los Angeles black community in the 1920s, was a recognition of the intense cultural life that enlivened the community from the 1920s through the late 1950s. Central Avenue, also called simply the Avenue, was its cultural heart, home to a thriving music scene. After the Supreme Court struck down residential segregation in 1948, people started moving south and west. The Los Angeles black community remained relatively united and culturally dynamic until the 1960s, when the area was transformed by the destructive effects of middle-class and white exodus. The slow decline of Central Avenue, starting in the early 1950s, mirrored the black community's transformation. As Kamau Daáood, a black poet-musician-activist born in 1950 testified, "Central Avenue was gone by the late sixties. There were a few clubs left in the community.... We had to go out of the community more and more to hear our music" (Cross 1993, 103).

It was only after Central Avenue's hour had passed that the community's great jazz musicians became objects of local as well as national pride. The Watts Towers Art Center organized and hosted an annual jazz festival in the mid-1970s and '80s.

It was designed to celebrate the Watts neighborhood by paying homage to African American music past and present, as well as to the community's art and history. In 1979, the third annual festival took place under the aegis of "Charles Mingus, who grew up in Watts." Over the years, the festival honored famous local musicians both dead and alive as unifying figures and symbols of community pride. These included such names as Eric Dolphy, Esther Phillips, Buddy Collette, Horace Tapscott, Billy Higgins, Johnny Otis and Red Callendar. John Outterbridge, who directed the Center and founded the festival, summed up the meaning of this event[28]:

Some years ago I produced the jazz festivals. This coming season it will be fifteen years ago, to look at heritage and some of the great names that grew out of the region. And that region expands itself, because you start to talk about personalities that have had national and universal application: Charles Mingus, Esther Phillips, Eric Dolphy...you just go on and on.

The evocation of the local jazz greats assured recognition for Watts, but only retrospectively, indeed almost posthumously, as all of the musicians cited were, like Central Avenue, already dead.

Far from Outterbridge's spirit of reverent and optimistic commemoration, Lynn Manning personifies the harrowing evolution of his neighborhood over the course of almost a century in this somber poem:

The Clark Hotel

Wagon red and pigeon shit gray,
It clings to the soil of Central Avenue
Like the last root of a dying tree.
Critically wounded by fire,
Its charred bowels spill into the filthy streets.

No historical societies rally to its rescue:
There are no concerts to save the Clark Hotel –

First to let to "Coloreds"
(When the word was in vogue),
A pre-war "Harlem West" sanctuary
Where The Count, and The Duke and Sammy put up
While they bopped The Avenue.
Kitchen mechanics and cotton pickers
Had the joints jumpin' til 'n
And The Clark was really swingin'.

But that's old history.
The soil's depleted and the tree transplanted;
Only the dying roots remain...
The Clark Hotel,
Where Momma crashed on a raggedy Murphy bed
With springs that cried
And she was too numb to care;
Where naked lightbulbs illuminated
The latest words of wisdom on piss-stained walls,
And the carpets were crusty
With blood from trapped rats and voided hypodermics.

Slow death clung to the skin like sweat
And The Clark didn't care: It had history.

Now it has nothing.
It stands, dead and deserted
Like a dilapidated whore
Remembering the days of fifty dollar tricks.

Mirroring the decline of Watts, the poem is all the more dramatic when one considers that Manning had to recite it from memory, because he was blinded by a gunshot.[29] The poem opens, unfolds and closes with the Clark Hotel in ruins and images of dilapidation, trash and garbage: vegetal rot, excrement, filth, soot and cinders, regrets of the fallen and aging prostitute. The poem's circular structure intensifies the despair; the decline is just as desperate as the days of glory were splendid.

With neither indulgence nor nostalgia, Manning reflects on a disenchanting history. He mixes three time periods: the impersonal, distant past of Central Avenue's Golden Age, associated with Harlem West and music; the personal and more recent past of his mother, a resident of the hotel whose dismal poverty is evoked by a few objects ("raggedy Murphy bed," "naked light-bulbs," "piss-stained walls," "carpets crusty/With blood from trapped rats and voided hypodermics"); and finally, the present of the narrator (speaking in the 1980s). For Manning, history was at best a hoax that had turned against African Americans. Twenty years after the 1965 riots, Manning suffers profound disenchantment. He knows firsthand the desperate reality of the ghetto, and his conclusion is, unsurprisingly, bitter.

The 1965 Watts Rebellion and the Black Arts Movement

The 1965 "uprising" or "rebellion," as it has been dubbed by Watts inhabitants has taken on an increasingly important meaning over the years. It was the largest in a series of inner city upheavals that started in New York in 1964. The Watts area became "a symbol of urban violence whose shadow still clouds the judgement of outsiders," wrote Leon Whiteson (1989, 33). At the same time, Watts and the whole of South Central by extension[30] acquired great visibility in the eyes of America and Los Angeles. The riots have become a rare shared point of reference in the city's history. The explosion of violence broke through the isolation and abandonment of the south central black communities. It was the subject of intense media attention, as Johnie Scott portrayed in his long poem, "Watts: 1966," reading in part:

On, on come the all-seeing
    eyes of the television cameras
controlled by the probing, insensitive
    hand of the detached reporter who
    purports to relate the news to millions

while there, in the eye of the madness,
    he quakes in his boots and wonders
when his turn to be beaten shall come.
        (Left bleeding like a brutalized ragdoll
        that has outlived its usefulness and

a child's curiosity.) Relating the news
    while the reality perpetuates itself.

Scott's disgust for the white media – and its indifference, igno-
rance and arrogance – is personified in the character of the
reporter. The onlooker's curiosity, represented by the cameras'
eyes and the reporter's hand, is set against the visceral fear of a
human being immersed in chaos and overwhelmed by events.

After the media came the money and the involvement of
Hollywood personalities, beginning with Budd Schulberg, a
novelist (*What Makes Sammy Run?*[31]) and Hollywood screen-
writer (*On the Waterfront*[32]) who went to Watts soon after "the
holocaust that began as a riot, developed into a rebellion, and
then settled down to the longer, harder task of constructive revo-
lution," (Schulberg 1969, 24). The uprising had politically galva-
nized artists and writers on a broad scale for the first time since
McCarthy's 1950s; they took an active role in the reconstruction
of the devastated neighborhoods, and tried to bring the various
Los Angeles communities together and make up for the past
indifference. Schulberg, for instance, understood the writer's
role in a progressive way, rejecting the apolitical, individualistic
American literary tradition:

I held to the old-fashioned notion that an author has a special
obligation to his society, an obligation to understand it and to
serve as its conscience.... The responsible American writer
makes it his duty to report on his corner of the nation. Los
Angeles is my corner. I was raised here. I had gone to Watts
in my youth to hear T-Bone Walker and other local jazzmen in
the honky-tonks.... I was self-appointed to Watts while the fires
were still smoldering (Schulberg 1969, 2–3).

Schulberg added to these ideals something more specific to the United States: an attachment to a given region. As the witness and conscience of a time and place, the author-citizen was responsible for making his corner of the nation known to fellow citizens. He was compelled to help Watts and its people, to whom he felt indebted, because he himself was an Angeleno, and recognized south central as an integral part of Los Angeles' cultural heritage.

The Watts Writers Workshop, which he helped found, published its first anthology, *From the Ashes: Voices of Watts*, just two years after the riots. The book's title suggests the wish for reconstruction, for the black community to be reborn from its ashes, as does one of its best poems, Blossom Powe's "Black Phoenix":

And so each day
Became a nightmare...
With no place else to run:
Picket fences falling down,
Sidewalks crumbling on the ground,
Hunger crawling all around...
Waiting for tomorrow!
And then Time...running swiftly,
Stopped to sift through the ashes
With barely visible picks
And such weak hands –
Crying! Brooding! Trying somehow
To create...from dreams archaic...
From old edicts and empty places!

And so each day
Became a nightmare...
Torture under the sun:
Picket fences falling down,
Sidewalks crumbling on the ground,
Hunger marching all around...
Waiting for tomorrow!

And then Time...walking quietly,
Stooped to lift the burnt ashes,
Wondering how it could fix
The broken Bands –
Crying! Brooding! Trying somehow
To create...a thing prosaic
From kindling sticks and shoeless laces!

And so each day
Became a nightmare...
But, what is done is done:
Picket fences falling down,
Sidewalks crumbling on the ground,
Hunger running all around...
Waiting for tomorrow!
And now, Time...crawling slowly
Starts to sift through the ashes
Of this black kind of Phoenix
With trembling hands –
Crying! Brooding! Trying somehow
To create...a new mosaic
From broken bricks and charcoal faces!

Powe's poem can be distinguished from Manning's "The Clark Hotel" by its tone, meter, grammatical person, references, point of view, and conclusions; but most of all, by the generations of which the two poets are members. Powe, who was born in Saint Louis in 1929 and moved to Los Angeles after high school, was thirty-six years old and had six children in 1965; Manning, born in 1955 and raised in the Los Angeles area, was only ten at the time of the uprising. "Black Phoenix" is written in a fairly traditional mode, something like a ballad – with its story, and its repeated, refrain-like verses. It retraces the black community's recent history, its misery and its hopes for a rebirth. Powe expressed the dreams of the community in the days following the violence through allegorical figures such as "Hunger," associated with past suffering, and "Time," in which present and future healing can take place. The poem moves from echo to variation, from past to present, from the idea of a nightmare with no exit to the still uncertain affirmation of action and renewal, without ever turning away from the injustice that provoked the violence. Despite the poem's pessimism,[33] the fact that it was published at all was a tangible sign of the battle fought against despair and exclusion, and of the mobilization of certain Angelenos in the struggle against the inevitable.

Thanks in large part to his connections, Schulberg succeeded in making the Watts Writers Workshop, in his words, "the most famous workshop on the West Coast." He obtained the financial support of an impressive number of figures in the world of letters and entertainment to pay for the Workshop's home, the Frederick Douglass Writers House.[34] Other celebrities became involved in the area; Bill Cosby, for example, was involved with Studio Watts, and financed the books and tuitions of some of its young artists, like Eric Priestley.

THE RIOTS ALSO MOBILIZED local progressive artists. Many organizations had been developing in Watts through the early '60s, mixing artistic practices, social programs and political militancy, including the Ebony Showcase Theater, founded in 1950 by Nick Stewart and his wife, and Studio Watts Workshop, a black arts center set up by Jim Woods, Guy Miller and Jayne Cortez in 1964. One of the first, and longest lived, was Horace Tapscott's The Underground Musicians Association (UGMA), which he set up in 1961. It became The Pan Afrikan Peoples Arkestra (PAPA) in 1971, as part of a larger organization called The Union of God's Musicians and Artists Association (UGMAA). UGMA was founded on "the struggle by many artists to rediscover and rebuild community, to forge an ethic [and an aesthetics] of community involvement..., an expansive, inclusive, noncompetitive vision of the arts and the role of the artist" (Isoardi, 2006 xii). Tapscott based the group in part on the iconoclastic, militant spirit of free jazz:

We got started on the free jazz out here in '59, tryin' to get a point over about what's really happenin'. A lot of cats didn't like the Arkestra because it was far out.... So the music became a message, a pipeline, by bringing all the arts together (Cross, 95).

After the riots, new groups sprang up around these established organizations. There was more or less peaceful coexistence between political groups, like the Black Panthers and Ron Karenga's us organization; the Watts Happening Coffee House, an abandoned store converted into a cultural center, from which the Mafundi Institute grew, specializing in theater and dance, and where the Watts Writers Workshop also made its home before 1967; the Watts Towers Arts Center; The Aquarian Bookstore, which transformed itself into an artistic center after 1965[35]; and the Inner City Cultural Center ("the first arts institution in the United States exclusively devoted to [multiculturalism]" (Breslauer 1991a, 5), which allowed groups like Teatro Campesino, the East-West Players and the Bilingual Foundation of the Arts to use its theatre.[36] The African American poets who lived through this period and participated in these organizations were profoundly molded by the education and vision they received through that participation.

In addition, the nations' first underground paper, the *Los Angeles Free Press* was created in 1964 by Art Kunkin, a journalist originally from New York, who worked for various leftists newspapers. Thanks to his articles on the riots in 1965, the *Free Press* succeeded in expanding its readership (Peck 1985, 26–7). Here, the city had a forum for minority voices that the *Los Angeles Times* and other large press organs had never provided. As Wanda Coleman noted in a 1987 interview[37]:

[The Watts riot] was a riot in which Blacks literally started burning and looting and tearing down most of South Central Los Angeles. Places they burned to the ground.... That happenstance created an interest in the community by forces outside who wanted something positive to come about the ashes of

Watts. So they started pouring money into the community to reduce the tension, the racial tensions.

The artists' enthusiasm was contagious, especially in the tumultuous political climate of the time. Studio Watts Workshop, which was founded in 1964 (and should not be confused with Schulberg's later Watts Writers Workshop) articulated the African American artist's philosophy in the following, which is both a mission statement and a profession of faith:

> Studio Watts Workshop is a community arts institute. It is also a catalyst in a continuing effort to engage the urban dweller in the revitalization of his community. In establishing Studio Watts Workshop we expressed our belief that the strength an individual develops through participation in creative activity is a major force in the renewal of the city. Creativity is positive; through creation the individual can begin to recognize himself as a resource for his community's improvement. Through participation in arts programs such as those developed and implemented by Studio Watts Workshop, he gains both a sense of himself and another route to understanding his society and the ways in which he can use its resources (Studio Watts Workshop 1971, cover).

The artists, like other inhabitants of Watts, hoped to revitalize their neighborhood on new foundations. The ideals that Schulberg brought with him were already indigenous to South Central: community members who felt that the artist was also a militant and citizen, a participant in the city's life, responsible to the community, and these artists found themselves at the heart of the area's revitalization. Art was understood to contribute to the development of both individual and community, promoting unity, freedom and autonomy.

Studio Watts Workshop was in many ways an exemplary cultural center. It succeeded thanks to the diversity of its programs and the way that they attracted the community, including many black poets. It was an art studio and provided art spaces; a learning and community resources center that put professionals and students in contact with each other in a master-apprentice relationship; it offered school and pre-school artistic discovery programs, academic scholarships, and exchanges between diverse neighborhoods; organized festivals, competitions and art exhibits; sponsored dance, theater and music productions; provided theatrical spaces; mediated between various community organizations; partnered with and counseled local, federal and international educational and urban institutions; and finally participated in rehabilitation and construction of housing and art workshops. It aimed to participate in the "process of cultural democracy in the community" (Studio Watts Workshop 1971, 27) by helping to build lasting and self-sustaining artistic infrastructure. Fiercely independent and ethical, Studio Watts members refused to accept subsidies that did not conform to their own objectives. For example, they declined subsidies from the federal Teen Posts program, the (unspoken) goal of which was, they complained, "policing and containing the youths in Watts" (ibid., 5) rather than promoting the blossoming of individuals and community. The organization's moral guidelines testify to the maturity of this approach, which offered a truly participatory democracy:

The structure for continuing a program must be placed in a setting beyond Studio Watts Workshop and must not require the establishment of an institution which is specifically designed to perpetuate only that program. The programs developed and implemented through Studio Watts Workshop must be absorbable into another existing organization or must help create a multi-purpose structure capable of diverse development.

To facilitate programs which have a major concern in training of apprentices....

To facilitate programs which leave behind a trace in a continuing community organization, an atmosphere of cooperation, and freedom for the participants to follow their own creative directions. In short, the output of Studio Watts Workshop must leave behind a network of creativity, a structure of cultural democracy. (ibid., 1)

Studio Watts Workshop, like the other cultural organizations in the 103rd Street area, attests to the fluidity which existed among places, activities and disciplines, allowing people to circulate freely from one place to another, from one art to another. These groups awakened the sleeping artistic talents of many of the area's young people and provided the foundation for numerous careers. Like other poets, Wanda Coleman recognizes the debt she owes to them:

I was influenced greatly by that, the fact that there was an art studio for me to get involved in…. And I went to that art studio, I had my first plays done there, I got involved in dance and theater there. I did my first poetry reading the first couple of weeks I was there. I took a couple graphic art workshops there so I'm tied in.

Like other artists in Watts, poets saw themselves as being at the service first of their community. Their art was deeply committed and political; it forged bonds within the community, particularly with the organized revolutionary movements, as Horace Tapscott said:

The Black Panthers, the us group (Ron Karenga's), all these groups were in the community, functioned in various ways for blacks, we were the only music they had, was the Arkestra. We played at all their things, there was tribal things every now and then. But the Arkestra would bring them together, let's put it like that. It would bring all the people together and they would start realizing other things (Tapscott 2001, 98).

The cultural organizations had to stay attentive to the community's needs in order to create a space where frustration and negative energy could give way to creativity and sharing. Tapscott continues:

It [the house where the Arkestra was based] didn't really have any straight-in, downright military purpose, it played many parts, it brought people together and helped them relaxing from going wild cause they had a place to talk and meet people, and concentrate on creating things together now (ibid., 98).

And like the other artists, those working with the cultural organizations were united by their opposition to the "culture industry" and the Hollywood star-system – a system from which they were excluded from the start anyway.

KAMAU DAÁOOD ARGUED that Hollywood and community people were opposites: "The idea of the community artist is really a noble concept, you serve the community rather than star status, you really serve people" (Cross 1993, 105). Stardom and the black community did not go together, because success in Hollywood, and its recognition, were white and inaccessible to blacks. However, the presence of Hollywood was inescapable from the beginning, despite the standing of artists like Tapscott and Daáood, who refused to play the system's game.[38]

The community's ambivalence toward Hollywood and the white liberal establishment is obvious in their attitudes towards Schulberg. For some, he was the Academy Award Winner for *On the Waterfront*, who had had the courage to come to Watts when it was still burning and try to help talented black artists. For others such as Wanda Coleman, Schulberg, though she did not name him specifically, was one of "the white males [who] were running the workshops, and [who] put all their focus and attention on the black males." And Father Amde of the Watts Prophets admired Schulberg's courage and determination in bringing "hungry" black novice writers together, but was disappointed by Schulberg's departure and return to New York a few years later.[39] His time in Watts looked like a brief parenthesis in the life of an Angeleno who was a New Yorker at heart. Finally, his connection with Hollywood, which was lauded at first, was ultimately a stigma that separated Schulberg from the black community.

His ambiguous reputation is revealing in several respects.[40] Here we see on the one hand the tensions between whites and blacks and the limits to possible cooperation between them, compounded by gender, intergenerational, aesthetic and ideological differences. And on the other hand, we see at least a perceived lack of long-term white commitment to the area after the riots.

The Watts Writers Workshop, a Milestone Similar to Venice West

But these reservations about Schulberg himself in no way diminish the importance of the Watts Writers Workshop for black writers and poets in Los Angeles. The Workshop's motto, "write only what you know," gave confidence back to what Schulberg called "young men of mysterious depths, of talents neglected," (Schulberg 1969, 22–3). Many of them had previously associated writing with frustration, humiliation and exclusion. Johnie Scott, who went on to become a professor and director of the Pan African Studies Writing Program at California State University, Northridge said of the Workshop that:

> Writing saved my life. The two-way exchange of opinions at the workshop was vital to me, just having the opportunity to hear other voices and to know I wasn't alone, that I was part of a serious dialogue taking place that would have impact nationwide.... The Watts Writers Workshop allowed us to voice what urban, black America was thinking, feeling, and seeing and to get that out to the rest of the country. Before that, we had no voice; no one was listening (NEA, 2005).

The Workshop was also a revelation for Anthony Hamilton, later known as Father Amde. In 1966, fresh out of prison, he met Odie Hawkins, one of the Workshop's writing instructors, while waiting to get a job at a poverty program in Watts. Hawkins noticed that Hamilton was writing all the time, and asked him to join the Watts Writers Workshop. Hamilton was a high school drop-out;

he had never thought of himself as a writer, let alone thought he would be seen as one by others. The Workshop revealed his own talents to him and helped him develop as an artist. It had an encouraging, friendly atmosphere; everyone was welcome, no matter how poor. To writers like Scott and Hamilton, the Watts Writers Workshop was a sanctuary, a magical space leading to conversion and healing. In fact, the Workshop was as important for these young writers as Venice West had been for the poets who congregated there. Like Venice West, the Workshop created a literary identity for participants – an exceptionally difficult task for Watts writers, thanks to the neighborhood's negative image. Unlike Venice, however, the Watts Writers Workshop was eventually important for black writers outside the immediate neighborhood as well. And this was despite the fact that the population of Watts was not representative of Los Angeles' black community.

OTHER POETS were more skeptical about the workshop. Wanda Coleman, for instance, downplays its role in her subsequent career; but she admits that she worked in opposition to the Workshop's less attractive aspects:

> I just hide that [the fact I went through the Watts Writers Workshop]. See, I hide it because when I went through there, there was a very strong element of sexism.... And the women were just, we were totally ignored. And I rebelled against that, because I wasn't getting any benefits from them, so therefore I don't allow them to claim me, now that I've established a voice and a reputation. It's bogus. I owe them nothing. Because they did nothing for me! Maybe it was good that they ignored me because I was so hungry to learn that I started looking [elsewhere...]. I'm almost as good a writer as a man, see. That was the kind of thing I was getting. They did not do anything to encourage me or feed me. If anything, they would have killed me off.

In "Poetry Lesson Number One," Coleman related in a subtle and comical way this formative episode:

Cleveland and them hung out in that Watts cafe used to be
    across the
tracks on a diagonal north of the workshop off 103rd. No
    women were
allowed at that table unless being schemed upon, or of
    exceptional beauty.
But I was a stubborn little mud hen at the fringe of the clique,
    starved
for approval.

So one day Cleveland and them was sitting at the table. Cleve
    and maybe
Eric and one other brother. I boldly intruded on their
    exclusivity with
my neat little sheaf of thin poems.

"And so you write?" and "Let us see one!" And the other
    brother took it and
read it out loud and they passed it around the table.
    "Hmmmm" and "Ahhhh."
And I blushed and my stomach tightened twice for each of my
    19 years.

"Oh yeeeaahhh," said Cleveland. "You *are* a writer, young
    lady. As good a
writer as a man!"

And I caught the bus home, carrying his words with me,
    clutching my thin
little poems to my heart,

glowing in the dark.[41]

The young poet is thrilled to be recognized by an established
writer, but the Cleveland's authority is deliberately undermined:
it is arbitrary and patriarchal. He speaks in an almost ridicu-
lous drawl, and explicitly makes writing like a man the standard

for which the young, female poet should reach. This is conde-scending self-congratulation, as vain as it is thoughtless. The initiatory rite is in fact a rite of submission. The poem asks us to question whether artists need this kind of validation at all. After an attempt to meet others, without blending into the "we," the lyric "I" returns to a still greater solitude, clutching her own work ever tighter. The last line is clearly ironic in the context of the rest of the poem. "Glowing in the dark," seems to imply a happy fairy-tale ending, but the speaker's naivety turns it into an explosive charge. Her understanding of the poem's events cannot be the correct one; she is needy, her poems are thin and little.

This is characteristic of Coleman's work as a whole. She often constructs disparate points of view and forces the reader to make up her own mind, to take a stand against prejudice – here sexism – which is presented as "natural." This example of her method sums up her relationship with the Watts Writers Workshop. Luckily, in Los Angeles:

nobody can corner the turf. See, because L.A. has no heart, no center. The city was not built around a plaza. It tried, but the plaza concept just did not happen here, and because it's such a massive terrain, no one has been able to come in and say: "I'm the big cheese. This is the way we're going to do things. Nobody else is allowed." What happens here, if so and so starts a game over here, someone else is going to start one over there, and someone is going to start one over there. L.A. is too big.

Richard Dedeaux, a Creole originally from Louisiana and one of the three Watts Prophets, was also uncomfortable with the dogmatic spirit of some members of the Watts Writers Workshop:

It was real interesting, see, when I went to the Watts Writers Workshop. I did my poetry there, because I had been with the Donnybrook Players [an Irish Repertory Theater who all ended up at the workshop]. So when I took my work to the workshop Ojenke and them was the ones that was evaluating the players. They was like man, this ain't black enough, you got to get more vicious than this.... See what was happening at the workshop was there was only one flavor of poetry at the workshop (Watts Prophets 1993, 1993, 115).

But whereas Coleman distanced herself from the Workshop, Dedeaux re-committed himself to it:

The diversity of the Watts Prophets, Anthony [Father Amde] has always been the fire of the group and Otis [Smith] is the love poet of the group, and I'm always trying to find some good in all this bullshit.... It's the diversity of the group that makes us unique.... So we tried to work it. Anthony would go out there and talk about tearing up the world and we'd try to put it back together in some way (ibid., 116).

THE CONCEPT OF A LITERARY SCHOOL is generally absent from the Los Angeles poetry scene, as the communities are too far-flung and heterogeneous to be grouped together. That said, the Workshop was so strong that some members did in fact call it a "school." Kamau Daáood used the term proudly:

There's a school of poetry that has blossomed up from this area in terms of Watts. I was part of the Watts Writers Workshop at a very young age, and there were some great writers that came through there, that were very very dynamic in terms of performance and in terms of their delivery. Names like Ojenke, which many people have probably never heard of but is very much like a legendary figure in this area. Eric Priestley, Quincy Troupe, K. Curtis Lyle.[42]

In another interview Daáood described the period's two styles more precisely:

There were two basic styles of poetry developing at that time: one centered around rhyme, bluesy, out of the tradition of Langston Hughes; the other school leaned more towards imagery, phrase lines of poetry more like a saxophone solo, out of the tradition of Amiri Baraka. I wanted my work to sound like Coltrane riffs and sheets of sound (Daáood 1993, 102).

The names Daáood invokes restore the Watts poets to a cultural tradition. As musical as they are literary, the Watts poets echo the genres, movements and seminal artists in their traditions. These traditions range from Langston Hughes and the Harlem Renaissance of the 1920s, to pop culture and rhymed poetry; from Amiri Baraka[43] and the Black Arts Movement to John Coltrane. Daáood includes Watts poets in this tradition, but also affirms their distinctive, local identity. The Watts poets are unique in their stress on orality and the creation of an oratorical poetic style.

Despite criticisms of the Workshop, it was a place of flowering, friendship, artistic exploration and community participation. Many black youths from Watts (or South Central) passed through the workshop and discovered poetry there. It incorporated as a non-profit organization, changed directors and renamed the Frederick Douglass House the House of Respect, after some members split over ideological differences. Under the editorship of Quincy Troupe, the Workshop produced a new anthology in 1968, *Watts Poets: a Book of New Poetry and Essays*. Its longevity, its renown, and the number of poets who identified with it make Watts Writers Workshop the most influential group in the history of Los Angeles poetry, alongside Venice West. The Workshop's building was burned down by an FBI informant in 1975, with a devastating effect on the 103rd St scene as a whole.

Three Poets

Although many black poets belonged to the Watts Writers Workshop or some other writing workshop or cultural center, they were important differences among them. This can be seen in the lives and the attitudes of Wanda Coleman, Kamau Daáood and Father Amde, three of the best-known Los Angeles poets. They experienced the 1965 riots as adolescents or young adults, and took part in the creative and militant explosion that followed. They received much of their artistic training in the cultural centers described above, and all three produced work that was resistant to categorization and indifferent to the boundaries between genres.

THE CLOSE POLITICAL AND ARTISTIC collaboration between jazz musicians, black activists and artists of all disciplines in the 1960s had a permanent effect on black poetry; as Daáood said, "the music connected the community together" (quoted in Isoardi 2006, 271). Daáood's work is rich in the rhythms and structures of black music, unsurprisingly given that he was a member of the Pan Afrikan People's Arkestra. Daáood has stayed involved with Los Angeles' music scene: starting in the early 1980s, he helped to organize an annual drum festival, and he is often one of the masters of ceremonies at the Watts Jazz Festival. In 1989, with jazz drummer Billy Higgins, he founded a performance space in South Central Los Angeles called the World Stage, and in 1997 he recorded a CD called *Leimert Park*, for which he read his poems to jazz music.[44]

In his performances with the Arkestra, Daáood would improvise poetry just as the instrumentalists did music:

I used to read my poetry in the context of the Arkestra really as another soloist. The tenor player might take a solo, then I might take a solo, it would be that context and it was good training, 'cause very seldom was it a rehearsed kind of situation. Like many times Horace would be playing and he would just look at me and I gotta find something that's appropriate... (Cross 1993, 103).

He saw himself as a "musician of words" (ibid., 104), but was not the only word musician in Horace Tapscott's Arkestra: Ojenke, Quincy Troupe, Jayne Cortez and the Watts Prophets, among others, also played with them. All of them drew from jazz, particularly from John Coltrane:

The first time I read was at South Park. Ted, Lena Horne's son, had seen me some work and asked me to come on stage and read. Horace Tapscott and the full Arkestra were playing "Equinox" by John Coltrane behind the work, it was a heck of a debut. That was probably 1969 (ibid., 102–3).

Daáood stressed the importance of oral presentation, and likened it to the improvisation of a jazz soloist. He even used similar terms to define it–energy, rhythm and music. He saw the *ars dicendi* as a fully fledged art form, with the same creative source as the written poem. Daáood adapted his interpretation to the audience, rarely reading the same poem in the same way twice. He learned the oratorical art alongside musicians, as well as at the Watts Writers Workshop, which inspired his sermon-like style:

I don't like to put poetry from purely a literary standpoint, you know typewriter, pen, paper, publishing. To me, much of the life of what it is that I'm trying to do is taken away from that. I try to get my work towards performance, towards the movement, towards the value of words, towards the emphasis, towards the music and the dance of poetry, going back to a more ancient tradition. A book with a poem can sit on a shelf. But the poem that is performed, …there's just so much more life to it!

Daáood warns that the "word can heal and the word can cause disease," adding that a "lot of these cats be throwing out concepts and they really don't know the power while back in the sixties... there was a lot of good people that ended up in jail and dead for what they said" (Cross 1993, 105). Poetry must recover, according to Daáood, the ritualistic and spiritual dimension of art, and of life as a whole. To do so, the poet needs to delve into his African roots and recover his true function, that of the griot, "the oral historian, the emotional historian who captured the emotion of the moment, the cries and the stories and the tears and the laughter of a people, at a given time, and captured that for future times."

Then poetry can return substance and sacred power to the words that have been commandeered by advertising:

> Poets are here to put the meaning back into the word. I mean, we're bombarded with verbiage coming from everywhere. And words mean very much to us. Vows, taking sacred vows. I mean we lie at the drop of a hat now. The poet brings that realness, that truth hopefully back to the word. I think that's one of the functions of a poet in society.

The power of the word – in some lines meaning the usually capitalized "Word of God" – is the central theme of Daáood's "The Lip Drummer":

> with the raw edge of language
> he creates song,
> here where he lives where old cars come to die
> and streets soak up blood like sponges
> from the outer edge of thought
> from the bulleye center of the heart
> bucknaked in prayer to a God that is all so infinite
> here where agents from the devil's butthole
> suck the life from the soul of children
> and leave them with ears tuned to sculptured static
> and uzi machine guns firing at colors wearing people
> here in the mist of meditation and prayer
> and the sweating and searching
>
> with the raw edge of language
> he creates song
> word
> word as a force for lifting, resurrecting
> word
> word as a force for healing, awaking
> word
> word as the space around silence
> building blocks for the song he is trying to sing

this wind sucks and blows
this heartbeat that he must master
...
naked labor, meatass raw on the hook of industry
smoked booty in the fire of exploitation
wearing wooden nickel sunglasses
beer belly and television for your vision
plugged nostrils and siren pierced ears
the sound of rattling chains
from the tips of their timid tongues
mouth full of stone birds
lips dribbling like basketballs
words spilled on the earth like verbal diarrhea
words heavy as the hair on a baby's butt
mental rigor mortis

In this excerpt, we find a stylistic blend dear to the poets of the
Watts Writers Workshop: slangy, poetic, abstract and bodily regis-
ters, as well as lyrical, sermonic and prophetic tones. The poem
is built around the opposition of two worlds, each with its own
style and vocabulary. The first is the reality of the here and now,
the street, blood, the devil, industry, technology – a nocturnal
world, full of decomposition. The second world, that of the poet,
is associated with prayer, flight, God, the regularity of the beating
heart, and silence. The combination of the two worlds is often
explosive. The griot uses language like a sacred drum to trans-
form the desolation that surrounds him. Daáood looks a brutal
reality in the face, depicts it in all its sordidness, and intimately
blends it with his message of healing.

WANDA COLEMAN, like Daáood, sees poetry as tied to music. She
has dedicated poems to jazz musicians, and written blues songs.
She said:

I like to write to music, I like to listen to music when I write
if I can, you know, if everyone isn't asleep, sometimes I'll put
on the radio and put on headphones, and if I can't, it's OK. But

I find music can be a medium, and I'll enjoy that, it becomes an implement and especially when I want to time-travel. Time-travel means if I want to remember what a period or a certain year was like then I can take the music from that year, and it takes me to that place. That's another way it functions.

She also suggests that her poetry has a "musical idiom," so that her work must be heard, rather than read in silence. Coleman is known for her intensity and masterful elocution, which she acquired as a participant on her high school debate and public speaking teams.

I used to write my own oratory and go around in high school competitions, and I got my share of the medals and awards. I was in public speaking all the time when I was in high school. I learned how to do tricks, how to control an audience, how to project my voice–which sometimes I delight in using (Coleman 1979–80, 55).

Her works are like musical scores, while her oral presentations, which she adjusted according to her audience and her mood, are interpretations. To paraphrase Harvey Kubernik, her oratory comprises an intense energy, which she modulates to pass from a scream to a whisper, from a song to a snigger. She calls this technique of improvisation the jazz principle.[45]

For Coleman poetry should be at the service of the political struggle against racism and all other inequalities, even if the poetic act in and of itself is not enough:

I am a believer in the Power of the Word. Defeating racism/ethnocentrity will take more than writing about it, more than poems. Ideological war demands each soldier fight with the weapon he/she wields best–guns, words, money–*whatever* (Coleman 1987, 81).

She was progressively stripped of her youthful illusions after the 1960s. Her vision became more incisive, her thought and writing became a vehicle for her revolutionary militancy and her poems transformed into weapons – "them bullets, them A bombs, them neutron bombs on the page," as she liked to call them:

> I'm still a revolutionary.... I'm still an activist. I think even *more* than I was then. I think I'm more of a revolutionary *now* than I was *then*, because then I was still learning a lot, I still had a lot of illusions, and I was still very romantic about it.... I'm more a revolutionary now, I'm more an activist than I was when I was running in the paramilitary groups, and going to the underground meetings, and plotting to climb on top of the Arco towers or whatever, and blow people away with machine guns, see. So, I'm more than that now, than I ever was.

A materialistic perspective runs through her writing, which shaped the clarity with which she saw the world. "I feel black writing has to be functional first," she said, "it has to address the needs of the body, and the spirit, man, is just going to have to be taken care of and dealt with later." Coleman rose up against those who practiced what she called "the cosmic nigger trip," those who are "concerned with outer space and expressing some ultimate religiosity" (Coleman 1979–80, 57). She believed that "words have all the power, can kill or heal." For her, the poet's role is to restore truth and meaning to language, because "in this culture, language is used so manipulatively that people are intimidated."

THE WATTS PROPHETS GROUP was formed in 1968 due to a strong demand for readings by Watts Writers Workshop members. Father Amde recalls:

> There were so many writers and poets there [at the Watts Writers Workshop] and such large requests from all over the country for writers from the Watts area to go and speak and do their poetry that writers began to go out in groups; four or five writers would go together, two sisters, two brothers and from that the Watts Prophets formed. Richard, Otis and myself

started going together. At the beginning we didn't care much for each other's poetry.... But we started reading together and people started requesting us (Cross 1993, 108–9).

It was characteristic of all poets at the time to perform throughout the community, doing "hundreds of readings" (Cross 1993, 105):

At the time we was doing poetry, we did prisons, nightclubs, schools, worked with the Panthers, the Red Cross, they all called on us, the Boy Scouts.... We did poverty shows, with five or six people in the projects, to auditoriums (Cross 1993, 114).

The Prophets included musicians and singers in their shows, often accompanied their poetry with jazz, and frequently performed in clubs alongside musicians and comedians.[46] Jazz music and the jazz scene were thus an integral part of their poetic practice, and they saw poetry as an oral form. African American poetry and music were contiguous, since both found their roots in improvisation. Father Amde put it this way:

Well Don Cherry says one thing, that what happened with poetry is the constant growth of improvisation, as the jazz musicians have grown over the years and improvisation has grown more and more. And the same thing with the spoken word. If you know the history of black music in the United States, it was always about every twenty or thirty years a change. From swing to jazz to bebop, etc. But each time, it was always rejected at first. All jazz was only found in whorehouses, bebop... The only people who would publish us at that time were... [the] nasty labels, with all the cursing and the sex... (Cross 1993, 114).

The Prophets' oral presentation was a theatrical form:

We were theater.... We would act out each poem. Each poem was a total play to us. It had a beginning, a middle and an ending, it was dialogue.... We lived together in perfecting this form for two years in one house, and we practiced day and night (Watts Prophets 1993, 114).

They tried to create a popular art, that would blend a serious message with professional performance, identifying with the performing, rather than literary, arts.

One unintended consequence of this was the Watts Prophets' later reputation as forerunners (along with the Last Poets) of hip-hop:

The school [the Watts Prophets] rose from was a little different from the school that centered around Ojenke and Quincy. [The Watts Prophets] were pioneers in what we call rap today. Very street oriented lyrics, very heavily rhyme influenced... (Daáood 2004, 5).

Although it should be a mark of honor to lay the ground for a new art form, the Prophets tried to distinguish themselves from hip-hop culture in the 1980s. One difference was the absence of obscenities in their work. According to the Prophets, even the best rappers used obscenities so often that they became meaningless. They also wrote and prepared their work in advance, whereas rappers and DJs could seem primarily to be improvisers (though many of them do write their lyrics or compose their music).

But, despite these differences from rap, the Watts Prophets will always be associated with their descendents. After all, they were the first artists to include the word in a record title (*Rappin' Black in a White World*). Later artists learned Watts Prophets' lyrics by heart, and paid tribute to this heritage by sampling their records. DJ Quik recalled:

I heard 'em when I was a kid, it was scary 'cause it was too radical for me. I was like five though, when I got into it. I think the real reason I remembered it and the reason I wanted to use it was because of how blatantly scary and formidable it was, it was thought-provoking and fearful... They were the first rappers in the truest sense, they been doing it since the sixties. If what you consider rap is philosophizing over rhythmic African type beats, they paved the way for this shit (Cross 1993, 256–60).

The Prophets thought rap had originated in African "call and response" patterns, and the rapper/poet himself was a descendant of the griot storyteller. Their work brought these traditions up to date, and adapted them to the urban environment. Like later rappers, their art was self-consciously populist and from the street. Their understanding of poetry as prophetic was also picked up in hip-hop culture, as in Grandmaster Flash and the Furious Five's "The Message." Here the rapper is a messiah who "brings hope and denounces." Both the Prophets and later artists understood poetry or hip-hop as a way of life, a whole culture. The Prophets' techniques of composition and diction are also very close to later hip-hop: rhyme in rhythmic lines, chains of puns, and the use of black slang and street speak. They can all be seen in this excerpt, in which the Prophets list activists and musicians from the ghetto in the style of a nursery rhyme:

Yeh in the ghetto,
Where niggers fine vine, but ain't got a dime,
To defend Panthers against crime ...
Let H Rap rap,
Let Huey duey,
Let Bobby Seale deal,
Let Dizzy Gillespie.

Their political bent and social themes also unite the Prophets with hip-hop. The urban environment is often pictured as a dangerous jungle, and many rappers encourage black pride by asking the people to wake up and take action. This is familiar from the much earlier "Kill," in which Father Amde urges people to put an end to police harassment by rebelling and killing those who oppress them:

Hot rod policemen
Zipping through the ghetto streets in jetmobiles
Trampling niggers
Killing babies/Beating sisters/Into miscarriages...
Killing us whenever they want to.
Scared/Scared/Scared/Scared all the time.
Surrounded by guns in worse shape than South Africa
Brothers we better get hip and come off of this trip –
Warriors, come forth and lead our people to freedom
Like Nat Turner meant to do...
With an underground arsenal of terror
On those and anything in the way of our freedom
Kill/Kill/Kill
Until the sucker raises up off of you
And finds something better to do.[47]

Some twenty years later, NWA's "Fuck tha Police"[48] gave an even harder, if more nihilistic, edge to the Prophets' militancy.

BUT THIS MASCULINE, militant realism, whether of the '80s or '60s, was open to criticism. Daáood spoke of the "'negative' fiery words" that L.A. black poets used in the sixties, a practice which he broke from in 1974 with *Beyond the Blues Toward the Rainbow: A Suite from Bitter to Sweet*; in this book he "wanted to write everything that was beautiful" (Stein 1987, 45). Father Amde criticized the affinity for violence that he found in later rappers, who only wanted "that vicious type poetry."

And Wanda Coleman, in 1966, "want[ed] to write for the Movement...to write propaganda," but she was discouraged from doing it because, as a woman, she "didn't really have a brain, [her] function was to lie prone" (Coleman 1979–80, 53). She revolted against what she called "the black power poem," a stereotyped "rhetorical mode" of the 1960s, beyond which, she argued, black American poetry had not managed to go:

Most American black poetry is rhetoric, it's not really poetry! So that it's very boring to read it, because everyone is using the same language, they've taken a very rich language, and everyone is using the same clichéd imagery out of that language. So the "black pro poem" I call it, where the black man writes a poem about a beautiful black woman, which came out of the '60s. It was all right, every movement needs that initial thrust of rhetoric. But when it goes on and on and on and doesn't evolve into something else, something's wrong. And there's this peer group pressure sometimes and people respond to it.[49]

Watts, Defining a Territory

The Watts poets were aware that they had been shaped by their surroundings, and often consciously wrote of their neighborhood. Even Daáood, who did not generally make concrete and direct references to Los Angeles, thought that both he and his writing had been profoundly shaped by the city:

Los Angeles has a major influence on my work in that I was born here, and I've lived here all my life. It's the only thing in terms of living that I can really compare other things to. Where does the poet get the poem? He gets the poem from the living and maybe occasionally a book here, an album there, a film, a little travel, or some other experience, but basically it's from the living, it's from the feeling of the breathing.

And Father Amde's childhood in the ghetto of Watts validated his voice and his prophetic message. Because he, and the other Watts Prophets, were from ghettoized communities, they could be truly "grassroots," unlike the college set. They considered themselves the spokespeople of their neighborhood, as well as addressing all "those communities of this country where there is oppression, isolation, and disenfranchisement" (Peters 1976, unpaginated).

But Wanda Coleman provides the best case-study in the interaction between location and poet. The exclusions that she suffered due to her race, social class and regional origins led her to seek out a solitary path. She set herself apart and developed a very individual style that took into account her responsibility, as an artist-citizen, to her neighborhood. She refused to choose between individualism and solidarity. In Coleman's words:

> It is essential to the nature of poetry, of art, that it come out of the dialogue between the I and the we – and the I-as-the-we.... I have a sense of myself that is not an individual. I'm an entity, a force that's been shaped by other forces. I felt that way about myself – I, I, I, I – early on in my work. Now that's changed. I feel totally comfortable to say that my voice represents a great many voices. I don't mind assuming that responsibility at some point – of saying, I am a leader speaking for all of those who share my point of view or who don't have the vehicle or who can't find their tongue to do so. And since I have those capabilities here, I-am-as-we (Coleman 1979–80, 59–60).

The legitimacy of her voice, and thus the silenced people for whom she speaks, is based on her birth in Watts:

> I was born in Watts in the first place. I was born in a little house there. So that's what I've come out of. I feel compelled, and I feel capable of representing my community.

Coleman's community is spatial, ethnic, and social, with well-defined borders, a politics, ideology, aesthetic, and metaphysics, which Coleman described as "organic." This community differed from those of the white artists discussed above, whose communities were contractual, built on the mutual consent of all of their members. This is reflected in the term *voluntary* poverty.

But the community of Watts did not result by accident. It has a very clear history. For Coleman, who had an almost painful consciousness of the impersonal forces that produced her, the genesis of her identity was perfectly clear:

> I'm the product of two diasporas, you know, World War II and slavery. Two major events in world history. I mean my mother wouldn't have come, my mother, my people are from

the Midwest, and World War II opened up the job-market for Blacks on the West Coast. So my mother came West to California from Oklahoma looking for a job, found one, and met my father there. I'm a result of slavery, you know.

Thus when asked if she could define Watts, Coleman answered:

OK, OK, Watts, Watts. When I was a kid, Watts was a place on the other side of the railroad tracks, a ghetto, a place that it was undesirable to be from.

The spatial separation (Watts is "a place on the other side") is both positive, associated with childhood and adolescence, and negative, an "undesirable" territory isolated by outside forces. The separation encompasses any number of binaries: us and them, poor and rich, people of color and whites. Although landmarks such as the Watts Towers could symbolize the Watts community, the railroad tracks drew the physical line of exclusion into the landscape. And once the railroads fell into decline in the early 1960s, the community was increasingly cut off from the rest of the city.

Nonetheless, for Coleman South Central was home – even if she did not choose it. She belonged to it, it spoke her language, and she could be herself there, whereas elsewhere she had to play a role. She always felt that "one of the things about black life, [is] you have to be an actor...in order to survive, you have to."

That'll always be home to me no matter where I live really. I mean even living in Hollywood, sometimes, I get homesick to go back to Watts. Because it's nice to be home and that's home for me. It's nice to be among people who treat me like people because when I'm on this side of town, I'm not a person, I'm a phenomenon, I'm something other.

This homesickness was a proof of her unfailing loyalty:

Where I Live[50]

at the lip of a big black vagina
birthing nappy-headed pickaninnies every hour on the hour
and soul radio blasting into mindwindow
bullets and blood
see that helicopter up there? like
god's eye looking down on his children
barsandbarsandbarsandbarsandbars
where i live
is the gap filled mouth of polly, the old black woman
up the street whose daughter's from new orleans and who
abandons her every holiday leaving her to wander
up and down the avenue and not even a holiday meal, she
collects the neighborhood trash and begs kindness in
doorways/always in the same browns, purples
and blues of her loneliness—a dress
that never fades or wears thin
where i live
is the juke on the corner—hamburgerfishchilli smells
drawing hungry niggahs off the street and pimpmobiles
cluttering the asphalt parking lot. pool tables in the
back where much gambling and shit take place and
many niggahs fall to the knife of the violent surgeon.
one night me and cowboy were almost killed by a stray
bullet from some renegade low riders and me and
kathy used to go down and drop quarters
and listen to al green, and the dudes would hate
my 'sditty ways and call me a dyke
'cause i wouldn't sell pussy
where i live
is the night club working one to six in the morning.
cigarette burn holes in my stockings and wig full of
cigarette smoke. flesh bruised from niggahs pinching my
meat and feeling my thighs, ears full of spit
from whispers and obscene suggestions and mind full of
sleep's spiders building a hazy nest—eyes full of

rainbows looking forward to the day i leave this hell
where i live
avoiding the landlord on the first and fifteenth when he
comes around to collect the rent. i'm four months behind
and wish i had a niggah to take care of me for a change
instead of taking me through changes. this building which
keeps chewing hunks out of the sides of people's cars and
the insane old bitch next door beating on the wall, scaring
the kids and telling me to shut up. every other day she calls
the cops out here and i hope they don't run a make on me
and find all them warrants
where i live
the little gangsters diddy-bop through and pick up
young bitches and flirt with old ones, looking to
snatch somebody's purse or find their way into somebody's
snatch 'cause mama don't want them at home and papa
is a figment and them farms them farms them farms
they call schools. and mudflapped bushy-headed entities
swoop the avenues seeking death
it's the only thrill left
where i live
at the lip of a big black vagina
birthing nappy-headed pickaninnies every hour on the hour
the county is her pimp and she can turn a trick
swifter than any bitch ever graced this earth
she's the baddest piece of ass on the west coast
named black los angeles

The central metaphor represents her home neighborhood as a "big black vagina" of an almost mechanical fertility ("every hour on the hour"). This image refers to the idea of home, a space that is intimate, familiar, maternal, feminine and vaguely monstrous as seen from the outside. The comparison in the last stanza sums up the exploitation and subordination of black communities by white Los Angeles: it is like the relationship of a prostitute and her pimp. He is the county – the local governments that fostered political and social inequality.[51] The African American community is a fertile and formidable goddess, but also a sexual slave.

The poem's circular structure is suffocating, and this sensation is highlighted by repetition: "where I live," a chanted refrain marking the stanzas; the parallel structure; and the phrases like "barsandbarsandbarsandbarsandbars." The ghetto is a war zone destroyed by poverty, violence, decay and abandonment, but it is also overflowing with life, with color, exuberance and movement. Like the Watts Towers, the neighborhood is a mosaic, fragments of life, objects, dialogues, sounds, odors, colors, feelings, memories, places and people.

We move little by little into the merciless world of the ghetto, passing from the general to the particular, from the exterior to the interior point of view, going so far as to cross from the I to the other side of the mirror. Coleman uses devices borrowed from film (she was also a screenwriter), which she sometimes does to enrich her poetic palette:

I like doing all those kind of neat things with the poem, using scriptwriting techniques – camera angles, I do panning shots in poems, pov shots – point-of-view shots. When the camera is acting as the eyes of a specific character to give that character's point of view. I use a lot of cinematic technique (Coleman 1979–80, 56).

Poems like this one, "woven out of the fabric of [Coleman's] life" (Moffet 1982, 3), attempt to fill in the gaps and rectify the distortions and falsifications in the "official" literature and history concerning African Americans, especially when they are female, poor and Angeleno:

I remember being in high school in '64, taking World History and reading, "The negro race has made no major contribution to the history of the world." Uh – *right!* There's a whole lost history, and as a writer, I constantly think about the fact that no one's ever written, say, the history of Black Los Angeles...I've written 6 books and feel it might have been *16* books if I'd had the quality time to just do *that* (Coleman 1991, 119).[52]

But using the elements of her life was just a start—"it's not enough just to tell it." Ultimately poetry is about working the material, composing, presenting and manipulating it, with the result that "sometimes the poem, man, is a substitute for a machine gun" (Coleman 1979–80, 61).

The tone and style of "Where I Live" contrast with those in the poems on Watts by Powe and Johnie Scott from the mid-1960s. Their tones were austere, their ghettos were unrelenting hells, sterile and abandoned. Their careful and restrained language described the reality of the ghetto from the outside looking in. The "I" either did not appear or was a mere observer, isolated from the community. Scott describes "Watts, a womb," which Coleman's poem recalls. However, Coleman's principal metaphor is crude and vigorous, where Scott's is modest and simple. "Where I Live" manages to reproduce the rhythm, speech and the life of the neighborhood, while also creating its own poetic language. Coleman gave Los Angeles poetry a unique and recognizable voice.

She eventually depicted the whole city with the same ambivalence that "Where I Live" limited to Watts. The feeling of imprisonment is omnipresent:

Prisoner of Los Angeles

so this is it, i say to the enigma in the mirror
this is your lot/assignment/relegation
this is your city
 ...
i will never leave here[53]

But despite this horror, Coleman says:

I *have* to write about L.A., I *had* to be about L.A., I didn't have any choice, I couldn't get *out*! I couldn't go East when Jayne Cortez went. Or when Quincy Troupe went. I couldn't leave! I was stuck here. So I had to make the best out of the bad situation.

Coleman did, in fact, turn the fact of living and writing in Los Angeles into an advantage. She profited from the untapped material Los Angeles offers, and shaped herself as an ambassador, demanding that the world recognize her city and neighborhood:

Everybody I know is writing about Hollywood or Orange County or Beverly Hills, but they are not writing about the Los Angeles I grew up in. So in a sense I have a stake here (Moffet 1982, 3).

In addition to her attachments to Los Angeles, Coleman takes a lot from W.E.B. Dubois' more universalist conception of the black artist:

W.E.B. Du Bois is my man—he wrote *The Souls of Black Folk*. And even though the language is a little stiff and archaic, he's important because he identified our context: that we live in two worlds simultaneously. Everything in the dominant culture is ours also; ...So you're bicultural—and if you're smart enough, you're bilingual (Coleman 1991, 135).

She has perfectly integrated the concept of "double-consciousness" that Du Bois developed and expressed in these famous words:

The Negro is a sort of seventh son, born with a veil, and gifted with second-sight in this American world.... It is a peculiar sensation, this double-consciousness.... One ever feels his twoness,—an American, a Negro; two souls, two thoughts, two unreconciled strivings; two warring ideals in one dark body, whose dogged strength alone keeps it from being torn asunder.

The history of the American Negro is the history of this strife, – this longing to attain self-conscious manhood, to merge his double self into a better and truer self. In this merging he wishes neither of the older selves to be lost. He would not Africanize America, for America has too much to teach the world and Africa. He would not bleach his Negro soul in a flood of white Americanism, for he knows that Negro blood has a message for the world. He simply wishes to make it possible for a man to be both a Negro and an American (Du Bois 1989, 3).

Coleman made this the basis of her world view and expanded it to include everything that made her "what [she is] physically before you – black, female, a mother. And black not as in African black, but black as a direct product of the socioeconomic structure of America" (Coleman 1979–80, 51). She considered the African American to be an "entirely new animal," an original and unique product of American history and racism, defined by the duality of African Americans being both members of the black population and citizens of the United States. This allegiance was reaffirmed throughout her work, as in "Midnight Carries Me South Along Illusion Avenue":

> my story no different. brother love came up to see me,
> a sack of goodies and an empathetic ear. "most sistuhs
> who been through what you been through been dead
>   long time ago"
> uncaps the bottle, pours the song. we toast that
> bitch, mother america

At the same time, she said, "I consider myself in the tradition of *Western Literature!*" (Coleman 1991, 135). She saw herself belonging to, and participating in, the dominant "high" culture, not a separate "minority" culture. Coleman noted that such black biculturalism was more pronounced on the West Coast, particularly in Los Angeles:

I'm from the West Coast. Blacks are only 9% of the population in Southern California at this time anyway, and when I was growing up, we were a greater part of the population but not that much greater. I didn't *live* in a black world, I lived in a black world and a white world.... And so I grew up with white kids and all that's my heritage, but at home I lived a black midwestern upbringing. So that's my heritage too. And then all the other things came to me from outside of those arenas, outside in the world out there. I did not have any black poets to hang with, I could not hang with an Amiri Baraka or any of his crowd, I could not hang with Gwendolyn Brooks or any of her crowd.... I was isolated from the centers of black culture in this nation.

Despite strong territorial identifications, the lines between ethnic communities were a lot less rigid than those between social classes. Watts has always been a mixed neighborhood; Coleman was raised by a black Honduran woman, and interracial couples were common. Even during the most militant period, whites participated in the local art movements.

So it was hardly out of the ordinary that Coleman should belong simultaneously to a militant black world and to a hippie world of love-ins and rock concerts.[54] Coleman found inspiration everywhere:

I can criticize a movie or piece of fiction because I belong to both traditions. I'm affected by the literature I grew up with, which is: Edgar Allan Poe, Nathanael West, Nathaniel Hawthorne, Evelyn Waugh, Somerset Maugham, Albert Camus, Andre Malraux, Chekhov...these are all people I read, they're all my influences. I was privy to that literature; I read Plato, Aristotle, Kant, Emerson – all of them. But I also listened to the blues; I also know who my culture is. I read Richard Wright, James Baldwin...although I came to black literature late because I didn't have access to it until I became an adult (Coleman 1991, 125).

Despite all their apparent isolation, and despite all the injustices that their community has suffered, this eclecticism unites the Watts poets with the other "Communards" of Los Angeles.

Decline and Heritage
of the Black Los Angeles Poets

The Watts Writers Workshop was infiltrated and then destroyed by an FBI informant as part of the bloody campaign of repression against political militancy in the United States. The Watts Prophets, too, saw opportunities run dry all of a sudden in the early 1970s, thanks to the pernicious action of this same informant. The most important Los Angeles underground newspaper also suffered harassment and costly legal proceedings. *The Los Angeles Free Press*, whose circulation reached 100,000 copies at its peak, underwent a change in management and became essentially an adult newspaper.[55] Most of the cultural centers in Watts ceased their activities or were relocated outside the black community. Of those cited earlier in this chapter, only the Watts Towers Arts Center, the Inner City Cultural Center, the Aquarian Bookstore, and the Arkestra lasted into the 1980s.

Although FBI repression contributed to this decline, other factors were involved. The interest and sympathy aroused by the riots eventually lagged, and subsidies dried up. Moreover, attitudes towards public arts funding grew more conservative, and government subsidies would all but disappear under Reagan in the 1980s. As Daáood observed:

It was very fashionable to give money to the arts, especially the so-called minority arts, or the black artist, to pacify this whole, the scream and cry of humanity for a better existence. And when the media did its job on pacifying this voice, and the social climate was such that it didn't need to quiet, it didn't need to have to deal with these voices anymore, well then the money left, and the support left, and it became harder and harder to deal with it, and to maintain these organizations.

The causes popular in the '60s were eclipsed, while the music industry provided a different channel for youthful revolt, which weakened the underground press. The absence of any comprehensive public cultural policy in Los Angeles and the fragmentation of decision-making bodies made the community arts organizations, which were dependent on public funds, very vulnerable:

> Unlike San Francisco and some other communities, Los Angeles does not have a neighborhood arts program. Thus there is no official body to assist with funding and proposal development, coordinate programs, provide technical and research support, and help clear away the typical bureaucratic obstacles to local programming. Without this resource, it is hard to build permanence into the various community arts projects (H.S. Perloff 1979, 34).

BUT DESPITE THE DECLINE and repression, a lively heritage remained. The Watts Prophets went their separate ways in the 1980s (although they would re-form in the mid-1990s). They represented a direct connection between the ghetto culture of the 1960s and that of the 1980s, and their reputation as the founders of hip-hop ensures that they will stay relevant for future poets.

Daáood remained loyal to the cultural militancy of his mentor, Horace Tapscott, and continued to participate in community endeavors into the 21st century. Among these was The Gathering, a socio-cultural center, food co-ops, and alternative schools for children – all of which were financed with the help of artists. His poetry continued the styles of the 1960s, but he also adopted later technology, using video/digital recording as a poetic medium. In the early 1990s, he and Billy Higgins created a performance space in Leimert Park, a South Central neighborhood that was revived in part thanks to his presence.[56] Once again, he could put his conception of the community artist into practice:

> At this stage in my life I see my work as healing, mending psyches through the arts, [to] create space for this to happen, the ritual space of performance, the classroom, the one on one

magic, the World Stage. To produce, to perform, to educate.... I met Billy Higgins on this journey.... We founded the World Stage: Performance Gallery, a place where the community deposits its laughter and tears and transforms them into music and poetry. It has become a vital force in the creative community of South Central (Cross 1993, 105).

Wanda Coleman was deeply involved in the construction of a local poetry network. She took part in the Beyond Baroque Foundation Wednesday Night Poetry Workshop, out of which grew the first truly city-wide, organized generation of poets. She was a role model for important poets of the following generation, including Michelle T. Clinton and La Loca. Although she moved out of South Central, she continued to visit her old neighborhood as a "haint"[57] (a ghost or spirit). She eventually combined South Central and Hollywood into a single symbolic conglomeration, "hollywatts," that represented Los Angeles as a whole. With this, she renewed the myth of Los Angeles through her personal interpretation.

Despite the continued presence of some of these artists in South Central into the 1980s, there was no self-sustaining scene, as Daáood pointed out:

There are very few settings where the young can meet with the older and share information.... I read this article once, and they were talking about how a lot of older people think the younger generation has let them down, dropped the torch, and the young lady was saying, "Y'all didn't pass no torch in the first place." And that's the problem I think, it's that gap that happened. A lot of young people think they had to develop in a vacuum. It's not always easy when you have to start from scratch to do something... (Cross 1993, 103)

For the South Central poets, as for other scenes before them, it was difficult, or even impossible, to develop a native, independent, long-lasting scene across different generations.

CHAPTER FOUR

The Los Angeles Scene in the 1970s and 1980s

Howling Poems of the Beat Generation

Sometimes I be like Miss bad ass black chick
above and beyond anything left behind by some white man,
sometimes honky culture piss me off & wear me out
'cept when I'm checking out the Beats,
the bongo drum beats of the old time beatniks
& their pseudo jazz scene – hey
truth is, I'm into it
truth is, them wine-drinking poet types,
them knapsack-lugging zen-meditating poem-writers
give me a literary tradition
a language of resistance & bongos,
give me hope & spit & joyful ways
to avoid all the fearful tapdancing
that assimilation got the hearts of the mainstream.
The lie-eatin', lie-generatin' lifestyle
that makes this breathing process deathly boring.

Problem is, we ain't got no name for the scene of this age.
We not hippies, we not beatniks,
we got a touch of the punk
but the heck would give in punk the leadership.
Punk ain't got the spunk, not the spark
ain't got the know-withall insight
to righteously dish out the dirt

to the yuppie bluppy guppie materialist sell-outs
in this girl's city.

— MICHELLE T. CLINTON

The Scene in the 1970s –
Beyond Baroque Foundation

Beyond Baroque Center was the first institution devoted to
poetry writing and publishing in Southern California, and its
beginnings in 1968 signaled the development of a more orga-
nized regional framework. Thanks to its gradual institutional-
ization, its longevity and its uniqueness, what was to become
known as Beyond Baroque Literary/Arts Center finally provided
a stable base and a gathering place for poets, who until then had
been largely isolated and scattered. Beyond Baroque played many
roles, perhaps most importantly that of an institution of record.
Without a record, a movement is condemned to start over again
with every generation. But Beyond Baroque made it possible
for an independent local poetry scene to develop.[106] All through
the 1970s, its members worked to create a poetic community
founded on a regional identity. The project succeeded at least in
part because Beyond Baroque forged a bond between previous
generations – the Beats, the poets of *Coastlines*, certain Watts
poets – and new arrivals.

Created almost by accident, Beyond Baroque reflected the
openness and flexibility of late 1960s Los Angeles. Its devel-
opment in the 21st century is an example of the way non-profit
cultural centers have evolved since the 1970s, and its contradic-
tions embodied those of the scene as a whole.

IN THE BEGINNING, *beyond baroque* was a literary review. George
Drury Smith, a Santa Monica high school teacher at the time,
had dreamed of becoming involved in the local literary commu-
nity since 1964. When he could not find the "scene," he decided
to draw writers to him by publishing a magazine. But it was

four years before he had the funds (thanks to an inheritance) to publish the first issue of *beyond baroque, Quarterly Anthology Reflecting Nascent Literary Trends,* in December 1968. Its stated mission was to promote a national, even international, and avant-garde experimental poetry, the prelude to a literary, artistic and human renaissance – a conviction displayed at the beginning or end of each issue of the magazine until the early 1980s:

If you believe in an imminent literary flowering...

If you believe that man's re-conception of the universe in terms of space-time extends to the arts...

If you believe that the survival of writing as an art implies a re-evaluation (not a devaluation) of language per se, and of its use, significance, vision...

If you believe that man stands on the threshold of new sensibilities and modes of thinking, new relationships and new apparitions even within old structures and forms, new relevance and changed proportions in all things......

If you believe these things, and if these, your beliefs are reflected in your life-style...

THEN beyond baroque IS FOR YOU!

This profession of faith, with its utopian accents and New Age flavor, recalled the mystic humanism, grandiloquence and hope for a new era of the Beats and hippies. Like them, it suggested a need to revolutionize the senses and the arts and to shatter the barriers between art and life. These aspirations, combined with a concern for language and form, placed the magazine within the avant-garde. It "was considered one of five or six avant-garde literary magazines in the United States," Smith said in a 1987 interview.

Smith acquired a building to provide an office for the magazine and "Roneo" (mimeograph-like) equipment to print the magazine starting with the second issue. Others joined forces with him, including Jim Krusoe, Lynn Shoemaker, John Harris and Joseph Hansen. Vacant space in the building was soon filled with regular literary activities – a writing workshop and poetry readings. Bayrock Press was founded to finance the magazine and support Smith. An art gallery/performance space was opened for exhibits, concerts, dance performances, theater, performance art and even films that could not be seen elsewhere. Beyond Baroque became a true cultural center, with ever more diverse activities, but it always focused on literature, and particularly poetry.

In 1972 Beyond Baroque Enterprises was incorporated as a tax-exempt educational organization, Beyond Baroque Foundation. The Foundation could now receive federal, state and city grants, often on the understanding that they would obtain matching funds from other sources. Thanks to this increased financial stability, Beyond Baroque was able to continue its expansion and extend its educational work, instituting programs for school children or hosting readings by poets of national repute.

The same year, Alexandra Garrett, who had worked for *Trace* and *Coastlines*, joined Smith's team; she was to organize a public library. The Beyond Baroque Library of Small Press Literary Publications opened in April 1974, with an initial catalogue of 3,000 volumes (by 1978 it held 15,000 volumes). It became what *Poets & Writers Newsletter* called "the largest American independent [poetry] library to date" (Poets & Writers, Inc. 1977, 15). The collection has continued to grow, thanks to grants from the National Endowment for the Humanities (NEH). Garrett acted as the Foundation's librarian, fundraiser, treasurer, administrator, editor and even custodian at various times until her death on December 31, 1991.

Also in 1972, a second magazine, *NeWLetterS*, began to appear. It was less experimental and more local, devoted to the "writers West of the Rockies [whom we called] 'the Cismontane' writers," Smith recalled in the interview. Alongside poems and prose fiction, it published "commentary and news of the Western literary and cultural community (workshops, writers programs, grants, publishing, community arts)." *NeWLetterS* had its origin in notices sent to the few early subscribers of *beyond baroque,* to let them know that their magazine would be late and advise them of activities taking place at the new literary center. The weekly programs of poetry readings organized by Beyond

Baroque's co-director and associate editor Jim Krusoe were also listed and soon a few poems were added to the notice. The note-turned-*NeWLetterS* was much more successful than the original magazine; under the name NEW *Magazine* its circulation rose as high as 18,000. At the event "Forty Years of L.A. Small Presses," which took place during the 1990 L.A. Poetry Festival, Krusoe recounted:

> We continued running out of money so we were delaying and delaying the production of the next issue for our 15 subscribers.[58] So we started sending out notes explaining why their issue was delayed. We had extra space on the note, so we threw in an extra poem or two. Then about that time we also started the reading series.... Then we started putting the schedule of the reading series onto this apologetic note that was explaining why their magazine hadn't arrived yet. It turned out that the circulation for our notes, and we started putting in other readings going on, was far more successful than the actual magazine [*beyond baroque*] ever was. So we got to the point where we had maybe 500 or a 1000 subscribers to our explanatory notes to the original 15 (Forty Years of L.A. Small Presses, 1990).

NeWLetterS answered a real need. Smith said its success was due to "the inability of the foundation and other groups to get consistent coverage of literary events in local newspapers and magazines." *NeWLetterS* reserved more and more space for the schedules of poetry readings in the region. And it started the idea of a publication with modest costs (using a cheap glue-bound newsprint format), large circulation and free subscriptions. This was the trademark of Beyond Baroque publications into the 1980s. Krusoe continued:

> Eventually we stopped doing the magazine in the limited traditional form and decided... to go for a high circulation, not charge any money whatsoever, give the magazine away but print on newsprint. And in those days it cost us 8 cents or a

dime to print each issue and we printed poems, short stories; we listed readings and we'd leave them around movie theaters and places like that. And that's in fact the height of it all.

In 1976, the Foundation started sending books to anyone wanting them free of charge, as well. The men and women of Beyond Baroque wanted to assume responsibility for the literary scene, and this encouraged them to emphasize accessibility – both geographic and financial – above all else. Smith recalled in his 1987 interview:

We sometimes had a hundred people who came to events and we had seating for only 50 or 60 at most.... We often put loudspeakers outside so people who couldn't get in could hear the poetry readings. Just all sorts of things were done to try to accommodate more people.... Sometimes people came from 35, 100, 200 miles away for poetry readings.

CONTRADICTORY ASPIRATIONS presided over the birth of Beyond Baroque. Smith had an avant-garde understanding of art and poetry.[59] He hoped that poetry could be renewed by an encounter with other art forms:

My original hope was that I'd see some sort of a renaissance in poetry and the first thing that I saw was that the really exciting writing was being done in fiction as far as I was concerned, not poetry. And frankly, I don't think that my expectations were met as far as seeing some resurgence in creative writing and poetry. I had the hope to see some fascinating experimental poetry and I think that what I saw was a lot of good poetry, but nothing that I felt was really great.... I originally had the notion that at Beyond Baroque there would be some sort of interplay between the various arts, a synesthetic sort of thing where art and poetry and music would come together in different kinds of forms, and I didn't see it at all. That didn't seem to be happening. Even though we had activities in most of the arts. The poets would come and lean their greasy heads against the paintings, and they wouldn't come to the music. And the artists who tried to dabble in literature usually failed miserably. So that thing simply didn't seem to be happening.

Smith's ambitions could seem detached from his local context. He saw literature as a private and individual art form. Los Angeles literature could not be distinguished from that of other cities except through the assertion of the poets themselves. Smith sought to publish quality writing that was aware of its history and its consequences. "I hoped to find works written by literate writers who love language and write well," he said. But his modernism conflicted with some earlier Los Angeles writers, who attached more importance to autodidacticism and freedom from formal constraints than they did to high art traditions. The mid-1970s version of *beyond baroque's* credo nonetheless concludes with "the belief that the role of High Art is to seek Truth, reach towards Cosmic Consciousness, and find ways of transmitting the highest levels of emotional and spiritual experience through Works of Beauty."[60] The explicit reference to art's ethical, aesthetic and spiritual role, and the suggestion that art should elevate subjective experience into something universal, suggest an allegiance to academic, rather than independent, poetry – a sign of the growing institutionalization of the Foundation.

But eventually the Foundation moved away from its founder's original plan, and became a regional poetry center. It "developed its own roots right in the area [and became] a base where [poets] could teach and converse as artists" (Cardona-Hine 1979, 148). Although he never abandoned his high aesthetic standards, Smith's desire for literary community, his generosity (he spent his entire inheritance on Beyond Baroque), and his sense of humor (some thought many of Beyond Baroque's programs and activities bore "New" in their title in homage to Smith's cat, which was called NewCat) made him an ideal leader. He knew how to work with a team of people, and the relaxed atmosphere of Beyond Baroque attests to this spirit of tolerance. Those who were involved, like Alexandra Garrett, remember it with a certain nostalgia:

When I first walked in Beyond Baroque, there was George, sitting at his desk, which was piled three feet high with the most incredible pile of mail and God knows what, and I saw this odd thing hanging from a string in a shoe-box top. It was strung from the ceiling and it turned out to be the telephone! ...In my estimation, things were a great deal funkier in those days.... People walked in off the street and there was a great deal of charm, something that I don't like to see lost and in fact I think that still exists here where people feel free to walk in off the street. That's really nice and George and Jim [Krusoe] and the original people really created that and the whole idea of putting [loud]speakers outside – I mean people pressing their noses against the glass – is something that won't happen again I don't think, but it set the tone for what's still going on at Beyond Baroque.[61]

The progressive transformation of Beyond Baroque Foundation into an institution distanced it from bohemianism. The Foundation, in "settling down" and in "federating" the city's scattered poets, came to be the guardian of the past. For example, it enabled the few remaining Venice Beats to perform their work for younger writers, which established continuity between generations for the first time.

Which is not to say that there were no changes at the Foundation itself. *beyond baroque* became *beyond baroque/newforms,* continuing into 1980. *NeWLetterS* became NEW *Magazine* in 1976, then NEW *Magazine: Arts & Letters*, and finally NEW. Then, starting in 1980, these were all replaced by *Beyond Baroque Obras* (which had several issues, edited by Manazar (Manuel Gamboa [1934–2000]), and in 1981 *Magazine* and *Poetry News* (both edited by Jocelyn Fisher). The *NewBooks* series published six titles in 1976 and 1977. The NewComp Graphics Center, equipped with "modern phototypesetting equipment...for the use of non-commercial literary publishers and arts groups," assisted and trained many local publishers.

A local and regional orientation now marked most of Beyond Baroque's activities. The State of California recognized Beyond

Baroque as a "conduit organization," which could oversee grants to organizations that lacked official "non-profit" status; the Foundation even lobbied elected officials and representatives to influence the state's arts policy.

This commitment to the region became ever stronger over time. The January/February 1975 mission statement spoke of serving the literary community "West of the Rockies." An editorial from February 1976 narrowed the focus still further:

> We believe the West Coast has begun to receive some of the literary recognition and attention it deserves, and we believe the wide circulation of *NeWLetterS* helped. Beyond Baroque Publications will now focus its attention more specifically on an area that still desperately needs focus – Southern California.

Much of Beyond Baroque's activity was governed by the unique nature of Los Angeles, as *beyond baroque 752 Newforms* suggested in 1976:

> [The Center] believes few, if any, areas in the nation have as much creativity per capita as Los Angeles. Yet the city has great difficulty in maintaining a cultural identity that reflects this creativity.
>
> The very diversity of talent and the enormous geographic space of Los Angeles pose special problems which do not exist in compact areas such as New York or San Francisco. For over seven years Beyond Baroque has offered a unique and ever expanding set of solutions to some of these problems.

Finally, the 1978 version of the credo (in *beyond baroque 783*) was aimed very precisely at "the entire greater Los Angeles community." The city may be huge and its artists dispersed, but the development of better communication could help create a unified community: at "the base of [Beyond Baroque's] program is a commitment to communication and to the importance of regional centers for the creative arts within the metropolitan area."

Beyond Baroque was pushed by local artists toward local writing, rather than modernist universalism. These writers, and the institutions they formed, helped to create an extensive, active network of literary production and distribution.

HARRY NORTHUP recalls the importance of Beyond Baroque's Wednesday Night Poetry Workshop:

> In February of 1969, the free Wednesday night poetry workshop began; I was one of its original members. That was where many of us here in L.A. got together. There was Leland Hickman, whom I had known from New York City, Bill Mohr, Wanda Coleman, Kate Braverman, Krusoe, all those people in the late '60s, early '70s. It was a gathering place.[62]

Jack Grapes described the scene:

> We used to go to Beyond Baroque on Wednesday nights and there were 20 of us sitting around a room. And that was it! We were the scene. And we were part of it and we believed in it…. We thought then and still think that some of the best poetry being written in the country is being written here, in Southern California. We wanted exposure and a wider audience for ourselves and for our fellow poets (Forty Years of L.A. Small Presses, 1990).

The workshop was initially co-directed by the poet and novelist Joseph Hansen (who died in 2004), and John Harris, who later ran Papa Bach Bookstore. It moved from the psychedelic shop The Bridge to Beyond Baroque in early 1969, where the co-directors played a valuable critical and pedagogical role, which became the basis of the workshop's success, as Hansen observed:

> At first, there were Wednesday nights when Harris and I had no one else to talk to or listen to. Some of those who did stray in out of the night became angry with us. We were after unity and brevity, directness, coherence, objectivity. We were after

craftsmanship. This implied self-discipline and in 1969 discipline was a dirty word.... However fed up he got, Harris stuck with the Workshop and so did I. And soon we were averaging a dozen poets a night, and after a few months had passed, two dozen. Sometimes, as many as forty packed the little room (Hansen, 1977–78, 136).

Drury Smith encouraged the workshop, and suggested splitting it into two: one for those whose goal was to share their poems with a kindly audience, the other for those who were looking for more critical discussions. Hansen thought Smith's tastes were "a far cry from what the Workshop was aiming at," but nonetheless several issues of *beyond baroque* were devoted to workshop members' work. These anthologies gave form to an emerging group of Los Angeles poets.

The Wednesday Workshop was important because, unlike earlier workshops, it brought together writers from different areas of the city. Hansen recalled:

Poetry workshops had existed in Southern California long before ours started in Venice.... But these pockets were mostly unaware of each other. Los Angeles sprawls. They could have remained out of touch forever. But Venice Poetry Workshop – tough and demanding as it was – drew crowds, and from all over, Watts to San Fernando Valley, Hermosa Beach to San Gabriel, people of all ages and backgrounds, willing to take bruises in order to learn to write. And slowly they began to shape a community of poets in Los Angeles (Hansen 1977–78, 139).

This new generation of Los Angeles poets went through the stages of artistic maturation – apprenticeship, writing, publication, recognition – at the same time and in the same place, and were able to encourage later generations as well. Wanda Coleman described it in these terms:

Between the years '68 and '73–'74, I used to go [to Beyond Baroque] pretty regularly. That's when I came across people that I feel like I more or less grew up with poetically in a sense, or I regard them as my peer group. And that would be Eloise Klein Healy, Holly Prado, Bill Mohr, Kate Braverman, Leland Hickman, Jim Krusoe, Jack Grapes – gosh, there's more – Greeny [Bob Greenfield], Bob Flanagan, people who were in the workshop that I came across. And Harry Northup also. So the workshop people, these became people that I regarded as my peers. And I kept running into them over the years as I went to read and do readings, and they were poets and we sort of all evolved in this miasma, this sort of cultural thing that was taking place. So those are more or less the people that I regard as the true basis of what's become [the L.A. poetry scene].

As Coleman noted, quite a few people connected with Beyond Baroque were originally from Los Angeles, and most of those who were not had settled there permanently. This put an end to the constant comings and goings that had characterized earlier movements in the city:

What was L.A. hadn't yet come into being. Because these people [the older poets] were not really committed to it, for whatever reasons, or they were going in and out of it, like Wakowski spent most of her growth in New York. Eshleman came from the Midwest. I don't know where John Thomas came from, he was just here (laugh). William Pillin came from Chicago. So these were people who came from other places. Dennis Phillips is another one who I regard as a sibling more or less, and actually Dennis Cooper. Those are two people who were born in Southern California.

Publishing Activity Around Beyond Baroque

The small presses and literary magazines that are essential to the emergence and expansion of a poetic scene were created around this time. Some attempted to "document what was seen as an emerging poetry movement," as, for instance, Jack Grapes'

Bombshelter Press. Others, like Bill Mohr's Momentum Press, wanted "to make the poets whom [they] knew and whose work [they] liked famous," (Forty Years of L.A. Small Presses 1990). And others aimed "to help build a community, to help introduce these various cliques to each other, to have them read each other's work," as Leland Hickman put it. Eloise Klein Healy described the importance of the connections these publishers helped to establish:

> When I first started to get involved with the writing community in Los Angeles [in 1974–75], there was only one thing going on, and that was at Beyond Baroque…. Some magazines in L.A., like *Bachy* or *Momentum*, have really contributed to developing an audience for poetry and an audience for poets, places to get more stuff out on the page and have some way to talk about it with each other…. I think that in this city in which so many things are spread so far apart, that this kind of network is really important to the writers (Healy 1979, 67).

During the mid-to-late '70s in particular, these small presses were almost exclusively devoted to writers of the Beyond Baroque workshop. At the 1990 L.A. Poetry Festival, Jack Grapes recalled:

> Here is how Bombshelter Press began. Dennis Ellman read a poem called "Tomatoes" one Wednesday night at the Beyond Baroque Workshop and said afterward that he was going to be reading at a place in Hermosa Beach called the Alley Cat. I went to hear him read and met Michael Andrews, the poet in charge of the reading. We started talking about publishing and decided to run the readings together and publish a series of anthologies to accompany them…. Since then we've published dozens of Los Angeles poets.

Bombshelter Press was created with the explicit goal of publishing poems by workshop members. In 1975–76 it produced five anthologies, with a circulation ranging from 300 to 1,000 copies, entitled *Alley Cat Readings*. They were based on a series of readings at the Alley Cat. The books included poetry, photography and draw-ings. Between 1976 and 1990, Bombshelter published 35 indi-vidual collections, and three Los Angeles anthologies including more than fifty works by students of the program Poets-in-the-Schools. They also produced limited edition books for collectors. In the late 1980s, they launched the magazine *Onthebus*, which broke into the national market. Bombshelter Press continued its regional strategy into the 1990s – the best way, the publishers thought, to gain recognition for poets. But they also published well-known authors from other regions or countries:

> Part of what we want to do is again we want to get exposure for the poets for publishing. Maybe 60% of the poets in here are from Los Angeles and another 40% are from around the country. So we don't want to keep it inbred, we want to get this out there.... Whether we know it or not, really the success of any individual poet and the success of any individual press rests on the success of the whole scene. I say that a lot and I don't say it because I'm generous. I believe that *I* will get the benefit if the group benefits. So it's selfish. And anything I can do for any other publisher, any other editor, any other poet, I think it's going to come back to me. So it is a little self-moti-vated. I think all of us have to think this way.

Thanks to his publishing and teaching, Jack Grapes became an authority and an institution of sorts, an essential figure in the poetry network. His work as an actor brought him income and visibility, so he could influence attitudes towards poetry in Los Angeles, as well as help direct the careers of a number of new poets. Bombshelter Press co-editor Andrews described their commitment to the poetry scene:

> Well, we started out with that attitude anyway, that L.A. poetry had something. This was '76.... We sort of thought it was different than anyone else's because it was accessible and concrete and people stood up and read it. And other people, plumbers, would come and listen to it. We thought

that deserved some recognition and Simon and Schuster wasn't going to print us[,] so *we* did. (Forty Years of L.A. Small Presses 1990).

These two poets and their press fit squarely in the "bohemia" tradition: their focus was on Los Angeles (during the 1970s) to the exclusion of the rest of the national poetry scene; they stressed accessibility, concreteness, simplicity and oral presentation; their audience was unsophisticated; they criticized commercial publishing; and they took Charles Bukowski as an aesthetic model. Grapes himself made this clear, openly aligning himself with the Beats, opposing "elitist" or "purist" poetry, and favoring "fun and interesting and spiritual" writing (Grapes 1979, 10).

Bill Mohr was also very conscious of the power that comes with publishing; he confided to the *Los Angeles Times* that he had started his own magazine and press so he could choose which poets would gain recognition (Mohr 1979, 5). Like Grapes, Mohr settled in Los Angeles in the late 1960s; like him, Mohr had been an actor. But Mohr and Grapes differed in important ways: where Grapes preferred accessible, entertaining poetry, Mohr had a taste for linguistic experimentation–he cited Whitman, Williams, and Olson as models, and called Holly Prado's *Feasts* "the *Tender Buttons* of the Los Angeles literary production of the last twenty years." At the same time, Mohr was politically involved; his opposition to the Vietnam War inspired his first reading. He believed that political dissent united Los Angeles' "best poets." His experimental bent and political vision led Mohr to a more universal understanding of poetry; Grapes preferred the local. And Mohr had academic aspirations, too; in 2011, his dissertation was published as *Hold-Outs, the Los Angeles Poetry Renaissance, 1948–92* (University of Iowa Press, 2011).[63]

But for all their differences, Mohr's Momentum Press was similar to Bombshelter. After he had directed the first two issues of *Bachy*, the literary magazine published by Papa Bach Bookstore, Mohr decided to found *Momentum*, to publish mainly "poets [he] knew from the Beyond Baroque workshop" (Forty Years of L.A. Small Presses, 1990), though he also included writers outside this circle such as Garrett Hongo. Nine issues of the magazine came out between 1974 and 1978, when he devoted himself exclusively to book publishing, because "what will last is books and a magazine is very transient" (Mohr 1979, 5). From 1974 to 1990 he published two dozen collections, including Leland Hickman's *Tiresias 1:9:B: Great Slave Lake Suite* (1980), which was nominated for the *Los Angeles Times* book prize in 1980. Mohr also started to work more with authors from other cities (James Moore and Alicia Ostriker, to name but two). But Los Angeles poets have acknowledged the role he played in the development of the local scene. Harry Northup considered Momentum Press "at the center of the poetry scene in Los Angeles for many years" (Forty Years of L.A. Small Presses, 1990), and Leland Hickman called it "a fount and a focal point in this town [that] has already become legendary" (Interview, Mohr 5).

Mohr established his reputation thanks to two very important anthologies: *The Streets Inside: Ten Los Angeles Poets* (1978), and *"Poetry Loves Poetry," An Anthology of Los Angeles Poets* (1985). *The Streets Inside* was composed at Beyond Baroque's NewComp Graphics Center and financed by a grant from the NEA. It "in some ways was an outgrowth of that [Beyond Baroque] workshop," Mohr said at the 1990 L.A. Poetry Festival, and the ten poets included – Leland Hickman, James Krusoe, Holly Prado, Deena Metzger, Peter Levitt, William Mohr, Kate Ellen Braverman, Eloise Klein Healy, Harry Northup and Denis Ellman – had all met at Beyond Baroque. In the introduction, Mohr justifies his editorial choices: to devote a work to poets living in Los Angeles, and to include only ten poets so a representative sample could be included from each writer. Mohr regretted the absence of black, Chicano, and Asian poets, and admitted that without them the book's map of Los Angeles was "poor" – but he hoped that "one day all of these streets will meet in a single huge book." His preoccupation was evidence of the spatial and racial segregation in the city that even the poetry scene did not escape. "The fact remains," he wrote, "that the white poets do not know the same streets that the Black, Chicano and Asian poets know in this city."

But Mohr's introduction affirmed for the first time in a poetry anthology the need for integration and foreshadowed the evolution of the poetry scene, and the city as a whole, in the 1980s. Nevertheless, Mohr was content merely to deplore this serious gap, and he did not take the steps that would have made his anthology more faithful to the city's diversity.

In *The Streets Inside* Mohr set out to undo the mythical image of Los Angeles, by publishing works that featured a more interiorized view of the self, and were concerned with human relationships, rather than the city's decentralization or Hollywood's ever-present vice and corruption. Mohr also sought to efface Charles Bukowski's imprint from Los Angeles' poetry:

> My initial impulse [was] that when I moved to Los Angeles, the only poet people seemed to talk about was Bukowski. And I like a fair amount of Bukowski's work. I think he's a pretty major writer. On the other hand, one gets tired of living under a shadow. And so I deliberately said this is going to be a book that doesn't even mention Bukowski. This is a book that's going to pretend as though Bukowski doesn't exist (Forty Years of L.A. Small Presses, 1990).

Mohr also set his anthology apart from the short, "confessional" poetry of university creative writing programs. He preferred long, experimental narrative poems, which he called "private self-narratives." These works often involved a speaker searching for keys to the survival of mankind, moving from the private to the public realm; they also explored the "rhythmic possibilities in the language" (Mohr 1979, 6–7). Leland Hickman's work is the best example of this.

HICKMAN WAS as committed an avant-gardist as Mohr. He became involved in the local poetry community in the mid-1970s. He was an actor, a native of Santa Barbara who had lived in New York and San Francisco before moving to Los Angeles in 1970. Harry Northup introduced him to the Beyond Baroque Workshop. Hickman became more central to the poetry scene in 1977 when

John Harris asked him to take over direction of *Bachy* from Bill Mohr; he made *Bachy* "a representative and permanent vehicle" for Los Angeles poetry, and Papa Bach Bookstore a venue for poets to meet. Most importantly, it was a forum for criticism. It became a cultural and political center, particularly for those opposed to the Vietnam War.

Hickman described his ambitions for the magazine in a 1987 interview:

> When I came on to the staff, ...I decided to use the magazine to help build the community, ...generally to build an atmosphere where people could become more sophisticated about each other's poetics and also to build an atmosphere where we would look outward and not be so insular – that is I had noted at that time that there was very little interest on the part of poets here in poetry that had happened in the United States – Charles Olson, Robert Duncan, Robert Creeley. I had to do it gradually, because I had to build up community first in a way. I had to help. There were a lot of people working at that time to build the same thing. And I succeeded I think for that magazine. And the poetry community did grow.

To achieve these aims, Hickman published long interviews with "various poets who [he] felt were representative of Los Angeles poetry, who had achieved a great deal, and who were outstanding on the scene" (Forty Years of L.A. Small Presses, 1990). The interviewees included authors who had arrived on the scene before the establishment of Beyond Baroque (William Pillin), or a bit later (Dennis Cooper, Dennis Phillips, Martha Ronk), as well as writers from outside the Beyond Baroque circle (Los Angeles-based novelist John Rechy, author of *City of Night;* and George Hitchcock, editor of the magazine *Kayak*).

Hickman also asked those who had been active before 1968 to write historical essays on the city's literary past. Among them was Alvaro Cardona-Hine, a Costa Rica-born poet who had been part of *Coastlines*. He had led a writing workshop from 1965 to 1975 for poets, some of whom went on to be prominent, such as Holly Prado. In 1978 and 1979 he wrote a two-part article for *Bachy* on his personal experience in the Los Angeles world of letters, "Poetry in Los Angeles: 1945 to 1975." Joseph Hansen brought the story up to date in three essays about *The Bridge*, the Beyond Baroque Workshop and its participants, and various other topics.[64] *Bachy*'s criticism section was devoted to publications that carried work by Los Angeles poets, and encouraged polemic. All this fostered a theoretical and critical dialogue in Los Angeles, and firmly established a regional, cultural scene. Hickman also tried to shape the tastes of local poets by exposing them to other modes of poetry. He published long poems in serial format, as well as large excerpts of work by contemporary foreign poets in translation.

But John Harris lost several thousand dollars each year on the magazine. *Bachy*'s final issue ran in 1981. It contained six interviews, forty poets (six in translation, including Aimé Césaire and Michel Deguy), eight authors of fiction, three portfolios of photographs and drawings, and three articles of literary criticism. In 1984, Harris closed Papa Bach Bookstore.

Hickman started to concentrate on introducing Los Angeles poets to new, more diverse forms and modes of poetry.

> I wanted to continue but I wanted to go into areas that I hadn't really done much research in. I was into more innovative and avant-garde poetry than generally was found here in Los Angeles at that time...So I asked Paul Vangelisti if he would be interested in doing a magazine with me (Forty Years of L.A. Small Presses, 1990).

Hickman and Vangelisti founded *Boxcar* in 1983. Hickman wanted it to "combine Los Angeles artists and poets from the avant-garde all around." Two issues appeared in 1983, including visual art, multimedia art, Language Poets and "poets whose work is innovative but maverick in style, no school."

Hickman started his own magazine, *Temblor: Contemporary Poets* in 1985. It was internationalist, rather than focused on Los Angeles, though he continued to publish Los Angeles poets who produced what he called "an emblematic poetry," requiring an active, creative critical reading, as opposed to an "expressionistic writing of poetry," "the passive consumption of someone's narrative or story or expression of emotion."[65] *Temblor* was a great success, though it was supported almost entirely by an audience of poets.

> One of the things I did with *Temblor* was try to make a magazine that would shout to poets: "Look, the editor is going to do what you want." You want a whole page for three words, you're going to get it.... So that the artists felt that they could design their poems, the pages themselves. So many of them wrote with that in mind (Forty Years of L.A. Small Presses, 1990).

Internationally distributed and subsidized, it broke even between 1985 and 1989, when the *Village Voice* declared it "an important American literary journal, which took its place alongside such great magazines as *Poetry Chicago, Evergreen Review,* and *Big Table.*"[66] In 1990 the University of San Francisco bought the magazine's archives.

Hickman also played an important role as a poet. In *The Streets Inside* he said he "avoided commitment to [his] poet-self until 1964." He then devoted himself to a single long poem, *Tiresias,* the first excerpts of which, written at the time of his stay in New York (from 1964 to 1970), were published in magazines (*Manhattan Review, The Hudson Review, New American Review*), and *American Literary Anthology No. 2* (Random House).

This long work, which he said in the interview "doesn't have a pre-established overall structure like Proust or Joyce," consisted of separate poems that overlapped each other and juxtaposed a chronological story of childhood—that of "a child growing up in a conservative town at a conservative time as gay"—with abstract and incantatory fragments of intense experience that blended violence, sex, Catholicism, homosexuality and incest. It included references to the Great Slave Lake region in Canada; the author's furtive sex life; and the Robert A. Harris case, which contributed to reinstating the death penalty in California. The following excerpt recalls Hickman's 1961 stay in Los Angeles, and his encounters with male prostitutes:

this song or segment of song for that flawd song Leland at
          26 in 61 tongue out dripping for
          balm in the corrupt
     land bereft angry hungry weeping
     male snake of that time in my dark those pale hard headlights
     wove
          over my dusty ceiling from
     cars beneath my window, wide open on selma my
          gay young hustlers
     lust bereft angry hungry weeping where
     Beckett Faulkner at a loss glare down that my
     strong song's urge
          hoist me higher in my malign
     fire this song or fragment of song for that snarld song Leland at
          26 in 61 isolate rubble down gutters shuffler in
     our thick spit pool of absolute freedoms against the law to be
          legal, heritage bilge trash, out still for
     balm in glutton land policemen to kneel to to pray to, mostly
          lone in Los Angeles aching
     all down selma vine to highland hardon bared icy in drizzle
     shouting
          four a.m. hank cinq at lung top get a guy
     fuck me in azaleas spit on my face slap me by the church at las
     palmas
          way we slay the blue temple/weird
     wanderings of my subtle body

He constructed his text as a musical suite, "an incredible
symphony of the tortured self," as critic Robert Peters called it
(Peters 1979, 141). Phrases recur throughout the work, as do
sections of the poem as a whole.[67] Through autobiographical and
linguistic exploration of the fictional self–what Hickman called
the "him writing himself at a different age"–he delves "all the
way through his experience into its mythic dimension" (Kessler
1979, 143).

As a poem, it is a prophecy. And since a lot of the impulses that guide the poem, and have guided it at various times, have to do with my feelings about America, about humankind at large, about history, about politics, that they all will be a part of it, as part of the prophecy. I had the gall to say to myself to keep myself writing, that what happened to the poem and what happened to my life, in terms of destiny, how my life worked out, had a lot to do with what was going to happen to America and to the world, in a time we live in, which is a very dangerous time.

Tiresias was the blind prophet of Greek mythology who changed from man to woman then back to man again and, having predicted his own death, drank from a fountain although he knew the water would kill him. Hickman would die from AIDS in 1991.

Other Rallying Points:
Individuals, Publications, Places

Some poets without ties to Beyond Baroque were also active during this crucial period. Paul Vangelisti was originally from San Francisco, but moved to Southern California in 1968. Vangelisti wore what Robert Peters described as a "quintuple hat – there's the poetry, there's the prose that you do, there's the criticism, there's the editing, there's the publishing, there's the translating, and then there's the entrepreneuring of these fantastic programs."[68] He tried to help create a literary environment like that he had left behind in San Francisco. For the greater part of the 1970s, he worked at the independent radio station KPFK; he helped turn it into what Cardona-Hine (in the second of his *Bachy* articles) called "one of the few centripetal forces bringing poets together." He invited poets from Los Angeles and around the country to read on his program, talk about themselves and discuss poetry. The first program was dedicated to the Watts Writers Workshop, while programs that followed were dedicated to poetry and jazz.

He also created a program of radio dramas, "Los Angeles Theater of the Ear" (L.A.T.E.), financed over the course of six years by the NEA, to "tap into this community of people and...bring the figure of the poet to the public in another way," as he said in our 1987 interview. And in 1971, he founded *Invisible City* with John McBride.

Like Hickman with *Bachy*, or Mohr with *Momentum*, Vangelisti used the media to promote local poets; he also helped to preserve Los Angeles poetic history by publishing some of the poets of Venice West (Stuart Perkoff, John Thomas) in his and McBride's Red Hill Press, as well as some that had been associated with *Coastlines* (Gene Frumkin, Cardona-Hine); he also interviewed writers from Watts. Finally, he brought together Los Angeles writers to perform marathon readings of great poetic works – William Carlos Williams' *Patterson* (five and a half hours), H.D.'s *Helen in Egypt*, Dante's *Inferno*:

> We take some major work and we all read it.... We did the whole *Odyssey* of Homer in an amphitheater – 13 hours with poets, and prose writers and screenwriters, etc. And everybody likes to do it because it's like the one chance they get to feel part of something cultural in Los Angeles.... The audiences have been good, that is, the people come and go, there's the 30 or 40 people that stay throughout the whole thing. The Pound thing was the best audience. Beyond Baroque was packed. It was at the highest 150 people. And it's a celebration. Something that I guess we don't get to do that much in Los Angeles, on a daily level. We don't walk into the café and argue about literature, and I guess that's an excuse for doing that. In New York I would see those things as more superfluous than here in Los Angeles.

In his work as a publisher, he showed a preoccupation with the avant-garde akin to Hickman's. This can be seen in his program for *Invisible City*, which he recalled at the 1990 L.A. Poetry Festival:

By 1975–76 we found that we did have a program and the program was essentially a three-fold one: 1) to publish as much poetry that we considered experimental as possible, and when I say experimental I mean precisely that. I don't mean necessarily avant-garde, though that also became a preoccupation. In whatever way experimental, be that politically, or in terms of gender or in terms of madness or hallucinations, whatever that idea of experimentation entailed. The second thing was to publish literature, that is throughout the magazine, in a collage style that came from my co-editor's experiments with graphics. We collaged in a lot of criticism that we found in European journals.... So we started running what I for a lack of a better word call literature, that is commentary on writing, that allowed us to look at work here in this country in a way that it wasn't usually looked at.... And we started publishing translation. That was the third program.... So we published things that weren't normally accessible.

Invisible City released twenty-eight issues between 1971 and 1982, "whenever enough good material [was] available," as was explained in each issue. The "tabloid...on decent paper" sought to be part of "some sort of perpetual avant-garde, ...essentially radical, ...open-ended and unfinished," Vangelisti said at the 1990 L.A. Poetry Festival. It published diverse works: there were European poets; sound poets; American poets; critical reviews; political philosophy; literary reflections; interviews (with Archie Shepp, Steve Lacy, and Kenneth Rexroth, among others); articles on jazz, contemporary music, feminism and the avant-garde; and finally drawings and photography. Red Hill Press' catalogue reflected this same diversity. It published local poets, two anthologies of Los Angeles poetry, foreign poets in bilingual editions (notably the *Edizione Geiger* collection, dedicated to Italian authors translated by Vangelisti), photo essays, and collages in limited edition.

Although Vangelisti's editorial policy was similar to Hickman's or Mohr's, they had their differences here as well. Vangelisti had strong ties to Europe, particularly the Italian neo-avant-garde; he had strong political convictions; and his broad theoretical and political approach to art set him apart. His broader understanding of the world of the arts (for him, including intellectuals and artists of various periods, ethnicities and nationalities) gave him a greater historical perspective and propensity for intellectual speculation, despite the unpopularity of this in Los Angeles.

Furthermore, his knowledge of Southern California's cultural and poetic history made him one of the most interesting observers of Los Angeles poetry. For him, the true meeting place when he arrived in the city was not Beyond Baroque, but rather Papa Bach Bookstore. Following the example of San Francisco's City Lights Books, Papa Bach split into a small press (Papa Bach Editions, which produced *Bachy*) and a place for public readings, making "the relationship between the poetry scene and the bookstore...critical for the success of the bookstore,"[69] said William ("Koki") Iwamoto, a poet who worked at the Free Press Bookstore and then at Papa Bach. Iwamoto left Papa Bach and in 1972 founded Chatterton's, a bookstore famous for its support of the poetry scene. Chatterton's closed in 1994 after Iwamoto's deather. The store would re-open in 1986 as Skylight Books.

Vangelisti argued that Los Angeles poetry needed to be considered in its Californian context, and beyond that its American context. In California and Los Angeles in particular some American characteristics were much more pronounced: the disregard for historicity and "formal aesthetic culture," and the tendency to make an immediate connection between subject and object. At the same time, Californian literature was characterized by its independence, its relationship with Europe and the Far East, the profusion of small presses, its indifference to the literary establishment and New York, and its eclectic individualism. Added to these American and Californian traits are those specific to Los Angeles, i.e., space, incommunicability and fragmentation. These factors led to a rich profusion of styles and subject matter among the city's poets, such that it was futile to categorize them or try to establish a canon.

In these ways, Vangelisti reconciled the cosmopolitan avant-garde with politically committed militancy. In our 1987 interview he said:

The beauty about living in Los Angeles is that it's sort of this void to fill up, in a sense one sits around and talks with one's friends about what's going on, and if you don't do it yourself, there's almost nothing there outside the mass media, there's nothing there on a cultural level to partake in. So that's why these things get done. One does them because one needs some life around one. This work I do here in Los Angeles...is local, and I was a politically involved person. And for me, it's my form of politics now, let's say, strictly in the cultural arena.... It was my idea of living here. If I'm going to live here, I'm going to help define some sort of cultural scene.... That's why I did it, in radio and in publishing, in organizing readings and things like this.

Like many other Los Angeles artists, he was indifferent to being accepted by the national intelligentsia, but understood art internationally: he thought globally, and acted locally. In 1973, for instance, he organized a monthly series of reading at the Pasadena Museum of Modern Art. This was an attempt to "spruc[e] up poetry's public image," wrote Gregg Kilday of the *L.A. Times*, by marrying poetry to other arts – jazz, dance, photography, film, and theater – in hybrid presentations close to performance art (Kilday 1978, 8). These readings were adapted to the space of the museum; here poetry could benefit from receiving "the same kind of public exhibition that music and the plastic arts are given," Kilday wrote. Vangelisti later published the readings as an anthology.

THAT ANTHOLOGY of the museum readings, *Specimen 73: A Catalog of Poets for the Season 1973–74*, was one of the four great Californian anthologies published in that decade, after the *Anthology of L.A. Poets*; Michael C. Ford's *The Mt. Alverno Review, A Quick Anthology of West Coast Verse* of 1971, and Momentum

Press's 1978 *The Streets Inside: Ten Los Angeles Poets*. A detailed examination of their editorial policies and their assessment of Los Angeles poetry helps us understand the aesthetic, ethical, and political attitudes of the poets involved, in particular through their relationship to the city and the prevailing notions about it.

The Anthology of L.A. Poets came out in 1972. It was co-edited by Vangelisti, Charles Bukowski and Neeli Cherry; despite the editors' diversity, it reflects many of Bukowski's views. The title simply and directly identified the poets with the city, unlike the later anthologies. Bukowski's foreword invites poets to meet at a discount store ("See you at zody's"); his tone is friendly (he starts the foreword, "You know"). He spoke of a Los Angles that was neither exotic nor mythical ("L.A. has its poor and L.A. has its real"), but instead worked as a point of reference for other urban experiences: "I have bummed the cities and I know this...the great facility of Los Angeles is that one can be alone if he wishes or he can be in a crowd if he wishes.... I must admit that I have gained a love for Los Angeles that forces me again and again to return to it once I have left." The city was defined by travel time, so that "Los Angeles is also Pasadena, Long Beach, Irvine..., any place you can get to within an hour drive or two. Technically, no; spiritually, yes"; clearly, then, the city was composed of various neighborhoods, each with its own history and its own identity. He did not become chauvinistic, and, far from denying the city's negative traits (its reputation as a cultural wasteland, as a shapeless conglomeration and capital of bad taste), he acknowledged these traits, sang them and attached a vitality to them that negated the usual simplistic images. This city combined sports, beer, sex shops and Hollywood with the self-sufficient freedom of the pioneer.

Bukowski's writing reflected his understanding of the city. He never shrank from vulgarity, bad manners, or contradictions. His work erased the separation between writer and character ("Henry Chinaski" in his novels, or the "I" in his poetry); its goals were "power," "clarity," "humor" and "feeling." His bohemianism was distinct from the academics' formalism and the cosmopolitanism and aestheticism of the avant-garde, as well as the gregarious and enthusiastic romanticism of the Beats and the hippies. Bukowski became the Los Angeles poet *par excellence* because he understood and used previously untapped aspects of Los Angeles life, and thus expressed the city's unique characteristics and limitations.

Many of the poets included in the anthology worked in Bukowski's colloquial style, deliberately rejecting classical and academic ideas of the poem. The collection could almost be read as an homage to Bukowski by his peers, admirers, friends and disciples.

The dominant motive of the anthology is debunking; it comes out as short fables involving mass cultural figures like the baseball player Lee Handley, actor John Wayne, Tarzan and Christ. "You, John Wayne," by William Pillin, is a "counter-hymn" to the famous cowboy, so symbolic of Hollywood, America, and its brutal past:

Sonofagun! In whose wake is silence!
...
All us American kids
who love Death
love you, John Wayne,
because You Made Good
and, unlike niggers and jews,
You Have Guts!
Your blazing guns still the bad man's lusty
       aliveness. Look how quietly he sprawls on
       the blood-stained ground! O kill him again!
Shoot the nesters, greasers, horse-thieves and
       cattle rustlers. The crows peck their eyeballs
       in the scrub and the sage brush.
...
Sonofagun! Gatherer of darkness and silence.
Rider into the bloody sunset.
Emptiness like a wind rushes in behind you.

The poem unmasks the America hidden behind Wayne's image: racist, sexist and anti-Semitic brutality, a thirst for death – in a word, barbarism. The poem's exclamations and its breathless rhythm capture the violent force of Westerns. The poet confronts the savagery of the hero with the power of fierce words and thus destroys the idol.

In other works, the poets offered a disenchanted, anti-romantic and even prosaic tableau of daily life, in the first person and generally in the narrative mode. Bukowski helped to inspire this mode, and the collection opens with three of his own poems, "Style," "if we take –," and "29 chilled grapes."

Los Angeles was present in only a few poems. When it did appear, it was as stereotyped scenery. Neeli Cherry's anarchic and parodic "Poem" was the only work to take Los Angeles as a subject, bringing together the commonplaces about Southern California and its literature:

> it was one of those long
> los angeles days that seem to last
> for centuries
> the palm trees
> were wilting
> for lack of air
> ...
> fatty arbuckle
> dead and buried
> it was the day
> crazy jack
> came to town
> we sat under the pine tree
> in griffith park ...
> the norsemen
> had left their tracks at venice beach,
> ...
> i caught the trolley car
> on hollywood blvd and rode to the santa
> monica station –

...
i saw the mahatmas
with their peace signs bathing on the shore –
...
evening never came –
it never does in los angeles
thats why we live here –

i swam for awhile then
hitched a ride to silverlake, an
old section of town where i was living
saw some hippies pass
from my window
watched chaplin movie –
    and felt the afternoon descend
        and faced it.

MICHAEL C. FORD originally conceived *The Mt. Alverno Review*, in 1962, as a fundraiser to help Kenneth Patchen pay for an operation, but only appeared in 1971, a year before the death of the poet it honored. It was not primarily a Los Angeles anthology, but most of the authors it included lived in, or were born in, the city. The twelve poets were fairly heterogeneous. No particular theme or style stands out, other than political commitment, and friendship for Patchen.

Ford attended readings at the Concert Jazz Hall, founded by Jack Hampton; those readings blended poetry and jazz and later inspired *A Quick Anthology*, as he recounted at the 1990 L.A. Poetry Festival:

The first thing that I did was *The Mount Alverno Review*. You have to go all the way back to 1959. I was at a place called the L.A. Jazz Concert Hall and a guy who was subsidizing the arts – Jack Hampton – brought down Kenneth Rexroth and Kenneth Patchen from San Francisco. Brought in the Beat refugees who had already come down from San Francisco and were hanging out in Venice. And they read their poetry. And that's really the first time I heard people reading their work outloud to the music of Shorty Rogers and his Giants and in the case of Kenneth Patchen, Alan Ferguson's Chamber Jazz Sextet from Palo Alto.

Mt. Alverno Press would go on to publish nine issues of *Sunset Palms Hotel* between 1973 and 1983. The graphics, the choice of Los Angeles poets, the references, the veiled quotations, and even the vibrant colors of the magazine all testify to the way that Ford was inspired by popular culture. Harry Northup described the magazine:

The *Sunset Palms Hotel*, vol. 1, nb. 1, published in the Spring of 1973 has poetry by Koertge, Locklin, John Kay, Steppenwolf, Eloise Klein Healy, Joe Hansen and me amongst others. The magazine is stapled with a bright orange cover. It has a subscription by Raymond Chandler: "If I had any sense I would pick up my suitcase and go back home and forget all about her." Stated on the back covers, first issue: used cars, suburbs, obituaries. Second issue: more used cars, more racket gals exposed. The last *Sunset Palms Hotel* was published in 1983 (Forty Years of L.A. Small Presses, 1990).

Ford also used media of all kinds to nourish his poetic imagination, which gave him an original style of expression:

I started to get involved more and more with media. I suppose, when I think about that, I guess I have taken the whole of media and allowed it to get kind of a hammerlock on my imagination. By that I mean billboard signs, radio, comic book covers, paperback mysteries, television, black and white b-movies.

Southern California in particular and the Western United States in general were at the center of Ford's poetry. He wrote about a Los Angeles that was ignored or unrecognized in the prevailing understanding of the city: though Hollywood was central to his work, he wanted to put forgotten or unjustly ignored actresses in "the spotlight they deserve," as he said in our 1987 interview. He also wanted to recoup the city's traffic jams, polluted skies and sprawling, monotonous suburbs. He told Barry Alfonso: "I worship the neglected regions, the destroyed landmarks, ... there's beauty in a traffic jam and in the way a blanket of radiated poison lays up against the San Gabriel Mountains."

He described this, as well as his interest in baseball and West Coast jazz, as "subversive nostalgia."[70] He called back to life places, people, moments, films or events that had disappeared from Los Angeles' memory, but only once they had come through the "very complicated, multi-layered funnel of the poetic imagination" (quoted in Stewart 1986, 20). He expressed the Los Angeles psyche both individually, and archetypally. And it is in this light that we should understand his use of media events or figures: Cleo Moore, an actress who never made it big; or Betty Grable, dying in Venice of cancer. His style oscillated "between the states of classical elegance and colloquial squawks."[71]

Grounding Out in Southern California

Clouds descended
       over our hometown houses
       & swam all the way to Pasadena
       as to coil around Brookside Park
       like choruses from a
       1949 movie sound-track

How long has it been
       since Nelly Fox caught a ripple
       punching a long single to the right corner;
       later got picked-off,
       as Chico Carrasquel forcing an out
       put him on a leash between 2nd & 3rd
       in the bottom of the 9th
       w/ Bob Rush hurling a 6-hitter,

when the Cubs clipped the White Sox
about 2000 miles from familiar turf?

It rained yesterday
    the same way it did then
    that springtime
    a long time ago,

    when we were begging for bubblegum
    on benign streetcorner universes

    ...& begging for the moon
    to spend a little more time w/ us
    near the foothills
    on nites free from the drag of discipline

    ...& begging for the chance
    to bag one in *Deep Center*
    just like Handy Andy Pafko

So now does it seem strange
    that all of us
    are still into
    some weird kind of
    pre-season exhibition?

    ...& could we be called on account of rain?

This poem, from the *Quick Anthology*, includes Ford's char-
acteristic themes and stylistic devices: childhood moments, the
present of a now-adult generation, which come together thanks to
weather and baseball. Remembered times and places overlap. The
prosody often guides the poem's progression and is constantly
present in the onomastic sounds, and the surge in the middle
of the poem of iambic meters where alliteration and assonance
predominate ("when we were begging for bubblegum/on benign
streetcorner universes"). This musical approach to poetry is a

reminder of Ford's origins as a jazzman. He conceived of writing as playing a musical instrument, as he said in our 1987 interview:

> I treat each strophe as note clusters, each stanza-block as a chord change. And through that, my own personal ding ding ding cadence.... There's so much music inherent in the notion of poetry, whether it's on the page or whether it's doing what I do sometimes, talk, right through a microphone. Poetry is like an instrument you do. Kerouac called the lines blowing choruses. He listened to a lot of bebop. He listened to a lot of Catholic prayers and hymns too. The correlation of bebop and Gregorian chant might make for an interesting dialogue.

The allusion to Kerouac is revealing: among his generation, Ford was the poet whose allegiance to the Beats was the most explicit and the most direct. Following in the footsteps of the Beats, he violently rejected all compromise with academia and its "heartless" professors, and advocated poetic militancy, self-teaching, the importance of experience and subjectivity, and the expression of the self in poetry. His incorporation of popular culture allowed him to continue the Beat heritage while modernizing it and enhancing the possible role of a bohemia in the local poetry scene.

But the biggest name in Ford's *Quick Anthology* was Jim Morrison, the singer of The Doors. The rock star had released two collections of poetry in 1969 and in 1970, *The Lords, Notes on Vision*, and *The New Creatures*. He wrote short poetic prose pieces and brief poems in short, descriptive language, featuring visual, supernatural and nightmarish metaphors. For Morrison, modern life was symbolized by the corrupted city, hungry for blood and sex, and by film, figured as the new religion, the "central fact" of which was the "cleavage of men into actor and spectators," as he wrote in *The Lords*. His apocalyptic tone and images recalled science fiction, while the portrait of an irremediably corrupt and rotten city, and his critique of the capitalist system, brought to mind noir novels and films. Morrison's popularity during the 1960s and '70s, helped to open poetry up to new audiences.

Ford had met Morrison and Ray Manzarek (The Doors' cofounder) before the band had formed, at the UCLA Film Department in 1964. Ford often played bass with Manzarek before he turned exclusively to writing. Ford gave his first poetry reading at Morrison's urging, and Manzarek and Morrison provided financial help for the publication of *The Mt. Alverno Review* in 1971; moreover, they shared an understanding of poetry as "metaphoric imagination":

> I remember going out on Venice Beach...and Morrison and I would watch the sun in its move, its long slow death, and drop into the burial ground of the horizon. And it seemed to be very important to us. This was the metaphoric imagination, this was the brain of poetry, being a witness, watching this demise, this natural exhaustion. And Morrison was able to put a lot of that into his lyrics and his poetry, and I guess I did too coming from a different direction.[72]

The main importance of Ford's contribution was undoubtedly the connections he established between artists of different disciplines and generations. Even leaving aside Morrison, Ford performed with bands and musicians as diverse as Jello Biaffra of the Dead Kennedys, X, the Minutemen, Tom Waits, Charlie Haden and Paul Motian. This determined some of the scene's later eclecticism—and helped to bring in a greater diversity of participants.

THE APPROACH of *specimen 73*, edited by Paul Vangelisti, lay midway between the two slightly earlier anthologies. It identified itself with the city less than *Anthology of L.A. Poets*, but it was more overtly involved in the development of a local poetics than Ford's *Quick Anthology*. Vangelisti's brief introduction was faithful to his views on the importance of experimentation. In it, he also defined the situation of Los Angeles poets, placing them in a more global context:

> An Italian poet who, like me, also edits a poetry magazine, wrote wanting to know what line my magazine was pursuing.

I said that here much of what he might call "art" was mostly an accident and one couldn't afford a program or destination.

One plays hunches with work that demands to know what it is to make a poem and, in turn, welcomes the world acting on the poem. One tries not to swallow the American pitch about total self-expression or happiness through art, what the money wants one to swallow, what every used car salesman and corporate executive wants one to swallow.

The 12 poets in this catalog are presented as a question in the form of a statement, though certainly a tentative one. Their work sustains what I find are the most serious questions about the craft and song implicit in the words we inhabit here in Los Angeles.

From the outset, Vangelisti adopted the aesthetic values of the avant-garde. He championed a poetry that would be erudite without being gratuitously formalist, and he protested against capitalist compromise in art. In Los Angeles, the American preference for the direct, the ahistorical and the formless was all the more dangerously tempting. There were only individual, separate voices, indirectly reflecting the city through language. The city had generated a poetry to fit its image, that is to say a diverse one, without models or a common language.

And indeed the poems in the anthology were varied. Each poet possessed a distinct voice, so aesthetic or thematic generalization was difficult, if not impossible. The twelve poets chosen[73] had all been residents of Southern California for ten to twenty years, with the exception of Charles Bukowski (a Los Angeles resident since the age of two). The city appeared in fewer than ten of the more than sixty poems. But themes peculiar to Los Angeles were treated: Venice, Hollywood, traffic, the climate, and so on.

In Alvaro Cardona-Hine's "Driving in North Hollywood," the freeway is the scene of a mysterious meeting between a driver and a crow. In "Monarch Butterflies in November (Southern California)," Robert Peters treats the strangeness of Southern California's climate. The narrative recounts the mid-winter presence of butterflies that leave their cocoons to mate, only to end up in the mouth of the narrator's cat. The narrator is comforted by the disappearance of the butterflies, signs of an unnatural lack of seasons.

Ronald Koertge's "Dick Powell" was one of the "funny-but-serious poems" (Benes 1983, 266) of which Koertge was so fond. He recounts the explosive and bittersweet meeting between a disappointed television viewer and the aging actor Dick Powell, who is obliged to take TV roles that are beneath him. The narrator rails against the star, who, in his eyes, has betrayed him and brought disgrace to the virile heroes he used to play. Dick Powell responds to the verbal aggression of his pushy admirer by lunging at him. The brawl that ensues requires police intervention, and leaves the narrator obsessed with a macabre memory: that of feeling "those cold, yellow teeth in [his] bones."

John Thomas' "Old Man Stravinsky Rehearsing With Orchestra" treats Hollywood very differently. In this poem of varied rhythm, Thomas cast Stravinsky as a feeble old man spending the last years of his life as the conductor of a Los Angeles orchestra. In order to capture his larger-than-life subject, Thomas juxtaposed a sense of comedy and sense of the grotesque, using slang as well as meditative language.

I.
this
voice
so po
lite bene
volent & such
pa
tience
with these Los
Angeles mu
       si
           cians – be
comes (this
 voice) the
archetype of sweet old

          genius everyone's
          papa Jungian wise old
          man all of
          that...

Stravinsky's genius and legendary acrimony surpassed that of
any film villain: it was not Hollywood, but old age that had broken
the composer. Los Angeles-Hollywood-Disneyland were merely
the accidental setting for the composer's suave decrepitude. His
greatness had been attained elsewhere, but it was associated
with an amoral malignance that was kept quiet by the American
cultural establishment. Thomas approached the contrasts in
Stravinsky's character by adopting a shifting tone–by turns
mocking, confidential, accusing, burlesque, moralizing–and
censuring Stravinsky's scandalous private life.

     hearing Stravinsky now so sweetly patient
     working with his orchestra
     No I sd No I
     remember certain things / he is not
     like that
     & my mind held such very specific
     matters as: Stravinsky the Evil Unscrupulous
          Mephistophelian Mastermind who
          every time Nijinsky tried to break with Diaghilev
          somehow got the poor sod to climb back
     gloomily
          into D's socratical bed / poor
          Nijinsky he really wasn't that way didn't
          Dig all that suave & Arty cornholing he was
     getting
          from the prick of that prick of a
          secondrate impresario
          Stravinsky-Svengali his schemes ruining
     Nijinsky's
          married life just to suit his own devious
          purposes heh! heh! heh! he sniggers like the

villain in some old villain flick
Stravinsky yes one of that bunch – mad
evil silly cloak-&-dagger Tsarist emigres of
fifty years ago &
> now sounding for all
> the world like good old Papa Haydn
> rehearsing his toy symphony
somewhere in lollypop land

THE STREETS INSIDE: *Ten Los Angeles Poets*, published by Bill Mohr's Momentum Press in 1978, capped the series of Los Angeles anthologies that came out during the 1970s. It was welcomed by critic Robert Peters as "an impressive effort towards defining a hive-geography for Los Angeles" (Peters 1979, 138), and by Robert Kirsch of the *L.A. Times* as the sign of a "golden age" (Kirsch 1979, 4).

The title of the work set the tone. It was about interior landscapes, rather than exterior, in line with Mohr's belief that "most L.A. poets 'write in reference to the city, and in a psychological sense'" (quoted in Moffet 1980, 7). As in the other anthologies, there were few concrete references to the city, and neither the media nor urban culture were taken up as thematic or poetic material. Deena Metzger expressed this point of view when she told Penelope Moffett: "I guess my relationship to L.A. has been against it.... The city landscape does not interest me, never has."

This attitude was denounced by Stephen Kessler, who saw it as a sign of limitation and immaturity rather than originality or authenticity:

One kind of approach I was astounded not to find represented in this anthology is the streetwise electronics-educated young urban poet whose focus is on and through the native culture (including video/radio & cinematic folklore and techniques), and who by putting down roots within that culture enters into a passionate perception of the action on the streets outside which leads, through soulful and disciplined attention, directly to the human heart.... [To] overlook such examples of vital alternatives seems to limit the book's scope severely. This limitation is compounded by work (as here represented) of "ten Los Angeles poets" in which this extraordinary city scarcely figures as a field of action, as a cultural phenomenon of any historic or ecological meaning, or even as a physical setting for the poem's or poet's existence. The exceptions to this rule are by far the most interesting passages in the anthology (Kessler 1979, 142).

But these poets did use Los Angeles in their work, inasmuch as they opposed Hollywood, noir, and Bukowski's poetics. In their work "Los Angeles appears undistorted by boosterism and romance," (Kirsch 1979, 4). Most of the poets of *The Streets Inside* neglected the urban landscape and concentrated on their own experiences. Holly Prado said in an interview with Leland Hickman:

As a person living in Los Angeles, I drive all the time. Driving holds a real rhythm for me. My car comes up a lot in my dreams as a symbol of my energy.... I think the rhythm of driving, to me, is very powerful.... I think it has a connection with writing generally, both poetry and prose (Prado 1978, 7–8).

Kate Braverman was an exception among the ten poets of *The Streets Inside* in that she drew her poetic material from the urban landscape and Los Angeles mythology. Although she didn't come to Los Angeles until she was 21, she adopted the city, imagined a past there–childhood, adolescence, adulthood–and created an image of herself that was half idyllic and half nightmarish, exploiting the powerful fantasies of the city rather than holding them in contempt. She transformed her life into a mythical autobiography, tracing a descent into hell and the survival of an invented "I," "an archetypal creature" (Braverman 1980, 224).[74]

Faircrest Avenue

I return by bus
even when I walk
or drive my car.
It is the drained blue
of the blue buses
of my youth.
The Western Line
with the blue veins
of Pico, Olympic, Santa Monica.
The world neatly contained
      between three boulevards
winding down at the thin breakwater.

I stop at Pico Boulevard
my anchor, unchanging.
      Herbie's Fine Meats,
      the laundry, bakery and camera shop.
The seasons of Pico Boulevard
are white hot or stinging gray
at Christmas,
      with lights strung on poles,
      glitter in the palms,
      the shop windows brushed
      with machine frost.
Dust is a cold splinter
as I walk from the school bus
with the books I never read.
The deformed sun dissolves
at my back
      spitting sick orange blood
      on the pavement, the poinsettias;
      the cats just fed and exiled
      to side streets with trimmed bushes.

Up, wind brushed, up
a small hill,
a hump struggling from the curb
covered with thinning ivy
 planted by my father
 turning brown always, and dying.
The rounded sides of orange tiles
form a low domed roof on the garage
jammed with old newspapers
still with red rubber bands
across their throats
 tossed by little boys
 on bicycles
 who know better than to stop.

...
Faircrest.
What did it sound like to her?
 Collecting the down payment.
 Promising them anything
 after the Bronx childhood
 of cold stoops and red bricks.
 After the hospitals.
Faircrest.
 The curling of clear blue
 mountain air in a kingdom
 nestled between Pico and Olympic
 where the past overlaps.
And him? The master at last
 with built in barbecue,
 rainbirds, leaves to sweep.
A man of property
In a land of second chances...
But I am back,
back with a bus.
And everyone is coming.
 My father. The newspaper boys.
 My mother. The rabbi with his dog.

Yes, the dog is coming.
The bus is taking everything.
    The Christmas lights.
    The summers.
    The goddamn ivy.
It's all of Faircrest Avenue
In the blue bus of my youth.
And finally I am driving,
taking them all down Pico Boulevard
and not stopping.
    Do you understand?
    Not for popcorn or the highway.
    Scream all you want.
The bus is going out to sea.

By piling regional stereotypes one on the other in her imaginary childhood memories, mixing melodrama with the crudest realism and lyric romanticism with a total absence of sentimentality, Braverman found a style, and a Los Angeles, beyond clichés.

The State of the Scene
at the End of the 1970s

These anthologies were the product of the poets' common artistic commitment, their friendships, their involvement in the future of Los Angeles' culture, and also their own personal interests. After their release, more publishers, distributors and presses were established. These laid the foundation for a cultural network and assured its future development.

The number of outlets and performance opportunities for poetry increased, so more poets could perform for a larger audience, and expanded the availability of critical forums and meeting places. The community produced, little by little, a "canonical" body of work, and created an audience for that new canon, members of which would go on to write their own poetry. Publication remained the most popular way to achieve recognition, but public readings also became more important. Just as importantly, the generation of the 1970s was committed to their movement, and documented it.

The press slowly started to show an interest in local poetry, too. In 1974, Jim Stingley published an in-depth article, "The Rise of L.A.'s Underground Poets," in the *L.A. Times*. He emphasized publishing rather than readings; a photograph on the first page showed thirty local publications – magazines and books – spread out haphazardly, with the caption, "The underground press – odd-sized, odd-colored and generally operating on half a shoe string, these are the launching pads in Los Angeles for poets." His essay began:

> The names of the books scratch your curiosity. Like *Laugh Literary and Man the Humping Guns*. Or *POOP and other poems*. Or *Throb*. They are published by softcover presses that rise and fall with regular irregularity in the cities of Los Angeles. The people who write the things that appear in these publications are the underground poets of Los Angeles (Stingley 1974, 14).

He wrote of an "underground" scene under the patronage of Charles Bukowski – one of its most famous representatives. But he also showed that Bukowski's influence was limited, compared to Paul Vangelisti on the one hand, and minority poets, on the other (ibid., 16). He quoted John Harris' claims that the local scene had "no center, no focus" (ibid., 17); that it was independent (that is to say, non-academic); and that it was organized around active independent individuals, rather than literary "schools" or trends. He concluded that the "local poets [are] fostering a new style of American poetry...talky, listenable, lyrical...indigenous to here and void of excess difficulty, folksiness, sentimentality, rhetoric and politics" (ibid., 14).

By this point the idea of the "underground" had lost much of its political and subversive connotation. The anti-establishment movements had fragmented, and the counterculture's underground press had a diminished role. Instead, "underground" now suggested, above all, invisibility, indifference and limited dissemination.

Stingley's article was welcomed by poets, who sent many letters of congratulations, thanks and comments to the *Times*. It marked the beginning of a new literary policy at the big daily, which started to make an effort to follow and promote the local poetry community. Penelope Moffet, Roselle Lewis and Nancy Shiffrin wrote on the region's poetry until the late 1980s, and local poets like Eloise Klein Healy and Holly Prado wrote criticism. The poetry scene had achieved public recognition.

Other presses or magazines reinforced the expanding scene: *Caterpillar* and later *Sulfur*,[75] both edited by Clayton Eshelman, a nationally-known poet who lived in Los Angeles for about ten years; *Little Caesar* (1976–83) by Dennis Cooper, a young gay poet whose aesthetic was influenced by punk, pop and the New York poetry school and who was Beyond Baroque's director of programming from 1979 to 1983; *Electrum, the Poetry Magazine* (1977–87), a very eclectic magazine directed by Roger Suva from Orange County (it took over from *Bachy* during the 1980s with interviews, critiques of Los Angeles poets, and a calendar of readings); *Marilyn* (1975–80), a magazine put together by Peter Schneider, which became *Orpheus* in 1980 and then Illuminati (a press that released numerous Los Angeles poets and was also known for the graphic inventiveness and format of its books); *Chrysalis* (1977–80), a militant feminist art journal linked to the Woman's Building; and *CQ* (*California Quarterly*), the magazine of the California State Poetry Society, started in 1975.[76]

But the region's most important press at the time was John Martin's Black Sparrow Press. It was based in Los Angeles from 1966 to 1975, when it moved to Santa Barbara and then Santa Rosa. Black Sparrow published some 200 titles during this period, including most of Bukowski's work. His popularity helped Black Sparrow become a respectable mid-size press, distributed throughout the United States and Europe, as well as in Australia and New Zealand. In addition to Bukowski, its catalogue included Paul Bowles, Wanda Coleman, Robert Creeley, Ed Dorn, Robert Duncan, Wyndham Lewis, Jack Spicer, and Gertrude Stein, to name just a few. Black Sparrow was a success thanks to its eclecticism, longevity, profitability, editorial integrity, and its lasting collaboration with its authors. Although the press was not involved in the local scene, its very presence bolstered the city's growing influence. Martin's credibility was due, he said, to the fact that he was not a poet. Publishing was his job, a business from which he had to make a living:

> I'm not a writer. That's where a lot of small presses get in trouble; they are started to publish the unpublishable writings of the publisher and once you let those bars down, you let anybody in. As far as I know, this is the only small press in Los Angeles that has operated successfully and continuously just on the sale of books; no government grants, no millionaire backers, no benefactors (ibid., 16).

Other sub-scenes developed at this time, outside the city of Los Angeles. Laguna Beach had the "Laguna Poets" around Marta Mitrovitch. In Pasadena and Long Beach, poet-teachers at community colleges (e.g., Gerald Locklin, Ronald Koertge, Charles Stetler and Charles Webb) brought together writers and readers.

Long Beach in particular had been a literary center since the 1970s. Hubert Lloyd's Applezaba Press was the symbol of this. Created in 1976 to publish an anthology of poets from Long Beach, Applezaba Press saved money by relocating the manufacturing and stocking of its books; and, because its authors were faculty of the community college, some of its titles were on college curricula–which ensured big sales. It produced one to four titles each year, all by Long Beach authors, including Lloyd himself, and Gerald Locklin. Locklin's *The Case of the Missing Blue Volkswagen*, a burlesque parody of a Hollywood noir novel, was a surprise bestseller in Germany.

But these communities remained somewhat isolated. The only figure who unified Los Angeles poetry as a whole was Charles Bukowski. He was "the papa guru" (ibid., 14), "the scene's only big daddy" (Cooper and Watt 1978, 8). Leland Hickman said in our 1987 interview:

Every city has their major poet. New York has John Ashberry, and San Francisco has Robert Duncan. We have Charles Bukowski, who is a very fine poet, possibly a very great one. He's been very popular here amongst poets for years.

The discovery of his work was a revelation for numerous poets, such as Robert Peters:

When I happened on this book [*Crucifix in a Deathhand* by Bukowski] in the '60s it was a revelation to me. Drenched as I had been for years in academic poets, I was stunned, and had no idea that poetry could be written so frankly and so straight-forwardly. This book had a tremendous influence on me when I was first writing poetry in those years – Bukowski showed me some things about writing courageously about my own life, without needing to pretty it all up – and he taught me also that I didn't after all need all that academic poetry-lingo and lace on the poet-jockstrap (Beyond Baroque Foundation undated, 20).

Poets in Los Angeles had either to imitate or reject him; he was either a role model or an influence to be avoided. This was true for those poets who knew him in the 1960s and '70s, like John Thomas, Paul Vangelisti, Michael C. Ford, Robert Peters, Jack Grapes, and Ron Koertge; as for those who met him later, like Wanda Coleman and Richard Meltzer; and even for the poets of the 1980s, whether white youths affiliated with the punk and spoken word movements or "minority" writers like Marisela Norte and Michelle T. Clinton.

With his accessible, simple style – Harry Northup said in our 1987 interview, "Bukowski makes it sound like anybody can write about anything" – his themes of individual revolt, isolation and autodidacticism, and his legendary public readings, Bukowski attracted a large audience.[77]

But Sharon Doubiago interpreted his influence differently:

More in L.A. than anywhere one knows "existence precedes essence." Film is Queen Art there because it catches the moment, the present, the body before it's gone.... The instinct is self-actualizing.... In the Los Angeles poem this all transmutes into autobiography, the writing of the self, which is a giving of the self to the world, piece by piece, a laying out of the body and soul for the reader. This is the reason Bukowski is important (Doubiago 1987, 50).

Bukowski's fame was a double-edged sword: though he brought readers to poetry, anyone who took him as a role model would reject the institutions needed to sustain the local scene: his ferocious individualism, anti-intellectualism and opposition to institutions contributed, indirectly, to the fragmentation of the scene.

Some Aspects of
the Community Poetry Scenes

Wanda Coleman was frequently cited, interviewed and published in the daily newspapers as well as the literary press, but she was not included in the poetry anthologies of the 1970s. This was symptomatic of the division within the scene. On the one hand, there was the white bohemia and avant-garde. On the other, there were the many identity-based scenes, which flourished during the 1970s and 1980s, on the model of the Black Arts Movement.

These identity-based groups put a new face on the independent scene by creating alternative artist spaces, which the NEA labeled "artist-run organizations." These filled the void left by the community cultural centers of the '60s. Nancy Drew wrote:

These *spaces* were created for a number of reasons: the need to express, the desire to connect, the necessity to exchange ideas. They were answers to prevailing problems. They addressed the need for young artists and new work to be shown.... Alternatives were therefore born out of L.A.'s frustrated underground art world (Drew 1988, 9).

These artist-run organizations had three goals: first, revolutionary political change; second, the creation of political art; third, the development of new systems of distribution (Pritikin 1988, 14). Beyond Baroque was focused on the third. The most active and well-organized identity-based groups, feminists and Chicanos, though, focused on political change and political art.

Like the Black Arts Movement, the feminists and Chicanos were part of a wider activist scene, in which art had a social role. Loyalty to a specific community was the context in which artistic activity took place. Deena Metzger, founder of the writing program at the Woman's Building, evoked this loyalty to community when she opposed Robert Peters. Peters had reproached her for her prosaic and conversational writing:

> As a woman, a person involved in, committed to, the creation of a new culture, I must respond to the postulation of literary reality which is competitive and aggressive.... It is disaffiliation which Peters represents and affiliation which seems to disturb him (Metzger 1979, 151).

These organizations were multidisciplinary. Each art and each member contributed to a strong positive collective identity. Whatever the artistic form or genre, the essentials were content and commitment. Artists advocated and practiced an openness that favored performance art–the interdisciplinary form *par excellence*, the theatrical aspect of which made it ideal for political action. The official policy of the gallery at the Woman's Building, for example, advocated "diversity: from traditional crafts to experimental forms to political and social art to highly personal work" (Woman's Building 1988, 8). Art was an active influence on the world, it was a part of it and could not be separated from its context without losing its meaning. Sharing and cooperation were more important than originality, genius, and competition. Art was an instrument of individual and collective emancipation, a means of developing "identity and sensibility" (Woman's Building 1983, 2) for groups that had been silenced and invisible until then. These artists guaranteed their community access to tools of public expression. Using these, they would define them-selves, that is to say, to name themselves.

Language was at the heart of political liberation. Kirsten Grimstad, co-editor of *Chrysalis* (a feminist magazine published from 1977 to 1980) evoked language's vital role and power :

> The poetry was always like the beating heart at the center of the magazine...So much of what we now take for granted as insights and understandings that have political implications was first expressed in the poetry that gushed forth in the early days of the woman's movement...[for example] the whole under-standing that we have today of the sexual abuse of children and incest, which was first surfacing in poetry long before it rose to public awareness... At that time it was absolutely shocking... When we think about where we are today with the subject, it reminds me of how important those first poetic expressions were in terms of actually leading to awareness and social action. The feminist movement was about political change, and I think that this exemplifies that connection between the poetry and political change, and political action.... I think... the thing that was most important to me and to us about our magazine was the attempt to find a whole new poetry, a whole new language that could rename our own experience from the inside and to strip the veils of language away from experience that had been named for us (Forty Years of L.A. Small Presses, 1990).

So, for instance, SPARC (the Social and Public Art Resource Center), an institution founded by Chicana muralist Judith Baca was "dedicated to the production, exhibition, distribution, and preservation of public art" (Angelo 1985, 71), but also to airing and retelling, from their point of view, the experiences of commu-nity members that had been distorted, repressed, or excluded by the dominant culture.

For these identity-based groups, the plastic arts were often a major catalyst, just as music had been for Watts. Spaces, groups and initiatives came into being to remedy the fact that there was an almost total absence of exhibitions of Chicano and women artists in Los Angeles galleries and museums. The feminist artists movement was particularly active in Los Angeles during the 1970s and its adherents mobilized to protest the 1971 exhibition "Art and Technology" at the Los Angeles County Museum of Art, in which no women were included.

> As they began to meet to organize this protest, women discovered that each of them had encountered similar barriers to advancement in their careers as artists. This led to research, which revealed a systematic pattern of underrepresentation of women artists – in exhibitions, collections, critical appraisal, and historical documentation – that spanned the whole of art history. Out of this growing recognition, women in Southern California began to found their own artists' collectives, and educational programs (Woman's Building 1988, 6).

Reactions to the County Museum exhibition inaugurated a new phase for the visual arts scene and also triggered the opening of many new "alternative" galleries, which in a sense came to replace the alternative galleries that had folded in the '60s. Examples of the new alternative galleries were Self-Help Graphics (1972, in East L.A.), Womanspace (1973, feminist), LAICA (Los Angeles Institute of Contemporary Art, 1973, a blend of international avant-garde and local artists) and Brockman Gallery Productions (1973, multiethnic in South Central Los Angeles[78]). Another example was Asco, a multimedia group of artists from East L.A. founded in 1971, one of whose first works consisted in signing their names on the entrance walls of the Los Angeles County Museum of Art in order to protest the absence of Chicanos in the museum[79] (Gamboa 1986, 51). But the most important group set up in reaction to this exhibit was the Woman's Building.

THE WOMAN'S BUILDING was founded in 1973 by three instructors at the California Institute of the Arts: plastic artist Judy Chicago, graphic artist Sheila de Bretteville and art historian Arlene Raven. It was located in the former Chouinard Institute and housed the

Feminist Studio Workshop and many other women's organizations, including a travel agency, a bookstore, a café, the office for NOW (National Organization for Women), galleries and theater companies.

The Woman's Building existed "to make women's experience public through a multitude of creative forms," (Woman's Building, 1983). Its program was both utopian and pragmatic:

to provide with access to the necessary skills, equipment, and expertise to make their artwork; and to offer an avenue for professional work opportunities for women artists;

to develop an appreciative audience for women's creative work, by providing the public with information about historical and contemporary women artists;

to create an environment where women can find a balance of challenge and support, and in which they are encouraged to examine the meaning of their experience as women;

to assist women to be powerful and self-determining, and to foster a collective identity among women as *women*;

to be an active part of the historical and contemporary feminist movement;

and
to use artmaking as a vital and essential instrument for social change.

Each student was enrolled full time in a two- to three-year curriculum that included plastic arts, writing, performance, video, design and graphic arts. They created performance art groups: The Waitresses, the Feminist Art Workers, Mother Art, and Sisters of Survival, and collectives like Ariadne: A Social Art Network, and The Lesbian Art Project. They worked over several years on events, very often in public places, that explored the lives, images, and exploitation of women from various angles – as mothers; workers; women of color; artists; victims of incest, race, violence, and war; heterosexuals and queer people. Artists organized exhibitions, plays, installations, books, magazines, postcards and posters. These projects were often designed around specific subjects (The Incest Awareness Project, Cross Pollination, Madre Tierra, Public Announcement/Private Conversations). Lesbians played a particularly active role,[80] as the homosexual movement in Los Angeles did within arts in general. And the projects were, increasingly, multicultural.

The Writing Program, directed by Deena Metzger, began in 1975. She was a Jewish writer from New York whose mother tongue was Yiddish, and her father was Yiddish writer Arnold Posy. She had lived in Los Angeles since the late 1950s and had met the founders of the Woman's Building at CalArts (California Institute of the Arts), where she also taught in its Women's Studies program – one of the first in the country. In 1975, Metzger organized a conference of women writers, which she called "Women's Words." She invited thirty writers, from across the genres – journalism, poetry, theater, publishing and criticism – and the event was a revelation, proof that women's literature existed, both nationally and locally, and had its own special characteristics and culture. It had "forms, concerns, images that really were distinct... It was the completely absurd thought that women might have a different culture from men's culture," Metzger said in our 1987 interview. Many women drew from the conference the confidence they needed to assert themselves as writers and counteract the cultural prejudices perpetuated by the university, dedicated exclusively to "great men." As Eloise Klein Healy said:

The Women's Words Conference was probably one of the three major events in my life. Up until that time, I was just drifting around out there, not knowing anybody. [Deena] had to ask Michael C. Ford who were the women writing in Los Angeles because there was no way of knowing anybody. I had gone through universities, I had taken writing, I had sent stuff out to be published, but basically I didn't know any writers. I didn't know a single woman writer, except dead ones that I had read. And then, all of a sudden, [there was the Women's Words Conference]. There were 300 people from all over the country. It was like, my God! This is going around and we don't know each other but now we know each other. It was like overnight, all the things that I had been told by my professors turned out to be untrue.... That women can't be serious about their work, that women don't really write, they just kind of sit around in their kitchens and scratch around on pieces of paper. That they don't take themselves seriously, that all they really want to do is get married. That there haven't been any major women writers. That women have never had a community of shared writing experiences. Bla, bla, bla, bla, bla, bla, bla. I mean all of those qualifying things that make you feel like you must be totally strange to want to do this.[81]

Intimacy was at the heart of this literary culture. The writers and listeners brought together by the conference discussed the "secret words of women speaking intimately about the reality of their own lives," as Metzger put it, which contributed to their recognizing "what was then a truly new form."

Anaïs Nin's influence was decisive. A Los Angeles resident from 1948 until her death in 1977, her friendship with Deena Metzger began in the 1960s and Metzger considered Nin "a Los Angeles-French writer." The success of Nin's diary, published in 1966, helped to popularize journal writing. Her public performances, writing workshops, friendly ties with local authors, and the admiration she aroused among women writers of various generations and ethnic backgrounds (like Chicana poet Marisela Norte[82]) stimulated the emergence of feminist writing in Los Angeles. "Woman's Words" and the autobiographical writing workshops set up at the Woman's Building (and then elsewhere) helped establish to the intimate journal as a major literary form in Los Angeles. This reinforced a stylistic predilection for writing in the first person that was common in the local poetic tradition, as Metzger suggested:

If we think about the Women's Words Conference as being the moment when personal writing was discussed, and we realize that from that moment, the interest in journals expanded into the public world. And women began writing journals. Then journal classes began to be formed. A lot of the writing that takes place in Los Angeles that's written both by men *and* women is influenced by this remarkable phenomenon of people dedicatedly recording their lives. I think perhaps that's one of the major influences on L.A. literature.

This focus on a neglected genre was only one instance of the ways in which the workshops and classes at the Woman's Building encouraged students to reject the divisions between poetry, fiction, theater and diary.

But the Woman's Building was also important for its creation of networks for the distribution and production of literature. The Graphic Center, founded in 1973, provided artists with the means to publish and distribute their works in large numbers without compromising their principles. The writing, printing, engraving and design workshops complemented each other and multiplied, generating a creative surge. Students pursued their activities beyond "the Building," creating an artistic network distinct from Beyond Baroque's – although they did overlap at points. This new network added to the poetry scene the voices of women from varied social and ethnic backgrounds, for example, Terry Wolverton, a militant lesbian writer who came to Los Angeles in 1976 to take the degree course at the Feminist Studio Workshop. She was very involved in the writing program until 1991, and described its importance and multicultural reach:

I think that the writing program was tremendously important, that it was tremendously important to women writers in the city of Los Angeles, or at least to some women writers in the city of Los Angeles. That it was important to a lot of audience members. Both actually and symbolically that it had that importance. And I think it was important to the Woman's Building because it brought in a different audience. I think in a lot of cases it brought in maybe more of a multicultural audience than some of the other programs did.

And Healy stressed the importance of the Woman's Building including various communities of women:

> I think...that one of the differences between the Woman's Building and perhaps some other organizations that present theater or performance or poetry or whatever, there has been a real concerted effort to also find out what's happening in various ethnic communities. That is a basic commitment throughout the organization. So if you look for example at the reading series, the major reading series, what you will see is: every time that series comes around, you will have black writers, Chicanos, Asian writers, Native-American writers. You will find that balance all the time. It isn't that it happens specially this one year where maybe they'll have a black writer or two. It's an ongoing attention to the fact that there are all kinds of women and let's put their work out. I think that's a big difference.

THE MAGAZINE *rara avis* had been directed, since 1978, by the couple Aleida Rodriguez and Jacqueline De Angelis. In 1984 it published, as its last issue, the anthology *Southern California Women & Artists*. This was printed in part at the Woman's Building, and the authors selected for it were connected with the Building in one way or another. The anthology's foreword traced the magazine's history; this was followed by an introduction that discussed the familiar themes of the identity movements and collectives in the Woman's Building: faith in literature's potential for social transformation; "belonging to a loosely formed group of feminist, lesbian, and gay writers" who were excluded from other publishing circles; devotion to both political commitment and literary quality; social and multicultural sensibility; absence of hierarchies and compartmentalization of artistic disciplines and genres; the need to own the means of production; to combat the de facto "economic censorship" that plagued all minorities;

and the importance of the personal dimension—in short, the ambition to be "an alternative space for the under-represented and the disenfranchised, for the invisible and silenced factions."

The magazine's name is a Latin term meaning *a rarity* (literally *a rare bird*). As Rodriguez put it:

> Since I'm a Cuban exile, I got interested in writing in Spanish and in the bilingual work of this area...We started soliciting work from the Southwest. Jim Segal, Victor Valle...I think that the main thing that *rara avis* did was that we traveled in a lot of different circles. There was the bilingual circle, the gay and lesbian circle, the heterosexual writer circle, and so when they all overlapped, they created this little sort of tripartite area that we then called *rara avis*. Because we wanted to represent that. We didn't want to be just this or just that or just the other thing. We wanted to cover that because that's who we were (Forty Years of L.A. Small Presses, 1990).

Most of the writers of the Woman's Building, like other Los Angeles poets, belonged to several distinct circles at once. This allowed them great independence of action, thought and politics.

In their introduction, Rodriguez and De Angelis began with the geography and history of Southern California. They noted that the area had been characterized by sprawling space and transitory human populations until the desert was turned into an oasis, then the oasis into freeways, the "phase of construction, primarily built by first-generation and new-immigrant hands[, and which is] bent on giving some permanence to this shaky landscape."

For the editors, the women's art scene, like the region to which it belonged, was still in its early stages. It was characterized by fragmentation into small independent groups, of which the Woman's Building was "the most organized support base." The absence of a broader community could lead to anonymity and a lack of cohesion and dialogue. But it also allowed for freedom, eclecticism and audacity. The poets' relationships with Southern

California, and the ways they depicted it, were very heterogeneous. The introduction continues:

> All of the women in this anthology live in Southern California and yet it would be impossible to have any of them agree on what it is about this area that affects their writing and/or art. Some of these writers and artists are deeply influenced by this landscape. Some are native, while others have implanted themselves in this quick-rooting medium, and some never even attempt to describe the ground under their feet but look back toward past landscapes and memories for towns, countries, and cultures they are absent from.... As with anything that is still forming, it will escape from the frame of any idea about itself.

Sadly, the anthology marked an end to this movement, rather than an origin. It was the last compilation during this period dedicated exclusively to women of the region.

The writing in the anthology provides a range of themes and aesthetics, though often the texts were explicitly political. African American, Jewish, Chinese American, Japanese American, Puerto Rican, Cuban, Chicana, white, homosexual and heterosexual, bourgeois and proletarian writers dramatized moments in the lives of women from childhood to old age, for the most part in the first person. They evoked their family environment, their difficulty raising a child alone, their emancipation from marriage, factory work during the Korean War, the personal discovery of homosexuality, and immigration. Others denounced racism, the atomic bomb, machismo and the oppression of women in American culture.

The poems that were set in Los Angeles presented new images of the city. For Susan E. King, Los Angeles was hectic and media-heavy; stress and anarchy reigned there. You had to leave it to find yourself. From "For Blackwell's Press":

L.A.'s relentless pressure continued on
to three freeways until, on the last hill out of town, the

radio signal stopped. It was as if I had broken a barrier,
and could, at the crest of the hill, see clearly.

For Jane Thurmond, the metropolis was above all an ecological disaster. From "Pop Quiz":

The City of Illusion is a test.
The City of Illusion is testy.
Things may not be what they look like.
Things may not be what we call them.

These four lines preceded instructions for a sort of "game," in which readers had to match six captions with six photos of the city. The word "air" matched a photo of Los Angeles on an intensely smoggy day; the "river" was the completely dry Los Angeles River; "big news" was electric signs announcing a traffic jam.

In "If It Happens During the Day," Bia Lowe used imagery usually connected with disaster and apocalypse to portray the human catastrophe of nuclear war.

When the bombs hit will you be driving to work?
Will I have to climb onto the freeway
search every smelted steel box
until I find your hands?
I won't die right until I find your hands.
...
If this disaster drops like a wedge
into a day we can't undo
and our bodies blaze up miles from each other,
it won't matter that the telephone has ruptured to bits,
power lines melting into pavement like crayon drawings.
It won't matter if we fought that morning.
I'd meet your gaze at that instant in spite of the distance.
I'd rise over this city like ash blown from a chimney,
and settle against you, and blot out the sun.

She blends the everyday with shockingly realistic details of death, which are both transcended and transformed into a hymn of love.

"Se Habla Inglés," a narrative poem by Marisela Norte, presents yet another twist: here, Los Angeles is viewed from Mexico. The narrator, a Chicana from East L.A., is visiting her Mexican family on the occasion of a wedding in Chihuahua. On the eve of the ceremony, the women gather in the kitchen and prepare food while drinking, relentlessly asking the poet about life in the City of Angels.

We are all there. Laura, Xristina, Betty, Dora, Lilly, Patty, Lilly, Peggy, three aunts, unas cuantas comadres, the bride-to-be and me. Gathered together at a kitchen table in Chihuahua preparing empanadas, buñuelos para los ovidados and cuernos for the wedding.

...

"Oiga, dinos como es allá?" They are all at once pulling out old picture postcards I have sent and the dust settles heavy on my shoulders as they begin to cheer. "Disneylandia! Disneylandia!! Ra Ra Ra!!!"

Disneylandia 82? It was me that time wasn't it? ...And they are all attentive, nudging each other and watching me with quick pale eyes as they all at once begin to question the darkened eyelids, the red mouth ...

Oiga...a poco así se pintan todas la mujeres allá en el otro lado?" "Por qué usas tanto make-up?"

A white hand holds up an American magazine and proclaims: "que no sabes que el 'look' natural es el 'look' más in?"

...

Another shot and another.... Their laughter nears hysteria when suddenly Betty asks me if I have seen "E.T." yet.

...

They are all at once demanding an ending to a movie which I refuse to see. But E.T. has crossed the border successfully in

broad daylight in the form of bubble gum, No. 2 pencils, note-
books, candy cigarettes, baseball caps and bumper stickers that
only rival those that read "i love chihuahua." Little E.T. ironed
on those little T-shirts made in downtown L.A., yeah over there
on Mateo Street. Cut, sewn and sweated by manos mexicanas
and then shipped over to el otro lado para los niños mexicanos
...

But they are too convinced that things go better en el otro lado
home of el sueño dorado de Coors, things are easier, so much
easier diving from swimming pool to swimming pool. It's a
big city L.A. ra ra ra! La ciudad que nunca duerme. Where no
one really knows you, no one will catch you. Pero acá en el otro
lado, Olvídate!

Irony pervades her view of the relationship between Mexico and
the United States. The essential truth that everything depends
on where you are is shown through the recurrence of "here" and
"there." These two words also appear in Spanish, as well as the
phrase "El otro lado," which has a similar meaning (the other
side). These phrases determine the context of the speakers.

Norte is from Los Angeles (there, in the poem); she has
Mexican parents in Mexico (here, in the poem); she immigrated
there, and speaks to her family and friends about there while
she is here. The desire for the other side, for American culture
and its icons (Hollywood, Disneyland, E.T.) is internalized,
discussed, rehashed, dreamt, criticized or rejected, according to
the geographic situation and the context.

The poem's alternation between Spanish and English follows
the same logic. Spanish is used for direct speech: the women's
questions about Los Angeles. English, on the other hand, is used
for narration. Spanish is used for emotions, English for stereo-
types. The Spanish recalls that "there" was once "here." Finally,
the interweaving of both languages denounces the exploitation
hidden by cultural images and slogans. The desire to be else-
where is manufactured in order to serve and maintain an imperi-
alism which enslaves peoples and blinds them to their conditions,
so they become dependent on consumption, and their lust for it.

Like Norte, Terryl Hunter was born in Los Angeles, and in her "Prairies of Unbelievable Grace," she also subverts conventional images:

Grade school gives you that first vast itch
with a Sandburg ballad.
It tells you that sweet gold fields
are never boring. That the prairie is your birthright
as an American but you know damnwell
you'll never see one. You'll see stucco.
You figure out that America has been bored for years
with its prairiness. Too bland. They like to pave it
and place pedestrians there
They liven it up. They chop across the acres
while you sing Amber Waves of Grain
and they bring it all to heel. Tie it up
with tight gray streaks going everywhich way.
Then they dot it
with little automobiles.

As a child, she dreamed of endless prairies, like those in Sandburg's poems. But that America could not be found in Los Angeles, which was her only point of reference. She plays up the contrasts between the city's myths and those of America in general. The history she learned in school was inadequate to her reality in Los Angeles, and only by widening her field of vision could she tell a story that explained the gap between ideology and experience.

Some Poets from East L.A.

In the 1980s, African and Mexican Americans were the most visible of the minority poets. These communities were large, and had long histories; the Mexican American community has historical and geographical landmarks, just as the black community does. South Central is bounded by the railway tracks;

East L.A. is bounded by the Los Angeles river, as Marisela Norte suggested[83]:

> The poetry scene has grown.... It seems to be growing but yet it only seems to be growing on that side of the L.A. River. I don't know why things start and stop and matter once they're safely over that side of the bridge. There's a lot of territory here.

The river symbolized a strong territorial and historical identity. Whittier Boulevard, sometimes called the Hispanic Sunset Boulevard, played for East L.A. the role that Central Avenue did for South Central. The Zoot Suit Riots in the 1940s, then the Chicano Moratorium in 1970,[84] were landmark events for the Mexican American community; these are the Mexican American counterparts of the Watts riots.

Finally, in 1982, an anthology appeared that focused on the long-ignored voices of Latino poets. *Two Hundred and One: Homenaje a la Ciudad de Los Angeles/The Latino Experience in Los Angeles*. The authors overlapped with those of *rara avis*, whose editors, themselves Latinas, had had a "special [interest] in the bilingual work of the Southwest" (Rodríguez and de Angelis "Foreword"); Rodríguez led a writing workshop for Latinas in 1982.[85] The anthology was the result of the Los Angeles Latino Writers Workshop, as well as of two Chicano magazines: *Con Safos*, which dated from the very beginnings of the Chicano movement (1968), and *Chismearte* (also written *XhismeArte*), which replaced *Con Safos* in 1976.

The anthology brought together a number of authors, who were to remain active on the scene for years to come.[86] It included, as authors or subjects, working class men and women, activists, "homeboys," grandmothers, young women, children, illegal immigrants and exiles. Although these works reflected an aesthetic and concerns common to the whole of the Chicano cultural movement, the presence of Los Angeles gave the anthology a distinct flavor.

In their long introduction, the editors announced that the "social/political movements of the '60s and '70s gave birth to

the contemporary Latino literary movement in Los Angeles,"
(*Two Hundred and One*, 3). As in the Black community, there was
a Latino cultural renaissance alongside the local, and national,
struggle for civil rights. Their ethical and aesthetic principles
resembled those of the Woman's Building and the Black Arts
Movement, as can be seen in the 1976 mission statement of
Chismearte:

> *Chismearte* is an open forum for the development of communi-
> cation, ideas/concepts that will contribute to the arts and social
> struggle.
> This issue of *Chismearte* is dedicated to the Chicano/Latino
> arts and the various organizations that represent new direc-
> tions of public art.
> We are exploring aesthetic sensibilities as being an integral
> part of the daily life of the people. We will attempt to organize
> and develop communication that is progressive and supportive
> of the revolutionary process.

Though the editors of *Two Hundred and One* mentioned South
American authors and Latino literature in general, it neverthe-
less focused on publishing the works of Chicanos and telling
their history "since the conquest of California" (Mena et al. 1982,
3) in 1846.

> Los Angeles is a city that has come full circle. From a small
> Mexican cattle town overrun by successive waves of European
> immigrants, to the Mexican, Latino city it has gradually become
> since the 1920s. Yet, with over four million Spanish-speaking
> inhabitants, this city can barely speak of its own indigenous
> literary tradition. (Concilio de Arte Popular, 1980, 26.)

Los Angeles was Mexican before it was American–like
California and, on a larger scale, the American Southwest as a
whole. This was fundamental to Chicano identity. They consid-
ered themselves first and foremost as "internal exiles."[87] So they
had to reclaim the city, and reaffirm their continued presence, to

which the very name of the city attests. They defined themselves, even more than African Americans did, as essentially bicultural, between the United States and Mexico, which was itself a blend of Spanish and Indian. The audible manifestation of this biculturalism was bilingualism:

> Since the conquest of California, this city's cultural chauvinism has suppressed the participation of Chicano poets and journalists who were consequently forced to publish their works in scores of Spanish language newspapers (Mena et al. 1982, 3).

Just as *Southern California Women & Artists* did, *Two Hundred and One* strove to document "a still vibrant and youthful literary tradition" (ibid., 4). The introduction tried to include the members of the Los Angeles Latino Writers Workshop as part of an emerging writing community. The workshop "represented the first attempt by Latino writers in L.A. to organize themselves" (ibid., 3); it aspired to be for the Latino literary community what Watts Writers Workshop had been for the Black community. Like the earlier workshops, it was a center for writing, teaching, publishing and distribution. Oscar Zeta Acosta was its father figure; its important anniversary was the Chicano Moratorium; and it worked with a unique aesthetic, inspired by "the oral tradition in the Latino culture" and "the importance of the barrio in this city's literary tradition" (ibid., 4). The workshop stressed traditions and cultural continuity. A "historical and cultural consciousness," was given a central place, as is apparent in the titles of the four chapters of the collection and the descriptions of the work in them:

> Chapter one...is entitled "August 29th," because it is a recognition of the literary lineage this anthology is directly descended from.... Chapter two, entitled "Recuerdos [Memories]," gives unique insights into the barrio by capturing memorable incidents in a writer's life.... Chapter three, "Hechos y Raices [Acts/ Facts and Roots]," combines poetry, short story and oral testimony to create a broad panorama of struggle and resistance

by the Latino community of Los Angeles. Chapter four, "Street Words" reveals Latinos as citizens of a whole city and not just the barrio (ibid., 4).

Victor Valle's epic triptych, "Ciudad de Los Angeles," illustrates this historical perspective particularly well.[88] Valle (a founding editor of *Chismearte*), examined the history of Los Angeles–how it was settled, its population, its place in the region–from various angles.

"Ciudad de Los Angeles I" looked into the various faces of the city: a village of cattle breeders in the American West who bore the scars of past destruction–destruction of the Indians, of Mexican neighborhoods and of the Southern California ecology: "This was one stroke across the map, / recent impulse to unfurl a destiny / ocean to ocean" (ibid., 24). Then the territory is seen as a social and trading crossroads for the Indians who spent millennia following mountains and waterways from end to end depending on the season: "And the older impulse, always presence, / Not a frontier for those south." Finally, Los Angeles is a destination for Mexicans who "follow the same paths" (*Los Mexicanos siguen los mismos caminos*) as the Indians long ago–but are stopped at the border.

"Ciudad de Los Angeles II" comprises two historical counter-factuals: the annexation of Baja California and eventually all of Mexico by the United States; or, conversely, the transformation of all of California into an independent country.

The third and last movement, "Ciudad de Los Angeles III," revisits Los Angeles' past from the Mexican point of view. The poet shows that the American "victory" was ultimately colonial, then brings charges against the invaders by recalling the darkest episodes of Los Angeles Anglo-American history. Finally poem determines the victors and the vanquished:

La verdad fue
que nos derrotaron
con las tratados de Fremond,
con las manadas de mineros hambrientos,

con las siembras descuidadas,
las viñas hechas foraje para caballos enemigos,
con el robo de Ganado y una sequía,
con las deudas y Colton
quien se trepó de una hija nativa
para casarse tierras,
con cazadores de bisonte y
racistas de Arkansas y Missouri
llegando con la raíz de la esclavitud bien cundida,
cómo el Tejano Thomas Jefferson Green
... quien inventó The Foreign Miners Tax,
corriendo los Latinos de Mariposa,
Yuba City, Dog Town, Hang Town, Calaveras
So that Huntingtons
could carve haciendas with railroads,
open an ocean for a city,
so that Colonel Harrison Gray Otis
could conjure a newspaper fortress
and a union-busting refuge out of two dead Wobblies,
so that Harry Chandler could
pull off San Fernando realestate deals
by hijacking a river,
deleting another
along with Owens Valley farmers and Paiutes,
so that, later, Norman Chandler
could beget from L.A. Times editorials
generations of Nixons,
ruin reputations by baiting until red,
until shadow, until rapists and thieves,
until Zoot Suiters,
until alien those who were too numerous,
until makers of furtive years
that breed
la matamultitud,
el multiplicado nosotros,
las morenas voces de aumento,
los descendientes de Tiburcio y Murieta

crecidos 61 porciento,
la raza indígena superando un millón
por la primera vez en más de un siglo,
reclamando lo nuestro sin estragos,
con ejércitos de niños y obreros (ibid., 37).

Valle's point of view shifts throughout the poem, as can be seen in the alternating pronouns: Spanish "we" to render the stolen past of the Indians and Mexicans; English "they" to remind Americans of the exploitation, violence, and racism present in country's history. Valle's poem captures the mission and urgency of the anthology itself, which aimed to restore the "cultural heritage of this city's more than two million Spanish-speaking people who have stubbornly thrived like the nopal of our desert hillsides" (ibid., 3). The poem's short lines and accumulation of dates and events are almost overwhelming; the bicentennial is an exceptional, perhaps unique, opportunity to be heard by Angelenos.[89]

Less historically minded, and more contemporary, Dukardo Hinestrosa's protest poem, "Canto sin estrellas" ["Song without Stars"] denounced the American capitalist system by evoking the Hollywood neighborhood and film industry:

No tengo dollars, ni quarters, ni dimes, ni cents.
Hollywood enciende sus movies stars.
El tío Sam no cambia su vestido a rayas.
No parking, no smoking, no admittance, Don't walk (ibid., 56).

The anthology also included some "proletarian" poetry "with strong emphasis on political and labor themes [and] stylistically...utiliz[ing] traditional, popular and oral forms" (Bruce-Novoa 1990, 76), for example, Art Godinez's *corrido*, a Mexican ballad dedicated to the militant Tony Guzman ("Corrido de Tony Guzman"); and Juan Gomez-Quiñonez's incantatory "Canto al trabajador" ["Song for the Worker"], which celebrated the worker and "his hand...etched / in holy grime, / ...etched in cries and sweat [that taught us] who are we and who are they...who has built the cities/and wherefrom came the riches" (Mena et al 1982, 25).

THE ANTHOLOGY also included more recent, free form poetry, which blended the first wave of Chicano poetry with the work of Beat poets, *pintos* (Chicanos in prison) and political refugees from Central America. The central poet in this strain was Manazar (Manuel Gamboa [1934–2000]), a pen name that he said means "people's helper." Manazar's "Jam Session" shows prison life in an intimate, lively and human light. It re-creates an improvised rhythm-and-blues session, mimicking the session's call and response structure.

From cell number four
Sapo de la Loma yells out,
"Ese, Chuta,
ain't you vatos gonna jam tonight?"

"Yeah, Chuta,"
someone else hollers,
"we wanta trip a little taste."
"Let's do it for Switch, man,"
a homey from Hazard joins in,
"he got life today –
                    him and Little Jimmy."

...
"Sing it, Chuta, sing it!"
someone yells out.
"Ah say,
did you ever have a woman,
catch her
running-a-round?"
and on, and on
we sing and jam
into "Kansas City,"
"Pink Champagne,"
"All that Wine Is Gone,"
and more, and more,
until:
lock-up time

all prisoners to their cells
Iron doors clang shut.
We settle into our bedding
with heavy, heavy sighs.

After a while –
inside the silence –
a toilet is being flushed,
a truck is rumbling down Temple Street
someone is softly singing,
"Did you ever have a woman..." (Mena et al. 1982, 20)

Manazar was born in 1933. His parents had fled the Mexican
Revolution, and raised him and his eleven brothers and sisters in
the Los Angeles barrio, Chavez Ravine – called "La Bishop," it was
destroyed in the mid-1950s to make way for Dodger Stadium. The
neighborhood was 99 percent Chicano, and nestled in the heart
of Los Angeles, "three miles from the Civic Center," (Gamboa
1987, 32–5). But he went to high school in a white area. He was
the victim of racism, particularly due his Spanish language,
which became an identity and ideological issue:

We were the first group of Latinos who went [to Nightingale
Junior High in Cypress Park]. It was a cultural invasion. The
teachers would get on our case for speaking Spanish. They
would scold me. So I rebelled totally and would speak nothing
but Spanish (ibid., 33).

Later he and his family harvested apricots in the San Fernando
Valley, cotton in Bakersfield, and grapes in Fresno, which he
described in "Buttonwillow":

My family is picking cotton.
My mother drags a ten-foot canvas
sack behind her –
a white, giant worm glowing in the sun.
She stoops over to drag it,

her hands move rhythmically,
picking soft, cotton balls
from the low, claw-like plants.

It is hot...hot...hot...
I stoop behind her
dragging an old potato sack:
imitating.

When I tire,
I straddle her canvas sack.
She pulls white worm and brown child
along the long, dusty row.
Dark, Indian eyes determined;
her long, black hair a horse's tail;
swaying,
       and swaying,
              and swaying.
Slowly,
my head goes down.
I fall asleep
on the peaceful, cotton-stuffed
sack...
to the rhythm of the picking,
and the dragging,
and the swaying,
and the rays of the morning sun.

As a young boy he identified with his elders, the *pachucos* of the 1940s, and thought of himself as a *chicano*, "a person who roamed the streets of the barrios," (Gamboa 1980, 29). In 1947 he was put in juvenile detention for theft.

Manazar discovered his calling in prison, where he spent a total of seventeen years between 1954 and 1977, usually on drug-related charges. He said he saw his woman companion die in his arms of an overdose. At the time of his last sentence, he suddenly felt the need to change his life. He turned towards art, reading history and biographies. The discovery of Villon, Shakespeare, Pope, Yeats, and Coleridge persuaded him to become a poet, he said in a 1987 interview:

> I really was not trained as a writer. I had never had any work-shops or anything but I had a real motivation. I really admired poets, I admired their lifestyles. They were, almost as a whole, very rebellious and I really identified with them. They're very interesting people. So I decided I was going to write poetry.

He wanted to create new images of the Chicano, in a more interior, even lyric mode:

> I had always been interested in writing and I felt an urge, a real strong urge for me to express myself. And what I chose to talk about was the people in there have feelings just like the people out here. And I think one of the things that motivated me to do that was that whenever I saw a movie or read a paper, television, and it showed something about prison or jail, it was always negative and it was always lies. Then I would portray people as real human beings and that was one of the reasons why I got into it.[90]

So, at age 39, behind bars, he began to write. Thanks to the intervention of the Berkeley Writing Association, his first writings were published and widely read; his work revealed "the other side of the 'hardened criminal' image the media constantly presented to the public" (Gamboa 1980, 29).

On his release in 1977, he went to Beyond Baroque, where he attended the Wednesday Night Poetry Workshop and ultimately found employment. He worked in the graphics department, and "then probably one or two years later at the most, [he] was managing the place on an everyday basis."

In late 1978 he directed a special bilingual issue, *beyond baroque 783*, a first for the city. Manazar translated English language poems by local authors into Spanish, because he had not been able to obtain a single manuscript "in Spanish, mixed Spanish/

English, and/or translation (in both languages)" (Gamboa 1978, 7). Beyond Baroque's magazines simply were not read in the Chicano community, with which Manazar had not made contact.

Manazar intended to quit Beyond Baroque in 1979, to start his own magazine. But Drury Smith offered him the office of president. Manazar accepted, on the condition that he "was not going to be anybody's puppet," and would have free rein to implement his personal politics, which were concerned with identity. He wanted to make Beyond Baroque a more multicultural institution.

As president, he turned in particular toward the Chicanos. He used an interview in *Chismearte* to promote Beyond Baroque's new multiculturalism – just as the Los Angeles Latino Writers Workshop was coming together:

> I am in a place where I can be more effective. I'd like to see more interracial participation within the organization. We have so much to offer. We are now doing more bilingual presentations in our programs. I want to give people a voice by using our organization, that's why embracing the problem of the Chicano is important because they should be heard, and take advantage of our facilities. I'd also like to become more innovative, invite more Latinos to get involved in the visual, literary and musical performance areas of our centro. Monday through Saturday I'm here trying to make things happen (Gamboa 1989, 29).

He went on to create "the first multicultural reading series and literary magazine in Los Angeles' history" (Stein 1987, 44), and set up a bilingual writing workshop:

> I started the Third World Series, I published a variety of different people, I did readings – American Indian readings, Latino readings, Blacks, different kinds of groups. We had this...group of poets from Berlin and poets from Japan. So it was like the way that I was taking the organization.

He edited three issues of *Obras*, which presented a poetry by whites, Latinos, Native Americans, African Americans and Asians side by side. The Winter 1980 *Obras*, the "Los Angeles Cross Cultural Issue," was the best example. It included work by, among others, Kate Braverman, Wanda Coleman, Odie Hawkins and Luis Rodriguez. The foreword highlighted the diversity of Los Angeles, while insisting on the solidarity that united the city's inhabitants:

> Los Angeles is an area of many contrasts: valleys, mountains, deserts, beaches and concrete; equally as vibrant is the landscape of its people: old blood, new blood, faces of all colors, and voices accented by the accumulation of diversified experiences: soft voices that speak of love; angry voices that speak of bitterness and hatred; steady voices that speak clearly of a place where the sun will shine on both dreams and dirt.
>
> Here is a selection of some of those experiences expressed through the poetry, fiction and photographs of the community that is Los Angeles.

As the last issue's foreword proudly proclaimed, *Obras* published voices from all of the city's streets, not just the streets "inside" as Bill Mohr's anthology had done:

> To our critics who accuse us of publishing street poetry, we say, "You're damned right!" Not only have we aspired to publish writings of the street, we have aspired to publish writings from all the streets: The streets of the Barrio, Watts, Venice, the east side, the west side, the streets inside prisons, the streets of New Mexico, of Chinatown, of Boston, the streets of Hiroshima... the streets of the reservation.

Perhaps to show that he disagreed with these "critics," in the last issue Manazar published poets associated with SPARC (Social and Public Art Resource Center), an organization that helped "writers who have been overlooked and underserved by many traditional literary organizations because of their age, gender, ethnic origin, or political orientation" (Angelo 1985, 71). SPARC shared a building with beyond baroque.

This all led to a clash between Manazar and the Beyond Baroque Board, which was unhappy with his focus on minority writers, particularly Drury Smith, who deeply regretted that the original *beyond baroque* magazine was no longer being published. In our 1987 interview Smith said:

> Manazar became president and director after I resigned, for a year or more. But eventually the board of trustees decided that he was taking the organization in a direction different from what we wanted it to go. So he was asked to resign.... He really wanted to turn the organization as we saw it into one that served primarily minorities. And that wasn't our original focus, although we have always tried to have programs open to everyone and that embraced a wide spectrum of the cultural scene in Los Angeles. We didn't have any particular desire to focus on any particular segment of it.

The gap between Smith and Manazar was obvious in Manazar's bilingual *beyond baroque 783*. Smith's foreword conceded, unhappily, that 783 "reflected the less avant-garde contemporary literary trends," while hoping that it was "the beginning of a more international *beyond baroque*." In his preface, Manazar spoke of his loyalty to "Beyond Baroque's main motivating policy: 'experimentalism' – however accidental," and emphasized the emotional and subjective side of the endeavor, noting that "most of the poets whose works appear in this issue are, in one way or another, connected with Beyond Baroque, and some are even personal friends of mine. So...this magazine is home grown and love nurtured." But the poets and poetry that Manazar favored distrusted Smith's avant-garde values of formal experimentation. Manazar recounted:

> [The Board of trustees] asked me what were my plans [when I accepted the position of president at Beyond Baroque] and I said that one of the things that I wanted to do is to incorporate

Third World artists and have a more political slant to the kind of things that were shown there rather than just the experimental stuff which was a big part especially of the magazine.

For Manazar, the poet was above all a social role model. It was important to him to share emotion and a message with his audience and show how writing could explore, express and communicate. Manazar was committed to the most disadvantaged groups – gang members, jailed delinquents, the mentally handicapped, incest victims, Central American refugees – and literature had to be engaged in the face of their suffering. The poet was duty-bound to write poetry with social and political content and put his talent at the service of the people. Manazar belonged to his community before the art world, which, being inward-looking, might "tak[e him] away from the community," (Gamboa 1987, 35). Life was the raw material of poetry. Authenticity was essential:

One of the things that helped me on a personal level was to be honest. Realize what you're about. When people are honest with themselves and their situation, whatever they're writing about is gonna come through as sincere. It you write a line just because it's a neat line, it's gonna show and hurt your work. It's gonna hurt you as an individual – your character. Expressing the thing that only you can express: that's what makes it worthwhile for a writer to be a writer (ibid., 34).

Faced with these profound differences, Manazar was asked to resign, despite the fact that numerous artists supported him. Multiculturalism only returned to Beyond Baroque in the mid-1980s. The Foundation's next publication, *Magazine, Southern California Women Writers*, contained an overwhelming majority of white women poets.

Manazar then turned to the Association of Latino Writers, *Chismearte* and the Los Angeles Latino Writers Workshop. He co-edited *Two Hundred and One*, became editor-in-chief of *Chismearte*, and directed the Los Angeles Latino Barrio Writers

Workshop. Like Kamau Daáood, he devoted the rest of his life to his community and lived up to his pen name. During the 1980s, he worked in various artist organizations, including Concilio de Arte Popular, a California coalition at the service of Latino artists; Galería Ocaso, a multicultural performance space and gallery; L.A. Theatre Works' Arts & Children Project, which brought art to incarcerated, at-risk and underprivileged youths in L.A.; and finally Homeland, a community center he created in 1989 in the Long Beach "Anaheim quarter," a very poor and violent area where Chicano and Cambodian immigrant gangs clashed.

He remained involved in art and poetry, which he used as a therapeutic and social tool. He directed thousands of workshops in prisons, hospitals and social centers, and published the participants' works in some twenty anthologies. He published collections of his own in the late 1980s.[91] In a 1991 interview he said:

> One of the things that *I* try to do is..., I try to bring the voice of those kids to the public, to the regular poets. Like I have kids come out to do–not only kids but the people from Home and also adults–brought them to the Midnight Special Bookstore, to the Basement Coffeeshop, and several other places. We've done poetry readings on KPFK several times, a few things on TV–... and people are *always* impressed. People are always blown away with the power that comes through from these people who normally would not be listened to.

When he died in 2000, the *Los Angeles Times* published a lengthy obituary, and Homeland had a mural painted in his honor portraying him next to one of his poems.[92]

ONE OF MARISELA NORTE's first prose poems was published in *Two Hundred and One*. Born in East L.A. in the late 1950s, her upbringing in a cultivated Mexican family was marked by the personality of her father, who forbade the use of English in his household. But he had been a film projectionist in Mexico, and Marisela and her brother learned English from films and television. In a 1991 interview she recalled:

[My dad] lived for movies, God! To him, that was the way we would learn how to speak English, was at the movies! And he would take us to the walk-ins during the day or the drive-in on the week-end to see American movies, or TV, you know, he'd sit us in front of the TV, "Watch this!" So all these images are coming to mind of Dracula, Frankenstein, the Wolf Man, gangsters, prison movies, I mean you name it, and so our introduction to English was on the television or on the big screen.[93]

Norte was always wary of labels, including "Chicano," which she said in a 1987 interview had "too much political feeling behind it." She preferred "Mejicana," as she was "the first generation living here in Los Angeles," or more simply "writer and poet." But she had much in common with the Chicanos of the 1980s.

She began her career as a poet in the multimedia group Asco in 1982.[94] Asco–"nausea or disgust" in Spanish–was a collective formed in 1971 by four East L.A. high school students: Harry Gamboa, Jr., a political activist and writer; Patssi Valdez, a hairstylist and makeup artist; Willie Herrón, and Gronk, both painters. They were all "Jetters," a circle of "very high-style and artistic, intellectual [teenagers], as opposed to the *cholos*, who tended to be much more limited, conservative," as Gronk said in an article on Chicano art (quoted in Burnham, Durland, and MacAdams 1986, 51).

Self-taught and iconoclastic, they criticized and parodied the traditional Latino community as well as the Anglo avant-garde: "Unwilling or unable to wholly identify with either camp, Asco created work out of its own sense of displacement" (H. Gamboa 1986, 51). That work included videos, performances, plays, poems, photo novels, drawings, fashion designs on paper, murals and manifestos. All of it had a nihilistic accent.

The group, whose membership fluctuated, criticized stereotypes and "emotional schizophrenia" (Burnham, Durland, and MacAdams 1986, 53)–which they said the modern Chicano suffered from. They were inspired by their contemporary, urban and media-savvy surroundings:

A lot of Latino artists went back in history for imagery because they needed an identity, a starting place.... Where Asco has a more modern sense. We didn't want to go back, we wanted to stay in the present and find out imagery as urban artists and produce a body of work out of our sense of displacement. Latin imagery has a strong input, but we also had Daffy Duck and were bombarded by B movies. My character Tormenta is very Mexican, very melodramatic, but also very Hollywood (Gronk 1986, 57).

Norte wrote a play for the group, *Éxito* (*Success*), fashioned an altar called "Last Writers," and participated in Guillermo Gómez-Peña's border project. She also gave public readings of her prose poems, which were so popular that her friends nicknamed her "Ambassador of East L.A. appointed by the East L.A. Ministry of Culture." She was also regularly published in magazines and newspapers, and a compilation of her work appeared on CD in 1991, *Word/Norte*.[95]

Norte's long narrative poems, which she recites in a hypnotic voice, are usually told in the first person. Willie Loya's conga drums provide a "Latin beat backing up those words." The combination of voice and percussion was meant to take the audience "on a small journey using language and words, [over the course of which] the English mixes in with the Spanish":

EAST STREET/EACH STORY

Once it was like seeing the night for the first time. Only someone dangled black ice cubes in front of my eyes. Each street/each story melted on a page.

An upholstery shop opened past midnight. In the back a fading light bulb persists overhead as the men gather to drink. They talk about women. Women at bus stops with slits in their secretarial skirts. Catholic girls with too much lipstick—New Wave Santitas cuddling school books, teddy bears and suddenly religious boys.

muchachas bailando en bikini! I pass these joints and I must look. Possibly I am searching for those who search for the anonymous body in the pink bathing suit. I hear the trampling of their feet. Men knocking doors down to get a good look at a pair of fishnet stockings. And for every man laying out the family bills on the bar there is another one pale and miserable who simply wishes he wasn't there. And the juke box still plays "yo quiero una muchacha como tu."

...

Radios blast each other on the streets de Boss Angeles con salsa picante, sabado salsa y salsa el pato tambien. Musica con ambiente y una cuba libre. And in another corner of the city some chavalito sneaks out the screen door to play in the garage. He crawls into an old washing machine, sings himself to sleep only he never wakes up.

...

I feel myself spilling through my fingers breaking into little pearls of Mercury, praying for rain to soothe the hot pavement, our souls, some dying lawn in a Sub-Urban postcard. The heart breaks, it breaks like an old woman's arm, it breaks like Mother's china crashing like a hopeless silver jet hitting the ground like Hiroshima.

Sir Lonely puts his shades on. His imperials pierce the moon. So a page from the Puppet Zone falls over the blue night. Baby Loca carries 45s and checks out all the guys. Impalas slide around the corner in dangerous love as three stars hang heavy over the East.

Norte's dream was to direct films, and the influence of film is discernible in her visual style. Using images and words found in shop windows, snapshots, signs, billboards, flyers and popular song lyrics, she revealed the inner depths and the superficial exteriors along these streets, as well as the contradictions and aspirations of the poet and the streets' inhabitants. She observed this world with melancholy, astonishment and kindly amusement. The poem includes a number of registers: documentary, allegory, comic book, omniscient narrative, diary, in Spanish and English. The registers collide, as do the I and family, the neighborhood, East L.A., the United States, the planet, and another galaxy. Even when it starts to look like a cardboard film set, this universe remains deeply marked by Norte's intimate vision, inspired by her meetings and conversations with people.

> I like to observe a lot, I'm on the bus and I have a captive audience every morning and every afternoon.... The people that are on the bus, I mean we're all on this thing together, and I can look at them and write down, "well there's a lady in pink bicycle shorts, and there's a baby, and there's a guy with this and that" and they keep changing characters and I almost feel like it's being done just exclusively for *me.* I can be selfish and think, oh that person is here, and I'm going to have to sit and talk to this lady and this and that.

Her poems left room for the reader's imagination. She recalled this personalized and almost private relationship with her listeners in an early 1980s KPFK radio show:

> I get a repeat of some people, I mean, I don't want to sound presumptuous by saying that I have a following, but there's your friends that are loyal and they're your buddies and they show up and then there's people that you kinda "oh yeah, there's that guy again, wow, you know, he's there," and maybe this time he'll talk to you or whatever, or you'll see him here or there...I used to do a thing called "The Morning Reading" where I would read stories or poetry or whatever.... And they repeated those shows because my brother's friend was at work and he said "hey, I think this is your sister, you know," and he called him over, and sure enough, it was me. And somebody else heard it, and I remember at Gorki's once I was paying for my coffee and this guy Fred, the cashier, said, "oh yeah, I heard you on the radio the other day," and I said, "oh yeah, what did you think?", and he said "oh, it was great, I really liked that," and there was a guy sitting at another table who said, "are you

the woman on the bus?" And I said "yeah I am." He goes, "oh wow! I was in my darkroom, I was developing film, and I was listening to your story." And I thought, "oh, my God!" That was just an overwhelming feeling for me.

DESPITE THE HOPE of poets like Manazar and Norte, the Chicano literary movement in Los Angeles was short-lived. Manazar said in 1987, "I don't think there's much going on in the Chicano-Latino writing scene." Norte regretted the lack of places for poets to present their works in East L.A., even when poetry was booming elsewhere in Los Angeles:

> I see more and more listings now for poetry readings than I did before. It seems that it's not such an unusual thing to do on a Friday or Saturday night: go have a little dinner and then go listen to some words, or listen to music mixed in with words. It seems to be growing but yet it only seems to be growing on that side of the L.A. River. I don't know why things start and stop and matter once they're safely over that side of the bridge. There's a lot of territory here, and different neighborhoods should be cultivating that. But it always seems that any kind of scene or anything that's almost worth writing about, it always takes place on that side of town. I don't understand it, I don't know why that is.

This state of affairs continued in the early 1990s, perhaps because there was little publicity for poetry events in East L.A.

The decline in Chicano militancy, the waves of new immigrants who were indifferent to local Chicano history, and the dip in federal subsidies during the 1980s were terrible blows to the Chicano cultural renaissance. Living conditions worsened in the Latino neighborhoods, as they did in South Central. Like the African Americans after the Watts Black Arts Movement, writers included in *Two Hundred and One* did continue their literary activity during the 1980s, but their participation in the Los Angeles poetry community as a whole was limited and often sporadic.

They did, however, bring to light their specific vision of the city – historical, continental, political, bilingual and immersed in the street and the barrio. *Two Hundred and One*'s allegiance to Oscar Zeta Acosta revealed what Los Angeles Chicano writers aspired to: an iconoclastic and nonconformist literature.

The Spoken Word Movement:
Between Public Institutions and Mass Culture

The Woman's Building closed its doors at the beginning of the 1990s, driven to bankruptcy by debts owed on their real estate acquisitions. Beyond Baroque was protected by its occupation of a city building, and its status as a regional literary center. But even Beyond Baroque was forced to "professionalize" in the late 1980s, hiring a management specialist in 1988. And they were the fortunate spaces: thanks to decreasing government subsidies, many of the arts institutions from the 1960s and '70s could not survive.

> In the 1980s there was a shift away from the established organizations, a move away from "spaces" to "scenes." Work was being performed in clubs, exhibited in restaurants and galleries and there was a proliferation of happening-type events. A brand new body of work with completely new ideas connected to punk rock seemed to be exploding throughout Los Angeles (Drew 1988, 12).

But, at the same time, the city of Los Angeles was creating a prestigious cultural infrastructure. It aimed to be a multicultural capital and attract foreign investors. Museums were constructed, visual arts foundations were set up, and festivals were inaugurated, often thanks to private investment. But the city government's arts policy remained unbalanced: "Civic hype would have us believe that L.A. is becoming the Athens of the Pacific Rim. But the truth is that, compared to other urban centers, we are increasingly inhospitable to our artists – and to our artists' organizations" (Burnham 1988, 20). Even a special real estate tax designed to finance local art and encourage small emerging organizations could not really manage to compensate for this policy, which was especially unhelpful for literature – the "poor relation" of the arts:

> L.A. Poets are impoverished for lack of institutional support. This year the city's Cultural Affairs Department allocated $71,500 of its $3-million budget to the literary arts, in contrast with almost $400,000 for visual arts, $467,000 for theater, a whopping $586,000 for music. Corporations, which may give generously to the performing and visual arts, rarely support literature (Wolverton 1990, 39).

The city imported architects, artists and intellectuals of international renown to direct the new organizations, and neglected its local artists. Eclipsed by superstars and grandiose events, independent Los Angeles artists withdrew into themselves, creating many private and often transitory spaces.

One of the most notable movements at this time was spoken word. It brought together certain elements of the Los Angeles poetry scene. Its boom during the 1980s energized segments of the poetry scene. It was launched by Harvey Kubernik.

Born in 1953, in Los Angeles, Kubernik worked for MCA as an artistic director and as a journalist for *Melody Maker* in the 1970s and '80s. The advent of independent distribution in the record industry gave him the means to realize a project he had conceived in the 1970s: to record the diverse artists and personalities whom he had met and admired.

> 1970 to 1980 I probably made 85% of every connection I have now, just by knowing Michael. I met Michael C. Ford in 1958. He had a car I remember. I was 6. He was an older guy with a car. Then there was a 20 year gap. I met a lot of people that I would always say, maybe I'll get a record label that will let us record you. I spent 10 years knocking on doors, wanting to record these people. So, by the time we got to record, I had

5 albums already storyboarded to do. I mean I met Wanda Coleman in 1965 in junior high school. I remember when she won a BankAmerica Award in 1964. She was the hottest debater in the L.A. City Schools District... and you just knew that this person might be a writer when they grew up or something (Forty Years of L.A. Small Presses, 1990).

He named his record label Freeway Records, and released three important compilations between 1982 and 1984: *Voices of the Angels, English as a Second Language,* and *Neighborhood Rhythms.* The freeway was the central and defining metaphor of this vast "kind of aural mural of Los Angeles," performed by a "polymorphous and interracial array of voices... most of [whom] were born and raised in Southern California" (Hoskyns 1983, 17).

The LPS included more than eighty pieces each – conversations, lyrics, stories, monologues and poems – varying in length from a few seconds to several minutes. Each record recalled the assemblage art that Simon Rodia's Watts Towers embodied as a Southern Californian tradition. The resulting cacophony revealed that "the apparently barren landscape was in fact populated all along, it's just that no-one had bothered to make a map," as Hoskyns put it. *Voices of Angels* opened with a Bukowski poem. The third record, *Neighborhood Rhythms,* closed with Dave Alvin's "Prayer," which took in the human, historical and geographical diversity of Los Angeles:

El Pueblo de Nuestra Señora la Reina de Los Angeles de Porciúncula
Our Lady Queen of the Angels, Queen of Chumash
Indians, Gaspar de Portóla
Pío Pico, Kit Carson,
pueblo of sweating desert winds,
oasis of burning canyons,
I bow.
Downtown looming above unmarked founders' graves
Mestizos, Indians, Blacks who trudged from Mexico
to Mission San Gabriel, settled nearby Chaparral River

Flats,
their ghost haunt pawnshop store fronts, ...
no movie stars slumming the abandoned burlesque
houses.
Just men's throats slashed behind the midnight Mission,
...
I bow.
Dying palm trees streets of Raymond Chandler
Apartments of stucco and heat,
I bow.
Hollywood movie stars,
dead stars, rock stars, has-beens, hopefuls, directors,
producers ...
I bow.
The Boulevard of Musso, Frank's and Grauman's
Chinese,
where bible belt tourists try to fill the shoe prints of John
Wayne and Shirley Temple,
I bow.
The Santa Monica Boulevard street corner boys ...
Sunset hookers tricks pimps vice squad ...
I bow.
Religious cult apostles handing out throw-away
pamphlets
throw-away salvation to a city believing in movie plots,
... I bow.
Heavy metal white kids cruising identical
endless suburban streets
and sun burnt Pacific Coast Highway,
smoking joints, tempting their wild side,
blond girls with blond surfer boyfriends with eternal
tans,
I bow.
Lowriders cruising Whittier Boulevard,
past Silver Dollar Cafe, past ghost Ruben Salazar,
while eastside homeboys spraypaint boundaries on
hopeless walls,

I bow.
Watts, old riot growing new on streets of unemployment,
and hearts that can't forget a past that still exists,
I bow.
Victims of drive-by gang shootings,
Victims of nervous police fingers and chokeholds,
Victims of fire and landslide,
victims of dark freeways,
I bow.
Indians, Latins, Blacks, Asians, Anglos,
from Pacoima to little Tokyo to Little Seoul,
from Torrance to Bell Gardens,
from Fairfax to Boyle Heights,
trying to get over on the panoramic view
from the air-conditioned Arco Towers,
I bow.
...
The cars,
I bow.
Vanished Chumash, vanished ranchos, vanished orange
groves,
vanished Angel's Flight, vanished red cards, vanished
Garden of Allah,
I bow.
... As it comes to the sand directed by you
through moon and stars,
again and again, again and again,
world without end,
amen.

The boundaries between speech, poetry and music were blurred on all of the albums, as were the generational divides: they presented "veterans" of the scene like Bukowski, Ford, and Coleman; younger poets like Dennis Cooper, Michelle Clinton and Jack Skelley; punk poets like Henry Rollins, Exene Cervenka and John Doe of X, and Mike Watt from the Minutemen; performance artists, journalists, militants and comedians.

Kubernik called these "spoken word" records – a term the industry used to classify comedians in the 1960s. He put his industry contacts to good use: he had his records broadcast on alternative and university radio stations, placed articles in the music press, and produced a few television programs on cable channels, including MTV's "The Cutting Edge." He organized tours and public concert-readings intended for a new young audience, who were attracted by the connections to popular musicians. Finally, he used venues which lent themselves to the events he promoted: a concert room/guitar store (McCabe's), rock/performance/comedy clubs (the Anti-Club, the Lhasa Club), an art gallery/record store/stage (Be Bop Records), and a university café (Kerkhoff Hall Coffee House at UCLA). The coffeehouse phenomenon only grew with time: beginning in 1992, *Caffeine* was published both on paper and online. It listed all the coffeeshops in Southern California that held poetry readings: 248 of them in January 1994.

Kubernik's concerts were specially designed for each venue and, like the records, they brought together poets and musicians. The format suited everyone – the poets gained a new and larger audience, and the punk-rockers welcomed the freedom of expression. Some of the events were open to all – the forerunners of today's open mic nights. This network of venues was a nurturing environment for the nascent movements. Even if a given venue was not long-lived, the general strategy was reproducible. It responded perfectly to Los Angeles' unique characteristics: it was live poetry's answer to the impermanence, sprawl and decentralization of Los Angeles.

The movement would accelerate still more over the course of the 1990s, thanks to the popularity of rap, which gave greater media visibility to the spoken word.[96] Gabriel Baltierra, born in East L.A. in 1966, organized poetry readings in new spaces (a laundromat in Silver Lake, stations along the Blue Line). In our 1991 interview, he recalled hearing spoken word artists on the radio:

That was the big thing back then they just had like on KXLU and the different radio stations had "spoken word," and so, I was always listening to that, trying to find out who was who, and then trying to contact them and get them on my [cable television] show. I never had Henry [Rollins] do any of his spoken words on the show, but he did do an interview, and he did have spoken word videos, so we showed those.

Kubernik prospered through this period. Freeway Records became Barkubco in 1990; it success allowed him to live off the sale of recordings. He released new albums by Wanda Coleman, Marisela Norte, and the "black conceptual theater/performance/ poetry group" blackmadrid. Three new compilations rounded out his catalogue. On *Hollyword*, according to a press release, fifty poets, actors and musicians "both famous and obscure" presented a view of Hollywood very different from the one people got "from movies or TV." *Jazzspeak* featured orator-poets from beyond Los Angeles, including Amiri Bakara, Ishmael Reed, Michael McClure and Quincy Troupe. And finally, *Black & Tan Club*, an anthology which brought together twenty Latino, black and white Los Angeles poets to evoke the life of Los Angeles' largest communities of color.

Kubernik also continued to organize readings. Of particular note was a series in the restaurant Cafe Largo, owned by the former owners of the Lhasa Club. Here television and film stars, actors and writers, along with famous authors and well-known local poets, read their works.

Spoken word represented the new face of Los Angeles poetry – multiracial, polyvalent, theatrical. Kubernik had hoped to launch a new artistic movement; spoken word arrived when Los Angeles already had a mature, local poetry scene to act as a foundation. Spoken word as a whole drew its aesthetic and ethical principles from the Venice scene and the Beats, valuing readability, content, autodidactism and a rejection of formal constraints, and sought to represent all Los Angeles neighborhoods, as Manazar had done.

In addition, Kubernik tried to define spoken word against academic poetry on the one hand, and the standardized mass culture of television and film, on the other:

What I have done and what I do isn't really poetry. Although I will tell you there are poets all over the recordings. I brought this term "spoken word" in, and it brought in people, to the shows especially, who never felt comfortable with poetry readings.... This world has gotten so fucking boring, from the books out to the movies made to the horrible academic poetry, that people had to embrace us.... Many people are starting to find the answers more themselves than finding it in other people or television.... Maybe because there's so much entertainment focused here...there *has* to be some other people besides people who want to be in sitcoms.

But spoken word also lived with the omnipresence of mass culture. Even as Kubernik repudiated the giant recording industry's obsession with producing and distributing short-lived hits, spoken word artists sought out the media spotlight: unlike their predecessors, they did not wish to escape it, provided they didn't have to compromise their freedom of expression. They knew that, without the recognition of the media, they were doomed to obscurity. They believed that poets had to embrace mass culture, rather than reject it.

So, for instance, Jim Glaeser and Dennis Cooper founded the influential magazine *Little Caesar* in 1976. It mingled punk with popular, artistic and literary cultures, as could be seen in the foreword to the magazine's first issue:

I think there are already too many little magazines around, mostly uninteresting and virtually unread. So why are Jim and I adding this to the heap? Maybe we're crazy but we think there can be a literary journal that's loved and powerful. We want a magazine that's read by the Poetry fans, the Rock culture, the Hari Krishnas, the Dodgers.... I have this dream where writers are mobbed everywhere they go; like rock stars and actors. A predilection? You never know. People like Patti Smith (poet/rock star) are subtly forcing their growing audiences to become literate, introducing them to

Rimbaud, Breton, Burroughs and others.... We're not fifty year old patrons of the arts. We're young punks just like you.

Similarly, when Jack Skelley released the first issue of BARNEY, he asserted the new aesthetic strategy of literature absorbing mass culture:

Welcome to BARNEY: *The Modern Stone-age Magazine!* What I've tried to do here is, I think, pretty new. The emphasis is on literary takes on popular culture, and more often than not there is a totemic focus on various characters, events, attitudes, images or icons of the culture at large.... I'd rather celebrate the beauty, garishness, meaning and absurdity of popular culture than sneer at it. Sure there's lots wrong with American life, but it seems to me that a poet's job is to gather together his/her nation's scattered myths and images and refashion them, not with the pompous attitude of being above it all, or dismissing it as garbage, but with love, amusement, invention and social intent.

For some poets, this accommodation to mass culture continues into the present.

CONCLUSION

Beneath the illusion of order, this city is a spectacle of personal histories being enacted in the theaters of intersections and parking lots. And it is not the cacophony that sickens me, but the abundance. The sense of something overwhelmingly human, trapped and caged and trying to get out.

...

Beneath our arrogantly glistening, steel-reinforced monuments, there are human beings who will not fit into the machinery, who by reasons of undefinable idiosyncrasy or cunning will manage to refuse.

— KATE BRAVERMAN

In 1987, thirty poets organized a protest against the *Los Angeles Times* replacing poetry criticism with the publication of poems. That year also saw the city's first large poetry festival; these festivals continued into the new millenium. Here, poets discuss criticism, publishing, Chicano poetry, "the situation of poetry in Los Angeles,"[167] and much more besides.

Many poets of the 1970s are now well established. Wanda Coleman was a prime example:

Now, commercial places of business are opening their doors to us — restaurants — ... academia has finally started to embrace us, and our books are being carried in the university store. So that *some of us* are becoming *the* Establishment in a funny kind of way. Which really seems weird.... And now we're being taught in classes. I'm one of the few who's starting to have an international reputation. I'm probably one of the first...who's been translated.

New voices recognize the heritage of their elders, and follow them in making the urban Los Angeles landscape material for a unique poetry. Consider Rubén Martínez:

Maxifesto

Can you feel the earth shudder?
This generation's shakey, bro'.
It is 1990 and I live and die
in Guatemala, San Salvador, the D.F.,
Tijuana and L.A....
And what time is it in L.A. when
a guatemalteco wears an Africa Now t-shirt
and a Black kid munches carnitas and all
together now dance to Easy-E and bdp,
crossing every border ever held sacred?

But that's live ammunition
on the streets of Southcentral
and in Westwood and San Salvador
and East L.A.
This is war, the battle
will be block to block
wherever the We's and They's face off.
Third World in the First,
that's what time it is.
...
see how anglo and how indígena we are
and how black and español...
History is on fast forward
this is the age of synthesis
which is not to say
that the Rainbow Coalition
is heaven on earth and let's party;

all kinds of battles are yet to come
(race and class rage bullets and blood),
choose your weapons just know
that everyone is everywhere now—
so careful how you shoot.

Some important venues have disappeared—Papa Bach
Bookstore in 1984, Bebop Records and the Lhasa Club in the
late 1980s. But they were replaced by, for instance, the Highways
Performance Space and Gallery in Santa Monica, a multicultural
organization founded in 1990, dedicated to performance art,
dance, theater and poetry; or Electronic Café, where videophone
technology was used for simultaneous public readings in Los
Angeles and other American cities.

It was cool to be a poet, as Ellen Henderson, an organizer of
Beyond Baroque's open readings, remarked a 1991 interview:

In this town, poetry is the route. You want to prove that you're
an intellectual, that you read books—even though a lot of poets
don't read books [whispers]. But you wanna kind of say you do.
That's why I think they choose poetry. Because you just have
a pencil and a paper, and then you can, like write this "great
art." And then also it's really "cool," you know, you go to pick
up chicks, you're a guy, you know, like "yeah, I work at IBM in
the morning, but at night I'm a poet, babe," you know, like "oh,
take me I'm yours," since it makes women weak for guys.

The Los Angeles scene attracted poets from all over the United
States, as William Slattery observed in our interview in 1991:

There's an openness here to new voices, that in New York you
have to be somebody, you have to get somebody established
already to recognize you. There's not as many open readings,
there's not as many places for the unrecognized, the unwashed,
to go and get themselves washed.... I heard at the reading here
[at Beyond Baroque] last month, from somebody who was
in Arizona or New Mexico, that people there in the smaller

cities in the middle of the country, are interested in the L.A. scene more than any other scene, and I think that that must be because they sense that openness. They sense that if they went to New York nobody would listen but if they come here, it's easy to be heard and someone might even pay attention, and that there's a decentralized poetry scene here instead of an authority, or a group of authorities, or even an unorganized non-group of authorities.

The scene became more and more multicultural, integrating a growing number of Blacks and Latinos, now joined by Asians – who not long before were isolated and invisible – as well as other newer and less numerous groups.

> I think that especially with minority poetry, you know, they've become a very strong voice in the *whole* community, because before, they'd always been there, but they were more isolated within their own in-club. But now, it's like mixing much more, and people are beginning to respect it and understand it, and relate to it. (Interview with M. Gamboa).

Public performance had become ever more vital for the dissemination, publication, reproduction and recognition of poetry. The expressions "performance poet" and "performance poetry" were used more and more frequently. A kind of *cursus honorum* had emerged for young poets: first, writing workshops, open mics and publication in a local magazine; then organizing readings, publishing a magazine or being included in an anthology; finally, book publication or running a workshop. The most prestigious mark of success was a solo paid reading, concert or publication outside Los Angeles. Some readings are more theatrical, some less so; some involve music; some are "acted" by a troupe of poets. And Beyond Baroque remained one of the most sought after venues.

Mecca for Los Angeles area poets is a large, drab stucco building near the beach on Venice Boulevard. Once Venice's town hall, it now houses the Beyond Baroque Foundation, a literary arts organization where a poetry reading is the *sine qua non* of career building for local poets. But first you have to get there (Shiffrin, 1986, 3).

Shiffrin takes the example of poet Laurel Ann Bogen who, after ten years of reading "in nearly every other reading venue in the city," publishing her work and being profiled locally, finally got her reading at Beyond Baroque. In a 1991 interview, Bogen spoke of her first reading at Beyond Baroque as "the most memorable of [her] life."

The ideals of accessibility and responsibility to a community dominated over those of the avant-garde—even if the latter were also very much present, supported by Lee Hickman and Paul Vangelisti. And some authors—like Wanda Coleman and La Loca—moved closer to the avant-garde as they received more recognition. This current is well represented, for instance, in Bill Mohr's second anthology (1985), *Poetry Loves Poetry: An Anthology of Los Angeles Poets*.

The avant-garde features prominently in Beyond Baroque's programs, though the Foundation also presents bohemian poetry, spoken word, and community poetry. Under the direction of African American poets Michelle Clinton and Akila Nayo Oliver, several workshops encouraged minority and women poets to use Beyond Baroque as a resource, a decade after Manazar Gamboa's first unsuccessful attempt. In 1989, editors Michelle Clinton, Sesshu Foster and Naomi Quiñonez published the award winning anthology *Invocation L.A.* It included poems by over 30 Los Angeles poets of various ethnic backgrounds.

Unfortunately, the popularity of the spoken word scene also reopened the old breaches between oral poetry (associated with vitality and energy) and written poetry (associated with form and permanence).

THE POETRY SCENE grew continuously from the 1950s, when it comprised only a few dozen people, to the beginning of the 1990s, when this study ends. It gained in breadth, intensity and variety. The 1968 creation of Beyond Baroque Foundation made possible an organized scene. It gave Los Angeles a permanent base, taking the best of the Beats and underground poets from previous decades, and providing continuity through following generations. The Los Angeles poetry community has been nourished by this group of poets, and, just as importantly, enriched by the contribution of the feminist, black and Chicano networks that had all been relatively isolated until the mid-1980s. By the beginning of the 1990s the poetry scene was solidly entrenched in the city; it had developed its own means of production, presentation, distribution, conservation and validation. Local poets succeeded in creating what Paul Vangelisti called a "new, Californian and progressive poetic culture...[which] does not defer to official literary culture" (Vangelisti 1983, 69, 78). They did this in the face of the East Coast's dominance of literature, and Hollywood's unrivaled power on the West Coast.

During the 1990s, a dozen anthologies of Los Angeles poetry appeared. They repudiated Lachlan MacDonald's belief (articulated in a 1960 special issue of *Coastlines* magazine on Los Angeles) that language and metaphor could not capture the multifaceted reality of L.A. It might not be possible for a single poet, or a single anthology, but a profusion of poets could do so, working together. They expressed the city without falling into the facile mythical and ahistorical clichés.

For example, Wanda Coleman edited a special issue of *High Performance Magazine* immediately after the 1992 riots. It showed how poetry could embrace the whole city, by combining contributions from a diverse range of artists who "set aside their differences, across boundaries of aesthetics, age, economics, ethnicity, gender and sex-orientation to reflect on the moment in history uniting us" (Coleman, Summer 1992, 1). The issue portrayed an alternative history of the violence and its aftermath, as seen from the inside by those who took part in or witnessed the violence. Coleman, who had experienced the Watts riots in 1965, wanted to make sure that "this time, others are not going to speak for us," that she could "say to [her] grandchildren, '*This* is really what it was like.'"

In a city where regional fiction sometimes takes the place of official history, poetry worked as a sort of alternative memory that recorded and recalled an often somber past. Poetry helped Angelenos, as citizens with shifting identities and loyalties, to build bridges between the city's diverse populations and neighborhoods. Poets came to view language as an ideological battleground, perpetuating the city's tradition of dissent and nonconformity.

But thanks to the stress Los Angeles poets place on freedom, and authenticity, as well as the city's immensity and decentralization, the scene is constantly in peril of forgetting its own history and fragmenting into nothing.

Los Angeles

The angels here
have pigeons' wings
blue collars
washed in sweat
the common salt
in tears
tongues swirl
in a stew of cultures
singing asphalt songs
in the midst of seagulls
bebop atop
the San Andreas
a humble plate
of beings

— KAMAU DAÁOOD

NOTES

1 *Author's trans.*

2 "Make it new" here echoes Ezra Pound's famous precept.

3 See John S. Gentile, *Cast of One: One-Person Shows from the Chautauqua Platform to the Broadway Stage*, Chicago, University of Illinois Press, 1989.

4 James Boyer May, the first to compile a directory of the small independent presses in his magazine *Trace* (published in Los Angeles, see chapter 2) which merged with *International Directory of Small Presses and Magazines* in its last year of publication, dates the boom to 1964: "The first directory (1952), limited to magazines, had but 152 entries; yet that was a fairly complete world coverage of littles in English. By 1956, 247 mags were listed along with 165 presses; and in 1963, the combined total had reached 747. But the huge acceleration began with 1964. The *incomplete* 'Evolving Directory' in *Trace* 71 had 697 entries. Indexed projects and listings in this issue totaled 999," James Boyer May, "On *Trace*," *The Little Magazine in America: A Modern Documentary History*, eds. Elliott Anderson and Mary Kinzie, Yonkers, New York, The Pushcart Press, 1978, p. 383. Len Fulton (publisher of *International Directory of Small Presses and Magazines*, launched in 1965, and the magazine *Small Press Review*, in 1966; as well as founder of the Committee of Small Magazines, Editors and Publishers (COSMEP) in 1967 – a major reference book, publication and professional organization for the independent press) discerns another quantitative leap between the 1960s and 1980s. In 1965, when he first published the *Directory of Little Magazines*, it was 40 pages long, listed 250 magazines and small presses, and printed 500 copies; in 1978, it was 500 pages, listed 2,500 small presses and magazines and had a circulation of 10,000. See Len Fulton, "*Dust*: A Tribal Seed," *The Little Magazine in America*, pp. 434–5.

5 Brochure for "California Poets in the Schools, My Kid is a Poet," San Francisco, not dated.

6 This is the title of what was, without a doubt, the most famous manual of the New Critics: *Understanding Poetry*, by Cleanth Brooks and Robert Warren, published in 1938.

7 "The contemporary revisionist anthology is not a new *kind* of anthology," Golding notes, as it is a tradition of American poetry anthologies to push for a political or literary agenda. The difference in the recent ones is that they have "become so many and so vocal, and their number reflects the nonacademic anthologists' increased power to shift the canon." Golding adds that the university has embraced a more open canon out of self-interest – i.e., in order to renew its exegetic material and have enough texts to analyze and interpret for its students and faculty. See Alan C. Golding, pp. 300–1. On the survival strategies of the university, see Edward W. Said, "Opponents, Audiences, Constituencies, and Community," *Critical Inquiry* 9, Sept. 1982, pp. 1–26. Also see Jane Tompkins, "An Introduction to Reader-Response Criticism" and "The Reader in History: The Changing Shape of Literary Response," (pp. ix–xxvi and pp. 201–32).

8 See in *Creative Careers, Minorities in the Arts*, pp. 138–43 the example of the San Francisco Neighborhood Arts Program.

9 In New York City, starting in the late 1970s, the *NYC Poetry Calendar* kept track of more than 300 readings at some 70 venues, had a circulation of 4,000 copies and was funded both privately and publicly. In San Francisco, *Poetry Flash* posted close to 200 readings a month, and many other cities had their local poetry reading newsletters. For more detail, read Donald Hall. Poets & Writers, Inc. listed in 1978 505 organizations that were sponsoring literary programs and 32 regional newsletters. In *Coda: Poets & Writers Newsletter*, Vol. 5, no. 3, February/March, 1978, p. 26.

10 Chapters Two and Three of Bill Mohr's *Hold-Outs, The Los Angeles Poetry Renaissance, 1948–1992*, Iowa City, University of Iowa Press, 2011, pp. 27–85, provide additional information, excerpts and perspectives on Venice West poets and poetry and the literary magazines of the 1950s.

11 The names of these people (among others) are culled from John Arthur Maynard's book, *Venice West, The Beat Generation in Southern California*, New Brunswick, Rutgers University Press, 1991, as well as from *Fantasy By the Sea, A Visual History of the American Venice*, Tom Moran and Tom Sewell, Venice, California, Beyond Baroque Foundation, 1979.

12 For an in-depth study of the division between "high" and "low" art, see Lawrence Levine, *Highbrow/Lowbrow: The Emergence of Cultural Hierarchy in America* (Cambridge, Massachusetts, Harvard University Press, 1988).

13 Dick Hebdige, in *Subculture, The Meaning of Style* (London and New York, Routledge, 1979, 1988), explores more in depth (chapters three and four) the multiplicity of these symbolic ties between the black and white cultures in the United States and Great Britain.

14 The monthly stipend for students under the GI Bill was $75; combined, the overall benefits of the GI bill paved the way to college for many millions of Americans.

15 *Brother, the Laugh Is Bitter*, New York, Harper & Brothers, 1942, and *In Secret Battle*, New York, Appleton-Century, 1944. Lipton generously collaborated with his first wife, Craig Rice, a well-known writer of detective novels, on many of her books. He had also acted as editor of *Jewish Chronicle* in Detroit, and as advertising director for the Fox theater chain.

16 Kirsch's article concerned a posthumous collection of Lipton's poetry, *Bruno in Venice West and Other Poems* (Van Nuys, California, Venice West Publishers), and was published in 1976, three years after Lipton died.

17 The second part, which was to be composed by May, was never published, *Intro* having disappeared in the meantime. See James Boyer May, "Towards Print, (Where We've Been...Where We're Going?)," *Trace* 71, Winter 1969/1970, p. 270.

18 Lewis, the famous leader of the United Mine Workers union, had used the expression "I disaffiliate" in 1935, to signify his official resignation as vice president of the American Federation of Labor, after which he founded the Committee for Industrial Organization, which later became the Congress of Industrial Organizations or CIO. See Maynard, p. 51.

19 "America's Literary Underground," *Coastlines* n° 6, Winter 1956, Santa Monica, California; "Poetry and the Vocal Tradition," *The Nation*, April 4, 1956; "Youth Will Serve Itself," *The Nation*, November 10, 1956, pp. 389–92.

20 It was held at the Los Angeles Jazz Concert Hall, from December 4 to 7, 1957. These concert-readings (eight in all) enjoyed great success. See John A. Maynard, p. 79 for a more detailed description of such concert-readings. Lipton released a record in 1958 entitled *Jazz Canto: Vol. 1, In the Mainstream of Poetry and Music*, in which poems by Walt Whitman, William Carlos Williams, Dylan Thomas, Lawrence Lipton, Philip Whalen and Lawrence Ferlinghetti were read by actors over improvised jazz music.

21 *Trace* was the other important magazine published in Los Angeles, but its focus was not at all on the local area. Being interested particularly in international small press publishing, it could have been conceived anywhere. According to Alexandra Garrett, who, from her arrival in Los Angeles in 1949 to her death in December 1991, actively participated in Los Angeles literary life (she directed the last issues of *Coastlines*, worked for *Trace*, and then Beyond Baroque Foundation, directing its library and working as associate editor of its magazines) the two magazines were more recognized nationally than locally: "None of the *Coastlines* nor *Trace* were well known in Los Angeles at all. They were known in New York City, Chicago, they were known by libraries all over the country. But nobody in Los Angeles had heard of them, because there really wasn't any literary scene at that time at all." (Interview 1987).

22 In a letter published in the last issue of *Coastlines*, Lipton wrote retrospectively of the magazine: "Too bad it has to be your valedictory number. It needn't have been, in my opinion, if *Coastlines* had not pursued such a narrow sectarian policy. It may well have been the magazine of *the* West Coast renaissance since it was the first on the scene," "Editorial," *Coastlines* no. 21-22, *Adios, Final Issue: Los Angeles Writers*, Vol. 6, No. 1 & 2, 1964, p. 4

23 In his journal from the summer of 1959, Stuart Perkoff proposed that Lipton's book be called "Holy Horseshit," Maynard, p. 111.

24 See Gene Frumkin's article responding to an injurious piece in the *Hudson Review* on California poetry: "it must be dreadful to think the only readers of one's poems are professors and editors and fellow poets who immediately begin dismembering them, probably through habit, instead of keeping the poems whole long enough to feel them. That's

necropsy, man. Real dead," Gene Frumkin, "A Squawk About Squeal," p. 48.

25 *Poets of the Non-Existent City, Los Angeles in the McCarthy era*, ed. Estelle Gershgoren Novak, University of New Mexico Press, Albuquerque, 2002.

26 In the complex toponomy of Los Angeles, South Central (the south central region of the City of Los Angeles proper), or South Los Angeles as it has been officially but not universally called since 2003, is a vast entity with fluid borders that includes neighborhoods, more and more extensive, both west and east of Central Avenue, where the black population settled over the years. The Watts area proper, whose name was often used to designate in metonymic fashion the whole of South Central, and by extension the whole of the Los Angeles black community, is some six or seven miles south of downtown Los Angeles. Central Avenue, which begins near the Downtown section of the city around First Street, runs south from Downtown L.A. all the way through Watts. Between 1918 and the end of the 1920s, the central axis of this black community was around 12th Street and Central Avenue. The community was rapidly expanding south along Central Avenue, and from the late 1920s until the early 1950s, the block between 43rd Place and 43rd Street was the center of the community, around the Dunbar Hotel and a number of clubs. During World War I, the southern half of Watts (beyond 103rd Street–where land and houses were cheap) progressively became a black neighborhood. Before 1900 when it was renamed after a real estate developer, Watts was known as Mud Town and it resembled black communities in the Deep South, where the migrant Blacks had originally come from. In 1926 Watts was annexed to the City of Los Angeles, at the same time as Venice.

27 The figures for 1920 are taken from Lonnie G. Bunch, p. 110; those for 1965 are from Leon Whiteson, "Watts," p. 33.

28 Unless otherwise noted, all quotations from Paul Outterbridge are drawn from an interview I conducted with him in 1991.

29 "Lynn Manning was born in Fresno in 1955. He is second in a family of nine children who became wards of the court and grew up in foster

homes around Los Angeles County. He worked as a painter until he was shot in the face and blinded in 1978. He has a degree from Los Angeles Community College and is currently a first-degree brown belt in judo and the heavyweight champion in judo of the u.s. Association of Blind Athletes. He lives and works in the Wilshire District of L.A.," *Invocation L.A.*, p. 127. He is also an actor and a playwright.

30   In the same way that Hollywood represents Los Angeles, Watts represented for a couple of decades, due to the riots, the Los Angeles black community – until Compton, via rap, took its place in the 1980s.

31 The novel was published in 1941 and belongs to the Hollywood novel genre, portraying satirically Hollywood power and corruption.

32 A film treating unionism directed by Elia Kazan in 1954.

33 These works, and more particularly the poems, depict in a generally allegorical mode, in regular and rhymed metrics and a language of refined images and references, the life of the ghetto as an inescapable and inevitable hell from which all hope is forbidden.

34 Among whom Irving Stone, Irving Wallace, James Baldwin, Irwin Shaw, Richard Burton, Steve Allen, Ira Gershwin, Herbert Gold, Senator Robert F. Kennedy, Art Buchwald, Elia Kazan and John Steinbeck. See Budd Schulberg, "Introduction," pp. 20–1. For the media coverage, see p. 13 and p. 20.

35 "During the '60s and '70s, their small shop not only served as a bookstore and lecture center, but also offered small theatrical productions, classes in black history for children and various other projects." Juana E. Duty, "Age of Aquarian Book Shop, Bookstore Still Surviving in 'Starvation Business'," *Los Angeles Times*, 24 March 1982, Section v, p. 1. One of the first bookstores owned by blacks, it closed its doors in 1992, when its proprietors retired, after having been in existence for over fifty years. They had always had to supplement their income with another job in order to finance what they considered as "a community service,"(*ibid*, p.4).

36   The Teatro Campesino was a Chicano theater group, founded by Luis Valdez in 1965; East-West Players offered theater workshops to the

Asian-American community and is still in existence today as well as the Bilingual Foundation of the Arts, a theater group founded by Carmen Zapata in 1973.

37 Unless otherwise noted, all quotations of Wanda Coleman are drawn from interviews I conducted with her in 1987 and 1991.

38 Tapscott recorded in the late 1960s for only two white-owned labels, Prestige and Flying Dutchman. After those experiences, he backed away from the recording studios for some years, refusing to be produced by a studio that was not operated by blacks, to make sure his music – his gift to his community – would not "become something else" in the hands of Hollywood. See *It's not about a Salary*, p. 97. As for Kamau Daáood, in the late 1960s, he refused a contract with a studio, and declined the Last Poets' offer to join up with them – because he did not wish to leave Los Angeles. See *It's not about a Salary*, pp. 99 and 104–5. It was only in the late 1990s that he overcame his reticence and released a cd, *Leimert Park* (Mama Foundation, Simi Valley, California, 1997) which gave him national visibility. In a 2004 interview, he expresses some regrets at this past radical attitude that prevented him from getting recognition. See "Kamau Daáood: The Words of a Man" by Rex Butters, 8 December, 2004, *AllAboutJazz.com*.

39 Unless otherwise noted, all quotations from Father Amde are drawn from an interview I conducted with him in 1991.

40 Budd Schulberg himself was aware of "the ambivalence and ferocious complexity of my two years in Watts," and observed attitudes and feelings in the workshop, ranging from the mistrust of this white man on the part of the young nationalist separatists to the integrationist tendency of the older members, and everyone in-between, "even a few Uncle Toms." And he concludes: "I am not afraid of the angry young men of Watts. I am more afraid of greed and selfishness...of social dynamics that build concentration-camp walls around enclaves like Watts," *From the Ashes*, pp. 23–4.

41 This poem won the 1986 *Spectrum* literary magazine poetry contest, University of California at Santa Barbara, and is reprinted here with permission of the author.

42 Unless otherwise noted, all quotations of Kamau Daáood are drawn from an interview I conducted with him in 1987.

43 Born Everett LeRoi Jones in 1934, he changed his name to Imamu Amear Baraka, which later became Amiri Baraka.

44 In 2005 *The Language of Saxophones: Selected Poems*, published by San Francisco's City Lights Publishers, showcased a selection of his poetry from the previous four decades. In 2012, *Notes d'un griot de Los Angeles/Griot Notes from L.A.*, an English-French bilingual selection of his poems, was published in France, and a residency was provided in three French cities (Bordeaux, Paris and Marseilles), where he read his poetry, accompanied by different jazz bands.

45 Presentation text for *Hollywood*, prod. Harvey Kubernik, audio recording, Santa Monica, Rhino Records Inc./BarKubCo Music, Inc., 1990.

46 Like Richard Pryor, to whom Watts Prophets leader Father Amde frequently refers. Poets – at least the Watts Prophets – jazz musicans and comics, as well as strippers, were in this way a part of the same milieu of performers that evolved on the fringes of the entertainment world. Another dissident group, which united an eclectic bunch of black and white musicians, formed around Lenny Bruce, the famous comic, and alto saxophonist Joe Maini. The two men had met in a Los Angeles strip club where they performed. See Robert Gordon, p. 117.

47 *Black Voices on the Streets of Watts*, Ala 1970 (compilation disc), cited in *It's not about a Salary*, p. 50 and p. 9.

48 This song, from their recording *Straight Outta Compton*, Ruthless/Priority, 1988, sold millions of copies, and earned them the wrath of censors, provoking strong reactions from the police and fbi, so much so that certain cities like Detroit and Seattle forced them to cancel concerts. See, for example, "Wanted for Attitude," Dave Marsh and Phyllis Pollack, *Village Voice*, 10 October, 1989, pp. 33–7.

49 During the 1960s, she was a part of Ron Karenga's us Organization, a member of a paramilitary group and on the point of joining the Weather Underground – with her first husband, a white civil rights activist. He,

she explains, woke her political consciousness. She speaks of him at length in her interview in *Angry Women*, pp. 120–1, (and of course some poems are dedicated to him) and describes him thus: "My first husband was a troubleshooter for SNCC (Student Non-violent Coordinating Committee, a civil rights group) who came to Southern California with Jesse Jackson and Stokely Carmichael. He was a white guy who was part of Martin Luther King's inner circle," (p. 120).

50 *African Sleeping Sickness, Stories & Poems*, Santa Rosa, Black Sparrow Press, 1990, pp. 21–2. This poem previously appeared in *Invocation L.A., Urban Multicultural Poetry*, eds. Michelle Clinton, Sesshu Foster and Naomi Quiñonez, Albuquerque, West End Press, 1989. It is reprinted here with permission of the author.

51 In the Los Angeles County area, including the City of Los Angeles proper, it is the county and not the cities that provides public health and certain welfare services. As Luis J. Rodriguez recalls it in his autobiography, "Unincorporated county territory was generally where the poorest people lived, the old barrios, which for the most part didn't belong to any city because nobody wanted them. Most of Watts and a large section of East Los Angeles were unincorporated county territory. Sometimes they had no sewage system or paved roads." p. 38.

52 On page 123, she adds: "When I was a child I was reading all these tomes by these so-called 'great' writers, and every now and then I would stub my metaphorical toes on the word 'nigger' or 'negress.' And the hunger was always there to present my world view, because my world view didn't exist–it didn't even exist when Simone de Beauvoir wrote *The Second Sex*. She wrote about women allright, but what she wrote didn't apply to *me*." Since then, and particularly after 2000, scholarship concerning black Los Angeles has become a research field of its own.

53 This poem previously appeared in *A New Geography of Poets*, eds. Edward Field, Gerald Locklin and Charles Stetler, Fayetteville, The University of Arkansas Press, 1992; and *Poetas de Los Angeles*, ed. and transl. Juan Hernandez-Senter, Guanajuato, Universidad de Guanajuato, 1992. It is reprinted here with permission of the author.

54 "[Those were] *very* exciting [times], because I was living in two

worlds. We were living in the world of the black militants, but we were also living in the world of the hippies. So we would go from love-ins to underground meetings plotting the overthrow of the government! ... That was the other thing – the music was such a part of the excitement! We were always crashing concerts and doing things like jumping up on stage.... And when you went to Griffith Park, the families (there were several 'families' there, including the Manson family) would pitch tents, and you could go inside and sit and talk with them or share their food – it was great! Everyone was young and beautiful, and drugs were free, and it was a fabulous time," *Angry Women*, p. 121.

55 See Abe Peck, *Uncovering the Sixties, The Life & Times of the Underground Press*, pp. 132, 136, 190, and p. 288.

56 *Leimert Park: the Story of a Village in South Central Los Angeles* is a documentary film by Jeannette Lindsay made in 2008 about Leimert Park. It features Kamau Daáood, as well as the other spaces and artists that make up this exceptional neighborhood, which, during the nineties and to a lesser degree after 2000, offered a creative sanctuary for the Los Angeles African American community as well as all those who wanted to join in.

57 See the poem "Region of Deserts" on South Central in the late 1980s, *African Sleeping Sickness*, pp. 291–5.

58 Smith claimed there were over 200 by 1971, the majority of them libraries.

59 This aesthetic is explained by Joseph Hansen (longtime co-director of Beyond Baroque's Wednesday Night Workshop): Smith "favored anagrams, word play, free association of ideas, surrealism, concretism," "The Thursday of the Small Rains," *Bachy* 10, Winter 1977–78, p. 137. Smith was eventually able to apply his aesthetic principles and beliefs in the "modernist" mock autobiography he published in 2012, entitled *The slant hug o' time* (Crawfordville, Kitsune Books), and whose reading experience is described on the back cover as: "Howl meets Ulysses in a work like no other."

60 *Beyond Baroque 781*, Vol. 9, n° 1, Spring 1978, p. 5. However, Smith observed much later that he believed that neither this amended version of

his "credo"–nor probably any other version–was ever fully embraced by Krusoe or others involved, or that most people paid any attention to it. "They merely tolerated it," he said, "and it never appeared in NEW *Magazine*."

61 Unless otherwise noted, all quotations of Alexandra Garrett are drawn from an interview I conducted with her and George Drury Smith in 1987.

62 Unless otherwise noted, all quotations of Harry Northup are drawn from an interview I conducted with him and Holly Prado in 1987.

63 Making a living from typesetting since the early 1980s, he returned to graduate school at the University of California, San Diego, after "the computer industry had eviscerated typesetting as a career option" (*Hold-Outs* ix), and started teaching at California State University, Long Beach after graduate school.

64 Joseph Hansen, "Forgetting the Bridge," *Bachy* 9, Summer 1977; "The Thursday of the Small Rains," *Bachy* 10, Winter 1977–78, pp. 136–9; "Odd Sabbaths," *Bachy* 11, Spring 1978, pp. 136–9.

65 Unless otherwise noted, all quotations from Lee Hickman are drawn from an interview I conducted with him in 1987.

66 Cited in Bill Mohr, Harry Northup and Holly Prado, "Monday, May 13, 1991, For Leland Hickman," *Poetry Flash, A Poetry Review & Literary Calendar for the West*, July 1991, p. 18.

67 *Tiresias I:9:B: Great Slave Lake Suite* was the first part of a trilogy. Another volume entitled *Lee Sr Falls to the Floor* was published after Hickman's death in 1992. Both volumes were finally published together in 2009 as *Tiresias: The Collected Poems of Leland Hickman*, ed. Stephen Motika, Nightboat Books & Otis Books | Seismicity Editions. The above stanza, for example, is also the third stanza of "Hay River," the first poem in the first part. In fact, all the stanzas from the poem "O Blue Temple," like the other texts in the second part, can already be found throughout the poems of the first part.

68 Unless otherwise noted, all quotations of Robert Peters are drawn from an interview I conducted with him, William Iwamoto, and Paul Vangelisti in 1987.

69 William Iwamoto, interview, 1987. For a look at the history of Chatterton's, see Beverly Beyette, "Chatterton's Lovers Help Celebrate Its Reopening," *Los Angeles Times*, September 22, 1985. The store closed in the early 1990s.

70 Quotation attributed to Writers Conspiracy in Michael C. Ford's press kit established for Freeway/New Alliance Records.

71 Michael C. Ford, "Los Angeles Poets Survey–Ideas and Influences, Part vi," *Poetry News, Calendar and Reviews of Southern California Readings and Publications*, August 1981, Beyond Baroque Publications.

72 Unless otherwise noted, all quotations of Michael C. Ford are drawn from an interview that I conducted with him in 1987.

73 Stuart Z. Perkoff, Charles Wright, Holly Prado, Charles Bukowski, Alvaro Cardona-Hine, Ronald Koertge, Barbara Hughes, Jack Hirschman, Robert Peters, Gerda Penfold, Paul Vangelisti, and John Thomas.

74 For Braverman, there was a fine line between autobiography and fiction, life and writing: "[My work] is autobiographical in intent...intensity and feeling.... In terms of the actual facts of it I would say that much of it is totally fiction.... Kate Braverman is sort of a character that my mother and I contrived over the years. I am a creation.... I live my life as a mythic character," interview with Leland Hickman, *Bachy* 18, p. 221.

75 *Caterpillar* was founded in 1967 and was a famous magazine in the small press world. It was published in Los Angeles from 1971 to 1973. *Sulfur* was created in 1981 and financed initially by the California Institute of Technology (Caltech), where Eshleman taught.

76 For complementary information about the small presses in Los Angeles, see Bill Mohr, *Hold-Outs*, Chapter Five, pp.131–56.

77 Even though he disliked readings and mostly did them for the money, when he did perform, he gave a real show, drinking as he was reading. Ronald Koertge, a long time admirer of Bukowski, explains thus the success of his readings for the younger crowd: "Bukowski can [read at rock music clubs] because he's a fairy tale ogre come to life. So you go to see the ogre. It only costs you a few bucks. And he does his ogre act.

I'm sure he knows what he's doing. He gets so loaded he's out of control, but he gets loaded so he can be out of control.... He doesn't have some Michael McClure scarf around his neck. He isn't doing that pretty boy business. He's doing the ugly boy business. And I think he reads really well. God, what a spectacle.... Most poetry readings aren't spectacles." Ronald Koerge, interview with Dennis Cooper, *Little Caesar*, Vol. I.1, 1976, pp. 20–21.

78 The Brockman Gallery was actually founded by Dale and Alonzo Davis in 1967 in Leimert Park and soon became one of Los Angeles' most important sites for the exhibition of works by African American artists. Brockman Gallery Productions was created in 1973 with non-profit status to allow the Davis brothers to expand their program to include classes, festivals and film screenings.

79 See Harry Gamboa Jr.'s interview, p. 51, and Chon Noriega, "Your Art Disgusts Me: Early Asco 1971–75," *Afterall: A Journal of Art, Context and Enquiry* 19, Autumn/Winter 2008, pp.109–11.

80 See Arlene Raven's article, "Los Angeles Lesbian Arts," *Cultures in Contention*, pp. 236–41.

81 Unless otherwise noted, all quotations of Eloise Klein Healy are drawn from an interview I conducted with her and Deena Metzger in 1987.

82 "I know the books that have influenced me the most have been the *Diaries of Anaïs Nin*, only because she has been that disciplined in writing and has volumes and volumes and volumes of journals. And I began reading her book and I got inspired to keep books of my own," Marisela Norte, interview, 1987.

83 Unless otherwise noted, all quotes from Marisela Norte are drawn from interviews I conducted with her in 1987 and 1991.

84 A massive pacifist demonstration organized in Los Angeles on August 29, 1970 by the Chicano movement within the context of the Vietnam War. The demonstration turned violent when the police deliberately charged the crowd. In the panic that ensued, Ruben Salazar, a *Los Angeles Times* Chicano journalist, was killed.

85 She published a chapbook presenting a selection of their works in *Latinas Unidas, Manteniendo el Espíritu*, Los Angeles, Books of a Feather, 1982, a book which went very quickly out of print.

86 Respectively, and by order of appearance: Enrique Hank Lopez, Luis Rodriguez, Peter Fernandez, Marcia Gonzales, Frank Sifuentes, Mary Helen Ponce, Art Godínez, Manazar, David Valijalo, Jorge Alvarez, Victor Manuel Valle, Juan Gomez-Quiñonez, Jesús Mena, J. L. Navarro, Harry Gamboa, Naomi Quiñonez, Dukardo Hinestrosa, Marisela Norte, Fernando Rosel, Daniel Acosta, Max Benavídez, Felipe Chávez-Trejo, and Helen Maria Viramontes.

87 This is the title of an interview given by Judith Baca to Diane Neumaier: "Our People are the Internal Exiles," *Cultures in Contention*, pp. 62–75.

88 It was a characteristic of Latino poetry in general, as Juan Bruce-Novoa put it: "In great part, Chicano literature has been an attempt to rewrite u.s. history from our point of view," *Retrospace: Collected Essays on Chicano Literature, Theory and History*, Houston, Arte Público Press, 1990, p. 78.

89 For another analysis of Valle's poem, as well as the anthology, and other representations of Chicano barrios and space in Los Angeles, see Raúl Homero Villa, *Barrio-Logos, Space and Place in Urban Chicano Literature and Culture*, Austin, University of Texas Press, 2000, pp. 101–10. Thanks to Victor Valle for pointing out this enlightening study.

90 Unless otherwise noted, all quotations of Manazar Gamboa are from an interview I conducted with him in 1987.

91 Manazar Gamboa, *Una Calavera Con Lágrimas en los Huecos de los Ojos*, Los Angeles, Olmeca Press, 1988 and *Connection '89*, Los Angeles, Olmeca Press, 1990. He had previously published *Jam Session*, Los Angeles, Olmeca Press, 1983. He also published in 1996 *Memories Around a Bulldozed Barrio*.

92 In addition, a documentary entitled *Poetic License* was made by filmmaker Simon Schorno in 1999 to portray his life and the conflict surrounding the razing of the Mexican-American community of Chavez Ravine for Dodger Stadium; also, a fragment of a poem of his was

engraved in the Venice boardwalk, as part of an ongoing project sponsored by Beyond Baroque. Finally, in June 2011 the Manazar Gamboa Community Theater was inaugurated close to the Homeland Cultural Center he had co-directed in Long Beach.

93 Unless otherwise noted, all quotations of Marisela Norte are from interviews I conducted with her in 1987 and 1991.

94 For a more in-depth analysis of Asco, see Chon Noriega, "Your Art Disgusts Me: Early Asco 1971–75," Afterall: A Journal of Art, Context and Enquiry 19, Autumn/Winter 2008, pp.109–21.

95 Marisela Norte eventually published her first collection of poems in 2008 under the title: *Peeping Tom Tom Girl,* San Diego, City Works Press.

96 "I will tell you rap music has been helpful as far as the spoken word thing, because a lot of the rap music people are very articulate speakers, and getting on television shows and in the media, and predominantly white music media often quotes the lyrics and things like that. And they didn't quote rhythm and blues music as much. Do you know what I mean? So the fact that they've been taking some of the lyrics out of these songs like those by Public Enemy or Run DMC…So the rap thing has helped a lot" (Harvey Kubernik, in an interview I conducted with him in 1991).

WORKS CITED

Allen, Blair H. (ed.). *Snow Summits in the Sun: A Different Anthology of Poetry and Prose Poems*. Cucamonga, California: The Cerulean Press, I–II, 1988.

Allen, Donald (ed.). *The New American Poetry: 1945–1960*. New York: Grove Press, 1960.

Angelo, Nancy. "A Brief History of s.p.a.r.c." In *Cultures in Contention*. Eds.. Douglas Kahn and Diane Neumaier. Seattle: The Real Comet Press, 1985. 71–2.

Austin, Alan. "The Black Box Series/Some Remarks." In *The Poetry Reading, A Contemporary Compendium on Language & Performance*. Eds. Stephen Vincent and Ellen Zweig. San Francisco: Momo's Press, 1981. 247–50.

Baltierra, Gabriel. Personal interview. 14 July 1991.

Barth, Fredrik (ed.). *Ethnic Groups and Boundaries: The Social Organization of Culture Difference*. Boston: Little Brown & Company, 1969.

Barthes, Roland. *Mythologies*. Paris: Editions du Seuil, 1957.

Benes, Steven. "Roses Are Red, Poets Are blue..." *Los Angeles* (April 1983): 264–6.

Beyette, Beverly. "Chatterton's Lovers Help Celebrate Its Reopening." *Los Angeles Times* Part VI, 22 September 1985: 1, 14–5.

Beyond Baroque Foundation. *Beyond Baroque 691* I, 1 (December 1968).

——. "What is Beyond Baroque Foundation." *NeWLetterS* VI, 1 (January/February 1975): 4.

——. *NeWLetterS* VI, 3 (June/July 1975).

——. "What is Beyond Baroque." *Newforms 752* VII, 1 (February 1976): 62.

——. New Magazine: Arts and Letters VIII, 1 (January 1977).

——. "Beyond Baroque Foundation." *Beyond Baroque 783* IX, 3 (October 1978): 45–6.

——. *Poetry News–Los Angeles Poets Survey: Ideas and Influences*. Venice: Beyond Baroque Foundation Publications, undated.

Bloosten, G. "Donor Without Profit; Yet at a Few Big Houses Poetry Hangs On." *Publishers Weekly* (12 August 1983): 48–52.

Bogen, Lauren. Personal interview. 7 July 1991.

Bourdieu, Pierre. "Le marché des biens symboliques." *L'Année sociologique* 22 (1971): 49–126.

———. *La Distinction: critique sociale du jugement.* Paris: les Editions de Minuit, 1979.

———. *Les Règles de l'art: genèse et structure du champ littéraire.* Paris: Editions du Seuil, 1992.

———. *The Field of Cultural Production: Essays on Art and Literature.* Ed. Randal Johnson. Columbia University Press, 1993, trans. R. Swyer.

Braverman, Kate. Interview with Leland Hickman. *Bachy* 18 (Fall 1980): 220–5.

Breslauer, Jan. "A Trailblazer for Diversity." *Los Angeles Times*, Calendar, 31 March 1991: 5, 75–6. [a]

———. "Blooming Wordscapes, Beyond Baroque sneaks past the Reagan Legacy." *L.A. Weekly*, 28 June–4 July 1991: g17–g18. [b]

Brooks, Cleanth and Warren, Robert. *Understanding Poetry.* New York: Henry Holt and Company, 1938.

Brown, Elaine. *Seize the Time.* Vault SLP–131, 1969.

———. *Elaine Brown.* Black Forum BF 458L, 1973.

Bruce-Novoa, Juan. *Retrospace: Collected Essays on Chicano Literature, Theory and History.* Houston: Arte Público Press, 1990.

Bullock, Paul. *Creative Careers: Minorities in the Arts.* Los Angeles: Institute of Industrial Relations, University of California at Los Angeles, 1977.

Bunch III, Lonnie G. "A Past Not Necessarily Prologue : The Afro-American in Los Angeles since 1900." In *20th Century Los Angeles: Power, Promotion and Social Conflict.* Ed. Norman M. Klein and Martin J. Schiesl. Claremont : Regina Books, 1990. 101–30.

Bukowski, Charles, Cherry, Neeli and Vangelisti, Paul (eds.). *Anthology of L.A. Poets.* Los Angeles: Laugh Literary/Red Hill Press, 1972.

———. *Hostage.* Freeway Records/Rhino Records, 1985.

———. *Crucifix in a Deathhand.* New Orleans: Loujon Press, 1965.

———. *The Days Run away Like Wild Horses over the Hills.* Santa Rosa: Black Sparrow Press, 1969.

Burnham, Linda, Durland, Steven and MacAdams, Lewis. "Art with a Chicano Accent." *High Performance* 35 ix, 3 (1986): 40–57.

Burnham, Linda Frye. "Art in Limbo." *L.A. Weekly*, 18–24 March 1988: 20–4.

Candelaria, Cordelia. *Chicano Poetry: A Critical Introduction*. Wesport, London: Greenwood Press, 1986.

Cardona-Hine, Alvaro. "Poetry in Los Angeles: 1945 to 1975 – Part II." *Bachy* 13 (Winter 1979): 146–9.

Cervenka, Exene and Coleman, Wanda. *Twin Sisters*. Freeway Records/ Rhino Records, 1985.

Clinton, Michelle and Coleman, Wanda. *Black Angeles*. Freeway Records/ New Alliance Records, 1988.

Clinton, Michelle, Foster, Sesshu, and Quiñonez, Naomi (eds.). *Invocation L.A.: Urban Multicultural Poetry*. Albuquerque, New Mexico: West End Press, 1989.

Coastlines II III, 3 (Fall 1958).

Coleman, Wanda. *Mad Dog Black Lady*. Santa Barbara: Black Sparrow Press, 1979.

———. Interview with Leland Hickman. *Bachy* 16 (Winter 1979–80): 51–61.

———. *Imagoes*. Santa Barbara: Black Sparrow Press, 1983.

———. *Heavy Daughter Blues: Poems & Stories 1968–1986*. Santa Rosa: Black Sparrow Press, 1987.

———. Personal interviews. 24 March, 4 April 1987 and 13 July 1991.

———. "An Interview With Wanda Coleman." *Z Miscellaneous 1*, 5 (November 1987): 80–4.

———. "The Best Words in Their Best Order." *L.A. Weekly*, 22–8 September 1989: 57–9.

———. *African Sleeping Sickness: Stories & Poems*. Santa Rosa: Black Sparrow Press, 1990.

———. Interview with Andrea Juno and V. Vale. In Angry Women. Eds. Andrea Juno and V. Vale. San Francisco: ReSearch Publications, 1991. 118–26. Still available from www.researchpubs.com.

———. "Letter to Jamal." *The Verdict and the Violence, High Performance* (Summer 1992): 44–7.

——— (ed.). *The Verdict and the Violence, High Performance* (Summer 1992).

———. *American Sonnets*. Milwaukee: Woodland Pattern Book Center and Light and Dust Books, 1994.

Collins, Billy. "Literary Reputation and the Thrown Voice." In *A Gift of Tongues: Critical Challenges in Contemporary American Poetry*. Eds.

Marie Harris and Kathleen Aguero. Athens: University of Georgia Press, 1987. 295–306.

Concilio de Arte Popular. *Xhisme-Arte* 1 (Fall 1976).

———. "L.A. Latino Writers Workshop." *Xhisme-Arte* 6 (February 1980): 26.

Cooper, Dennis and Watt, Mark. "It's a Small World: Los Angeles Poets." *Gosh* (November 1978): 7–9.

Cox, Bette Yarbrough. *Central Avenue – Its Rise and Fall.* Los Angeles: BEEM Publications, 1993.

———. "The Evolution of Black Music in Los Angeles, 1890–1955." In *Seeking El Dorado: African Americans in California.* Eds. Lawrence B. De Graaf and Quintard Taylor. Seattle: University of Washington, and Los Angeles: Autry Museum of Western Heritage, 2001: 249–78.

Cross, Brian (ed.). *It's not about a Salary... Rap, Race and Resistance in Los Angeles.* London, New York: Verso, 1993.

Daáood, Kamau. *Liberator of the Spirit.* Los Angeles: Ascension Press, 1984.

———. Personal interview. 5 April 1987.

———. Interview with Brian Cross. In *It's not about a Salary... Rap, Race and Resistance in Los Angeles.* Ed. Brian Cross. London, New York: Verso, 1993. 102–6.

———. *Leimert Park.* Mama Foundation, 1997.

———. "Kamau Daaood: The Words of a Man." Interview with Rex Butters. 8 December 2004. *AllAboutJazz*.com. 25 August 2012 http://www.allaboutjazz.com/php/article.php?id=15768#.UDkY7aAR-uI

———. *The Language of Saxophones: Selected Poems.* San Francisco: City Lights Publishers, 2005.

———. *Notes d'un griot de Los Angeles/Griot Notes from L.A.* Eds. of translation: Nicole Ollier and Sophie Rachmuhl. Bègles: Le Castor Astral, 2012.

Davidson, Michael. *The San Francisco Renaissance: Poetics and Community at Mid-Century.* Cambridge, Massachusetts: Cambridge University Press, 1989.

Davis, Mike. *City of Quartz: Excavating the Future in Los Angeles.* London, New York: Verso, 1990.

DJ Quik. Interview with Brian Cross. In *It's not about a Salary... Rap,*

Race and Resistance in Los Angeles. Ed. Brian Cross. London, New York: Verso, 1993. 258–60.

Doubiago, Sharon. Review of *Poetry Loves Poetry: An Anthology of Los Angeles Poets*. *Electrum* 39 (Fall/Winter 1987): 50–4.

Drew, Nancy. "L.A.'s Space Age." In LACE *(Los Angeles Contemporary Exhibitions): 10 Years Documented*. Ed. Karen Moss. Los Angeles: LACE, 1988. 9–13.

Du Bois, W.E.B. *The Souls of Black Folk*. 1903. New York: Bantam Books, 1989.

Dujardin, Philippe. "Processus et propriétés de la mise en réseau : débat, problématique, propositions." In *Du groupe au réseau : réseaux religieux, politiques, professionnels*. Ed. Philippe Dujardin. Roundtable of 24 and 25 October 1986, Université Lumière Lyon II, Paris: Editions du CNRS, 1988. 5–27.

Duty, Juana E. "Age of Aquarian Book Shop, Bookstore Still Surviving in 'Starvation Business.'" *Los Angeles Times*, Section V, 24 March 1988: 1, 4.

Eliot, T.S. *The Waste Land*. 1922. In *The Norton Anthology of American Literature, Vol. 2*. New York: W.W. Norton & Company Inc., 1985. 1210–25.

Fabre, Michel. "Perspectives des littératures ethniques." In *L'Etat des Etats-Unis*. Eds. Annie Lennkh and Marie-France Toinet. Paris: Editions La Découverte, 1990. 187–90.

Field, Edward (ed.). *A Geography of Poets: An Anthology of the New Poetry*. New York : Bantam Books, 1979.

———, Locklin, Gerald and Stetler, Charles (eds.). *A New Geography of Poets*. Fayetteville, Arkansas : The University of Arkansas Press, 1992.

Fisher, Jocelyn and Garrett, Alexandra (eds.). *Southern California Women Writers*. *Magazine* XII, 2 (Fall 1981).

Ford, Michael C. (ed.). *The Mount Alverno Review: A Quick Anthology of West Coast Verse*. 1962, 1969. Los Angeles: Peace Press, 1971.

———. *Language Commando: Tape Box Transitions*. Freeway Records/ New Alliance Records, 1986.

Frumkin, Gene. "A Squawk About 'Squeal'." *Coastlines* 9 III, 1 (Winter 1957–58): 47–8.

———. "In the Tense Present." *Coastlines* 12 III, 4 (Spring 1959): 46–8.

————. "The Great Promoter: A Hangnail Sketch of Lawrence Lipton." *Coastlines* 13 IV, 1 (Fall 1959): 3–10.

Fulton, Len. "*Dust*: A Tribal Seed." In *The Little Magazine in America. A Modern Documentary History*. Eds. Elliott Anderson and Mary Kinzie. Yonkers, New York: The Pushcart Press, 1978. 423–37.

Funsten, Kenneth. "Bert Meyers (1928–79)." *Bachy* 15 (Fall 1979): 3–7.

Gamboa, Harry, Jr. Interview with Linda Burnham and Steven Durland. *High Performance* 35 IX, 3 (1986): 51–3.

Gamboa, Manazar. "Preface." *Beyond Baroque* 783 ix, 3 (October 1978): 7.

————. "Editorial." *Obras* XI, 4 (Winter 1980): 4.

————. Interview with Barbara Carrasco. *XhismeArte* 6 (February 1980): 29.

————. "Editorial." *Obras* XII, 1 (Spring 1981): 4.

————. *Jam Session*. Los Angeles: Olmeca Press, 1983.

————. Personal interviews. 25 March 1987 and 12 July 1991.

————. Interview with Michael Roth. *Electrum* 39 (Fall/Winter 1987): 32–5.

————. *Una Calavera Con Lágrimas en los Huecos de los Ojos*. Los Angeles: Olmeca Press, 1988.

————. *Connection '89*. Los Angeles: Olmeca Press, 1990.

Garrett, Alexandra and Smith, George Drury. Personal interview. 21 March 1987.

Gentile, John S. *Cast of One: One-Person Shows from the Chautauqua Platform to the Broadway Stage*. Chicago: University of Illinois Press, 1989.

Gilmore, Mikal. "The Musicians of Watts." In *The Watts Towers of Los Angeles*. Ed. Leon Whiteson. Oakville, Canada: Mosaic Press, 1989. 59–65.

Ginsberg, Allen. *Howl and Other Poems*. San Francisco: City Lights Books, 1956.

Gioia, Ted. *West Coast Jazz: Modern Jazz in California, 1945–1960*. Oxford: Oxford University Press, 1991.

Golding, Alan C. "A History of American Poetry Anthologies." In *Canons*. Ed. Robert Von Hallberg. Chicago: University of Chicago Press, 1983. 279–307.

Gordon, Robert. *Jazz West Coast: The Los Angeles Jazz Scene of the 1950s*. London: Quartet Books Limited, 1986.

Gramsci, Antonio. *Textes*. Ed. André Tosel. Paris: Messidor/Editions sociales, 1983.

Grapes, Marcus J. "Getting Around, Poetry in L.A." *Follies* (September 1979): 10–1.

Gray, Richard J. *American Poetry of the Twentieth Century*. London, New York: Longman, 1990.

Grandjeat, Yves-Charles. *Aztlàn: terre volée, terre promise, les pérégrinations du peuple chicano*. Paris: Presses de l'école normale supérieure, 1989.

Gronk. Interview with Linda Burnham and Steven Durland. *High Performance* 35 ix, 3 (1986): 57.

Gunn, Thom. "Is There, Currently, An American Poetry? A Symposium," In *American Poetry*, Vol. 4, no 2 (Winter 1987).

Hall, Donald, Pack, Robert and Simpson, Louis (eds.). *The New Poets of England and America*. Cleveland: Meridian, 1957.

———. "The Poetry Reading: Public Performance/Private Art." *The American Scholar* LIV (Winter 1984/85): 63–77.

Hansen, Joseph and Harris, John (eds.). *New Venice Poets. Beyond Baroque* 701 (1970).

———. *Venice Thirteen: Poetry of the Venice Poetry Workshop*. Venice: Beyond Baroque Foundation, 1971.

Hansen, Joseph. "Forgetting the Bridge". *Bachy* 9 (Summer 1977): 122–5.
———. "The Thursday of the Small Rains." *Bachy* 10 (Winter 1977–78): 136–9.

———. "Odd Sabbaths". *Bachy* 11 (Spring 1978): 136–9.

Healy, Eloise Klein. Interview with Leland Hickman. *Bachy* 14 (Spring/Summer 1979): 61–70.

——— and Metzger, Deena. Personal interview. 9 April 1987.

Hebdige, Dick. *Subculture: The Meaning of Style*. London, New York: Routledge, 1988.

Henderson, Ellen. Personal interview. 7 July 1991.

Hernandez-Senter, Juan (ed. and transl.). *Poetas de Los Angeles*. Guanajuato: Universidad de Guanajuato, 1992.

Hickman, Leland. *Tiresias I:9:B: Great Slave Lake Suite*. Santa Monica: Momentum Press, 1980.

———. Personal interview. 22 March 1987.

———. *Lee Sr Falls to the Floor*. Los Angeles: Jahbone Press, 1991.

————. *Tiresias, The Collected Poems of Leland Hickman.* Ed. Stephen Motika. Calicoon: Nightboat Books and Los Angeles: Otis Books/ Seismicity Editions, 2009.

Hoskyns Barney, "Riding the Freeways of Language." *New Musical Express,* 13 August 1983: 17.

Isoardi, Steven (ed.). *Songs of the Unsung: The Musical and Social Journey of Horace Tapscott.* Durham, NC: Duke University Press, 2001.

Isoardi, Steven. *The Dark Tree: Jazz and the Community Arts in Los Angeles.* Berkeley and Los Angeles, CA: University of California Press, 2006.

Iwamoto, William, Peters, Robert and Vangelisti, Paul. Personal interview. 28 March 1987.

James, David E. "Poetry/Punk/Production: Some Recent Writing in L.A." In *Postmodernism and Its Discontents.* Ed. Ann E. Kaplan. London, New York: Verso, 1988. 163–86.

James, David E. (ed.). *The Sons and Daughters of Los: Culture and Community in L.A.* Philadelphia: Temple University Press, 2003.

Jeffers, Robinson. *Tamar and Other Poems.* New York: Peter G. Boyle, 1924.

————. *Roan Stallion, Tamar and Other Poems.* New York: Boni & Liveright, 1925.

————. *The Double Axe and Other Poems.* New York: Random House, 1948.

Jones, LeRoi. *Blues People: The Negro Experience in White America and the Music That Developed from It.* New York: Morrow Quill Paperbacks, 1963.

Kahn, Douglas and Neumaier, Diane. "Introduction In *Cultures in Contention.* Eds. Douglas Kahn and Diane Neumaier. Seattle: The Real Comet Press, 1985. 8–13.

Kazan, Elia (dir.). Schulberg, Budd (scr.). *On the Waterfront.* Columbia Pictures, 1954.

Kessler, Stephen. "Inside the Streets: A Curb's-Eye Lowdown on L.A. Poetry." *Bachy* 14 (Spring/Summer 1979): 141–4.

Kilday, Gregg. "New Public Image for Poetry at Pasadena Museum Readings." *Los Angeles Times,* Part II, 24 December 1973: 8.

King, Martha. "Is Academia the Writer's Best Friend?" *Coda: Poets & Writers Newsletter* VIII, 5 (June/July 1981): 10–4.

Kirsch, Robert. "Venice West: Lipton's Last Stand." *Los Angeles Times,* Sect. IV, 11 January 1977: 4.

———. "Building Bridges Between People." *Los Angeles Times,* Part iv, 27 April 1979: 4.

Koertge, Ronald. Interview with Dennis Cooper. *Little Caesar* I, 1 (1976): 17–23.

Kostelanetz, Richard. *The Old Poetries and the New.* Ann Arbor: University of Michigan Press, 1981.

Kubernik, Harvey (prod.). *Voices of the Angels.* Freeway Records, 1982.

———. *English as a Second Language.* Freeway Records, 1983.

———. *Neighborhood Rhythms.* Freeway Records/Rhino Records, 1984.

———. *Hollyword.* Rhino Records/BarKubCo Music, 1990.

———. *Black & Tan Club.* New Alliance Records/Barkubco Music, 1991.

———. *Jazz Speak.* BarKubCo Music, 1991.

———. Personal interview. 9 July 1991. Lapassage, Georges and Rousselot, Philippe. *Le Rap ou la fureur de dire.* Paris: Editions Loris Talmart, 1990.

Lazer, Hank. "Poetry Readings and the Contemporary Canon." *American Poetry* VII, 2 (Winter 1990): 64–72.

Levine, Lawrence. *Highbrow/Lowbrow: The Emergence of Cultural Hierarchy in America.* Cambridge, Massachusetts: Harvard University Press, 1988.

Lindsay, Jeannette (dir.). *Leimert Park : The Story of a Village in South Central Los Angeles.* DVD documentary. Pasadena, California: Jeannette Lindsay, 2008.

Lipton, Lawrence. *Brother, the Laugh Is Bitter.* New York: Harper & Brothers, 1942.

———. *In Secret Battle.* New York: Appleton-Century, 1944.

———. "Secession: 1953: The State of the Arts on the West Coast." *Intro* 2 (1953): 31–43.

———. *Rainbow at Midnight.* Francestown, New Hampshire: The Golden Quill Press, 1955.

———. "Disaffiliation and the Art of Poverty." *Chicago Review* (Spring 1956): 53–79.

———. "Poetry and the Vocal Tradition." *The Nation,* 4 April 1956.

———. "America's Literary Underground." *Coastlines* 6 (Winter 1956).

———. "Youth Will Serve Itself." *The Nation*, 10 November 1956: 389–92.

———. *The Holy Barbarians*. New York: Julian Messner Inc., 1959.

———. "Editorial." *Coastlines* 21–22 VI, 1–2 (1964): 4.

———. *Bruno in Venice West and Other Poems*. Van Nuys, California: Venice West Publishers, 1976.

Long, Philomene and Thomas, John. Personal interview. 8 April 1987.

Lummis, Suzanne Webb and Charles Harper (eds.). *Stand Up Poetry: The Poetry of Los Angeles and Beyond*. Los Angeles: Red Wind Books, 1990.

MacDonald, Lachlan. "Poetry of the Non-Existent City." *Coastlines* 12 III, 4 (Spring 1959): 43–5.

———. "The Non-Existent City." In *Los Angeles: The Non-Existent City*. *Coastlines* 14–15 (Spring 1960): 3–4.

Machan Aal, Katharyn. *The Writer as Performer: A Study of Contemporary Poetry and Fiction Readings, Based in Ithaca, New York*. Doctoral Thesis: Northwestern University, Illinois, 1984.

Magistrale, Tony. "Doing Battle with the Wolf: A Critical Introduction to Wanda Coleman's Poetry." *Black American Literature Forum* 23. 3 (Autumn, 1989): 539–54.

Marcuse, Herbert. *An Essay on Liberation*. Boston : Beacon Press, 1969.

Margolis, William J. "In Memoriam: Some Immediate Impressions of a Studio Poetry Reading at KPFK, September 9, 1961." *Bachy* 4 (Fall 1974): 1–3.

Marsh, Dave and Pollack, Phyllis. "Wanted for Attitude." *Village Voice*, 10 October 1989: 33–7.

May, James Boyer. "Towards Print (Where We've Been...Where We're Going?)" *Trace* 71 (Winter 1969/1970): 217–24.

———. "On *Trace*." In *The Little Magazine in America: A Modern Documentary History*. Eds. Elliott Anderson and Mary Kinzie. Yonkers, New York: The Pushcart Press, 1978. 376–87.

Maynard, John Arthur. *Venice West: The Beat Generation in Southern California*. New Brunswick: Rutgers University Press, 1991.

McDonnell, Evelyn. "New Poets with a Rock & Roll Attitude, Native Tongues." *Village Voice*, 5 August 1993: 20

McGee, Lynn. "Poetry in Motion." *L.A. Reader*, 31 January 1986: 1, 19–21, 28.

McWilliams, Carey. *Southern California: An Island on the Land*. New York: Duell, Sloan, & Pearce, 1946.

Mena, Jesús, Navarro, J.L., Valle, Victor Manuel and Viramontes, Helen María (eds.). *Two Hundred and One: Homenaje A La Ciudad de Los Angeles/The Latino Experience in Los Angeles*. Los Angeles: Los Angeles Latino Writers Association, 1982.

Metzger, Deena. "Looking for a Path with a Heart." *Bachy* 15 (Fall 1979): 150–3.

Mingus, Charles and King, Nel. *Beneath the Underdog: His world as composed by Mingus*. New York: Vintage Books, 1971.

Moffet, Penelope. "Take Five: L.A. Poets Look at L.A."*Los Angeles Times*, Calendar, 10 February 1980: 6–7.

———. "Gutsy Poetry from the 'Mad Dog Black Lady.'" *Los Angeles Times*, Calendar, 31 January 1982: 3.

Mohr, Bill (ed.). *The Streets Inside: Ten Los Angeles Poets*. Santa Monica: Momentum Press, 1978.

———. Interview with Lee Hickman. *Bachy* 14 (Spring/Summer 1979): 3–8.

——— (ed.). *Poetry Loves Poetry: An Anthology of Los Angeles Poets*. Santa Monica: Momentum Press, 1985.

———, Northup Harry, and Prado Holly. "Monday, May 13, 1991: For Leland Hickman." *Poetry Flash: A Poetry Review & Literary Calendar for the West* 220 (July 1991): 1, 18.

———. *Hold-Outs: The Los Angeles Poetry Renaissance, 1948–1992*. Iowa City: University of Iowa Press, 2011.

Moran, Tom and Sewell, Tom. *Fantasy by the Sea: A Visual History of the American Venice*. Venice, California: Beyond Baroque Foundation, 1979.

Morrison, Jim. *The Lords and the New Creatures*. New York: Simon & Schuster, 1970.

Moss, Karen. "lace's First 10 Years: From El Monte to Industrial Street." In LACE *(Los Angeles Contemporary Exhibitions): 10 Years Documented*. Ed. Karen Moss. Los Angeles: LACE, 1988. 6–8.

Moulin, Raymonde. "Le Marché et le musée : la constitution des valeurs artistiques contemporaines." In *Sociologie de l'art et de la littérature*. Eds. Jean-Claude Chamboredon and Pierre-Michel Menger. *Revue française de sociologie* XXVII.3 (July–September 1986): 369–95.

Murphet, Julian. *Literature and Race in Los Angeles*. Cambridge: Cambridge University Press, 2001.

National endowment for the arts. "Writing Out of the Ashes: The Watts Writers Workshop." nea.com. 2005. National Endowment for the Arts. Highlights in nea History. 25 August 2012 http://www.nea.gov/about/40th/watts.html.

Napper, Michael and Levin Susan. "Spoken Words." *Arts/LA* 1 (August 1986): 11.

Nin, Anaïs. *The Diary of Anaïs Nin: Vol. 6: 1955–1966*. 1966. Ed. Gunther Stuhlmann. San Diego, New York, London: Harcourt Brace Jovanovich, 1976.

Noriega, Chon. "Your Art Disgusts Me: Early Asco 1971–75." In Afterall: A Journal of Art, Context and Enquiry 19 (Autumn/Winter 2008): 109–121.

Norte, Marisela. Personal interviews. 26 March 1987 and 9 July 1991.

———. *Norte/Word*. New Alliance Records/Barkubco Music, 1991.

———. *Peeping Tom Tom Girl*. San Diego: City Works Press, 2008.

Northup, Harry. *Enough the Great Running Chapel*. Los Angeles: Momentum Press, 1982.

——— and Prado, Holly. Personal interview. 22 March 1987.

Novak, Estelle Gershgoren (ed.). *Poets of the Non-Existent City, Los Angeles in the McCarthy Era*. Albuquerque: University of New Mexico Press, 2002.

N.W.A. *Straight Outta Compton*. Ruthless Records: 1988.

Onthebus 4 (Winter 1989).

Peck, Abe. *Uncovering the Sixties: The Life and Times of the Underground Press*. New York: Pantheon Books, 1985.

Peirce, Neil R. *The Megastates of America: People, Politics, and Power in the Ten Great States*. New York: Norton, 1972.

Perkoff, Stuart. *The Suicide Room*. Karlsruhe: Jargon Press, 1956.

———. *Alphabet*. Ed. Paul Vangelisti. Los Angeles: The Red Hill Press, 1973.

———. *Love Is the Silence: Poems 1948–1972*. Ed. Paul Vangelisti. Los Angeles: The Red Hill Press, 1975.

———. *How It Is, Doing What I Do: Poems and Drawings, Bowery n°21*. Ed. Tony Scibella. Denver: Black Ace, 1976.

————. *Voices of the Lady: Collected Poems.* Ed. Gerald T. Perkoff. Orono, Maine: The National Poetry Foundation, 1998.

Perloff, Harvey S. (ed.). *The Arts in the Economic Life of the City: A Study by Urban Innovations Group, School of Architecture and Urban Planning University of California, Los Angeles.* New York: American Council for the Arts Publications, 1979.

Perloff, Marjorie. "The Word as Such: L=A=N=G=U=A=G=E Poetry in the Eighties." In *The Dance of the Intellect: Studies in the Poetry of the Pound Tradition.* Marjorie Perloff. Cambridge: Cambridge University Press, 1985. 215–38.

Peters, Brock. "Introduction." In *Poetic Reflections.* The Watts Prophets. Watts: Watts Prophets Press, 1976. Unpaginated.

Peters, Robert. *The Gift to Be Simple: A Garland for Ann Lee.* New York: Liveright Publishing/Norton, 1975.

————. "Scribbling in Journals, and Other Poetry Matters." *Bachy* 14 (Spring/Summer 1979): 138–41.

————. *Hawker.* Greensboro, North Carolina: Unicorn Press, 1984.

————. *Ludwig of Bavaria: A Verse Biography and a Play for Single Performer.* New York: Cherry Valley Editions, 1986.

————. *The Blood Countess.* New York: Cherry Valley Editions, 1987.

Pillin, William. Interview with Leland Hickman. *Bachy* 16 (Winter 1979–80): 3–11.

Plagens, Peter. *Sunshine Muse: Contemporary Art on the West Coast.* New York: Praeger Publishers, 1974.

Poets & Writers, Inc. "Poetry Libraries: For Those Who Can't Get Enough." *Coda: Poets & Writers Newsletter* IV 5 (June/July 1977): 15–8.

————. "A Free Listing from Poets & Writers, Inc. – 32 Newsletters, 505 Sponsors of Readings." *Coda: Poets & Writers Newsletter* V, 3 (February/March 1978): 26.

Prado, Holly. Interview with Leland Hickman. *Bachy* 12 (Fall 1978): 3–14.

————. *Feasts.* Los Angeles: Momentum Press, 1976.

Priestley, Eric. *Raw Dog.* Los Angeles: Holloway House Publishing Company, 1985.

Pritikin, Renny. "Historic Issues of Artists Organizations." In LACE *(Los Angeles Contemporary Exhibitions): 10 Years Documented.* Ed. Karen Moss. Los Angeles: LACE, 1988. 14–5.

Quinn, Michelle. "A Special Post-Riot Forum for Los Angeles Artists." *Los Angeles Times*, 24 August 1992: F5.

Rachmuhl, Sophie (dir.). *Innerscapes : Ten Portraits of Los Angeles Poets.* 94 mn 3/4" NTSC video documentary. Rachmuhls Productions, 1988.

Raven, Arlene. "Los Angeles Lesbian Arts." In *Cultures in Contention.* Eds. Douglas Kahn and Diane Neumaier. Seattle: The Real Comet Press, 1985. 236–41.

Rechy, John. *City of Night.* New York: Grove Press, 1963.

———. *Numbers.* New York: Grove Press, 1967.

———. Interview with Lee Hickman. *Bachy* 17 (Spring 1980): 2–11.

———. *The Sexual Outlaw: A Documentary.* New York: Grove Press, 1977.

———. *The Miraculous Day of Amalia Gómez.* New York: Arcade Publishing/ Little, Brown and Company, 1991.

Reed, Ishmael (ed.). *Califia: The California Poetry.* Oakland: Yardbird, 1979.

Rexroth, Kenneth. "Disengagement: the Art of the Beat Generation." *New World Writing* 11 (Summer 1956).

Rodriguez, Aleida and De Angelis, Jacqueline (eds.). *Southern California Women Writers & Artists, rara avis* 6–7 (1984).

Rodriguez, Luis J. *Always Running, La Vida Loca: Gang Days in L.A.* New York: Touchstone, 1993.

Rolfe, Lionel. *In Search of...Literary L.A.* Los Angeles: California Classics Books, 1991.

Rothenberg, Jerome. "A Dialogue on Oral Poetry with William Spanos." *Boundary 2* III, 3 (Spring 1975): 509–48.

Said, Edward W. "Opponents, Audiences, Constituencies, and Community." *Critical Inquiry* 9 (September 1982): 1–26.

Schulberg, Budd. *What Makes Sammy Run?* New York: Random House, 1941.

——— (ed.). *From the Ashes: Voices of Watts.* 1967. New York: Meridian Books, 1969.

Scibella, Tony. Interview with Bruce Kijewski. Manuscript. 1987.

Shiffrin, Nancy. "Playing Politics in the Poetry Game." *Los Angeles Times*, Calendar, 23 February 1986: 3–4.

———. "Poetry: Is There a Los Angeles Sound?" *Los Angeles Times*, Calendar, 25 January 1987: 42–3, 79.

Silliman, Ron. "Is There, Currently, An American Poetry? A Symposium," In *American Poetry*, Vol. 4, no 2 (Winter 1987).

———. "Canons and Institutions: New Hope for the Disappeared." In *The Politics of Poetic Form: Poetry and Public Policy*. Ed. Charles Bernstein. New York: Roof Books, 1990. 149–74.

Slattery, William. 7 July 1991.

Small Press Conference. "Forty Years of L.A. Small Presses." Audio cassette. Los Angeles: L.A. Poetry Festival, Chatterton's Bookstore, 27 October 1990.

Smith, Elihu Hubbard (ed.). *American Poems: Selected and Original, Vol. 1*. Lichfield, Connecticut: Collier and Buel, 1793.

Smith, George Drury. *The slant hug o' time*. Crawfordville, Florida: Kitsune Books, 2012.

Sollors, Werner. *Beyond Ethnicity: Consent and Descent in American Culture*. New York, Oxford: Oxford University Press, 1986.

Staley, Eric. "Influence, Commerce, and the Literary Magazine." *The Missouri Review* VII, 1 (Fall 1983): 177–93.

Stam, Robert. "Mikhail Bakhtin and Left Cultural Critique." In *Postmodernism and Its Discontents*. Ed. Ann E. Kaplan. London, New York: Verso, 1988. 116–45.

Stein, Gertrude. *Tender Buttons*. New York: Claire Marie, 1914.

Stein, Julia. "L.A.'s Poet Innovators, Voices from the New Ellis Island." *High Performance* 38 (1987): 40–5.

Stewart, Zan. "Poet Ford Takes Jazz at its Word." *Los Angeles Times,* Part VI, 25 July 1986: 20.

Stingley, Jim. "The Rise of L.A.'s Underground Poets." *Los Angeles Times*, Part IV, 21 April 1974: 1, 14–7.

———. "Hustling the Very Sacred and Special." *Los Angeles Times*, Part IV, 5 May 1975: 1, 10–2.

Studio Watts Workshop. *Studio Watts Workshop: an Evolution*. Los Angeles, 1971.

Tapscott, Horace. *Songs of the Unsung: The Musical and Social Journey of Horace Tapscott*. Ed. Steven Isoardi. Durham, NC: Duke University Press, 2001.

Tercinet, Alain. *West Coast Jazz*. Marseille : Editions Parenthèses, 1986.

Tompkins, Jane P. "An Introduction to Reader-Response Criticism." In *Reader-Response Criticism: From Formalism to Post-structuralism*. Ed.

Jane P. Tompkins. Baltimore: The Johns Hopkins University Press, 1980. ix–xxvi.

———. "The Reader in History: The Changing Shape of Literary Response." In *Reader-Response Criticism: From Formalism to Post-structuralism.* Ed. Jane P. Tompkins. Baltimore: The Johns Hopkins University Press, 1980. 201–32.

Ulin, David L. (ed.). *Writing Los Angeles: A Literary Anthology.* New York City: The Library of America, 2002.

Vangelisti, Paul (ed.). *Specimen 73: A Catalog of Poets for the Season 1973–74.* Pasadena, California: Pasadena Museum of Modern Art, 1973.

———. Interview with Silvia Bizio. In *Los Angeles Babilonia.* Ed. Claudio Castellacci. Milan: la milano libri edizioni, 1983. 65–81. Trans. Sophie Rachmuhl.

——— (ed.). *L.A. Exile: A Guide to Los Angeles Writing, 1932–1998.* New York: Marsilio, 1999.

Varga, George. "Jazz Poet Combines Vision, Rhythm." *The San Diego Union,* 11 October 1986.

Villa, Raúl Homero. *Barrio-Logos: Space and Place in Urban Chicano Literature and Culture.* Austin: The University of Texas Press, 1990.

Walker, Franklin. "Abbot Kinney's Venice." In *Los Angeles: Biography of a City.* Eds. John and Laree Caughey. Berkeley: University of California Press, 1976. 235–9.

Watts Prophets (Father Amde, Richard Dedeaux, Otis Smith). *Black Voices on the Streets of Watts.* Ala Records1970.

———. *Rappin' Black in a White World.* Ala Records A1971. Re-published in *Things Gonna Get Greater: The Watts Prophets 1969–1971.* Water, 2005.

———. *Poetic Reflections.* Watts: Watts Prophets Press, 1976.

———. Interview with Brian Cross. In *It's not about a Salary... Rap, Race and Resistance in Los Angeles.* Ed. Brian Cross. London, New York: Verso, 1993. 107–17.

Weisburd, Mel. "The Merchant of Venice." *Coastlines* 7 11, 3 (Summer 1957): 39–40.

Weisman, Alan. "Born in East L.A." *Los Angeles Times Magazine,* 27 March 1988: 10–20, 25.

West, Nathanael. *The Day of the Locust.* 1939. New York: New Directions, 1962.

Whiteson, Leon. "Watts." In *The Watts Towers of Los Angeles*. Ed. Leon Whiteson. Oakville, Canada: Mosaic Press, 1989. 31–40.

Whitman, Walt. *Leaves of Grass*. New York: self-published, 1855.

Widener, Daniel. *Black Arts West: Culture and Struggle in Postwar Los Angeles*. Durham and London: Duke University Press, 2010.

Wolverton, Terry. "Rhyme and Reason, All Ears at the L.A. Poetry Festival." *L.A. Weekly*, 16–22 November 1990: 39.

———. Personal interview. 12 July 1991.

Woman's Building. *The First Decade, Celebrating the Tenth Anniversary of the Woman's Building: a Pictorial History and Current Programs*. Los Angeles: Woman's Building, 1983.

———. *Fifteen Years and Growing: Celebrating the 15th Anniversary of the Woman's Building*. Los Angeles: Woman's Building, 1988.

Other Titles from Otis Books | Seismicity Editions

Erik Anderson, *The Poetics of Trespass*
        Published 2010 | 112 Pages | $12.95
        ISBN-13: 978-0-979-6177-7-5
        ISBN-10: 0-979-6166-7-4

J. Reuben Appelman, *Make Loneliness*
        Published 2008 | 84 pages | $12.95
        ISBN-13: 978-0-9796177-0-6
        ISBN-10: 0-9796177-0-7

Bruce Bégout, *Common Place. The American Motel.*
        Published 2010 | 143 Pages | $12.95
        ISBN-13: 978-0-979-6177-8-2
        ISBN-10: 0-979-6177-8-

Guy Bennett, *Self-Evident Poems*
        Published 2011 | 96 pages | $12.95
        ISBN-13: 978-0-9845289-0-5
        ISBN-10: 0-9845289-0-3

Guy Bennett and Béatrice Mousli, Editors, *Seeing Los Angeles:
A Different Look at a Different City*
        Published 2007 | 202 pages | $12.95
        ISBN-13: 978-0-9755924-9-6
        ISBN-10: 0-9755924-9-1

Robert Crosson, *Signs/ & Signals: The Daybooks of Robert Crosson*
        Published 2008 | 245 Pages | $14.95
        ISBN: 978-0-9796177-3-7

Robert Crosson, *Daybook (1983–86)*
        Published 2011 | 96 Pages | $12.95
        ISBN-13: 978-0-9845289-1-2
        ISBN- 0-9845289-1-1

Mohammed Dib, *Tlemcen or Places of Writing*
        Published 2012 | 120 pages | $12.95
        ISBN-13: 978-0-9845289-7-4
        ISBN-10: 0-9845289-7-0

Ray DiPalma, *The Ancient Use of Stone:*
Journals and Daybooks, 1998–2008
>Published 2009 | 216 pages | \$14.95
>ISBN: 978-0-9796177-5-1

Ray DiPalma, *Obedient Laughter*
>Published 2014 | 144 pages | \$12.95
>ISBN: 978-0-9860173-3-9

Jean-Michel Espitallier, *Espitallier's Theorem*
Translated from the French by Guy Bennett
>Published 2003 | 137 pages | \$12.95
>ISBN: 0-9755924-2-4

Forrest Gander, Editor, *Panic Cure: Poems from Spain*
for the 21st Century
>Published 2014 | 304 pages | \$12.95
>ISBN-13: 978-0-9860173-4-6
>ISBN: 0-9860173-4-5

Leland Hickman, *Tiresias: The Collected Poems of Leland Hickman*
>Published 2009 | 205 Pages | \$14.95
>ISBN: 978-0-9822645-1-5

Michael Joyce, *Twentieth Century Man*
>Published 2014 | 152 pages | \$12.95
>ISBN: 987-0-9860173-2-2

Norman M. Klein, *Freud in Coney Island and Other Tales*
>Published 2006 | 104 pages | \$12.95
>ISBN: 0-9755924-6-7

Luxorius, *Opera Omnia or, a Duet for Sitar and Trombone*
>Published 2012 | 216 pages | \$12.95
>ISBN-13: 978-0-9845289-6-7
>ISBN-10: 0-9845289-5-4

Ken McCullough, *Left Hand*
>Published 2004 | 191 pages | \$12.95
>ISBN: 0-9755924-1-6

Béatrice Mousli, Editor, *Review of Two Worlds:*
French and American Poetry in Translation
> Published 2005 | 148 pages | $12.95
> ISBN: 0-9755924-3-2

Laura Mullen, *Enduring Freedom*
> Published 2012 | 80 Pages | $12.95
> ISBN-13: 978-0-9845289-8-1
> ISBN-10: 0-9845289-8-9

Ryan Murphy, *Down with the Ship*
> Published 2006 | 66 pages | $12.95
> ISBN: 0-9755924-5-9

Aldo Palazzeschi, *The Arsonist*
Translation from the Italian by Nicholas Benson
> Published 2013 | 232 pages | $12.95
> ISBN: 978-0-9845289-9-8

Dennis Phillips, *Navigation: Selected Poems, 1985–2010*
> Published 2011 | 288 pages | $14.95
> ISBN-13: 978-0-9845289-4-3
> ISBN: 0-9845289-4-6

Antonio Porta, *Piercing the Page: Selected Poems 1958–1989*
> Published 2011 | 368 pages | $14.95
> ISBN -13: 978-0-9845289-5-0
> ISBN: 0-9845289-5-4

Eric Priestley, *For Keeps*
> Published 2009 | 264 pages | $12.95
> ISBN: 978-0-979-6177-4-4

Ari Samsky, *The Capricious Critic*
> Published 2010 | 240 pages | $12.95
> ISBN-13: 978-0-979-177-6-8
> ISBN: 0-979-6177-6-6

Hélène Sanguinetti, *Hence This Cradle*
Translated from the French by Ann Cefola
> Published 2007 | 160 pages | $12.95
> ISBN: 970-0-9755924-7-2

Janet Sarbanes, *Army of One*
Published 2008 | 173 pages | $12.95
ISBN-13: 978-0-9796177-1-3
ISBN-10: 0-9796177-1-5

Severo Sarduy, *Beach Birds*
Translated from the Spanish by Suzanne Jill Levine and Carol Maier
Published 2007 | 182 pages | $12.95
ISBN: 978-9755924-8-9

Adriano Spatola, *The Porthole*
Translated from the Italian by Beppe Cavatorta and Polly Geller
Published 2011 | 112 pages | $12.95
ISBN-13: 978-0-9796177-9-9
ISBN-10: 0-9796177-9-0

Adriano Spatola, *Toward Total Poetry*
Translated from the Italian by Brendan W. Hennessey and
Guy Bennett, with an Introduction by Guy Bennett
Published 2008 | 176 pages | $12.95
ISBN-13: 978-0-9796177-2-0
ISBN-10: 0-9796177-3-1

Carol Treadwell, *Spots and Trouble Spots*
Published 2004 | 176 pages | $12.95
ISBN: 0-9755924-0-8

Paul Vangelisti, *Wholly Falsetto with People Dancing*
Published 2013 | 136 pages | $12.95
ISBN-13: 978-0-980173-0-8
ISBN: 0-9860173-0-2

Allyssa Wolf, *Vaudeville*
Published 2006 | 82 pages | $12.95
ISBN: 0-9755924-4-0